MW01676065

HOW TO TAKE BETTER PICTURES

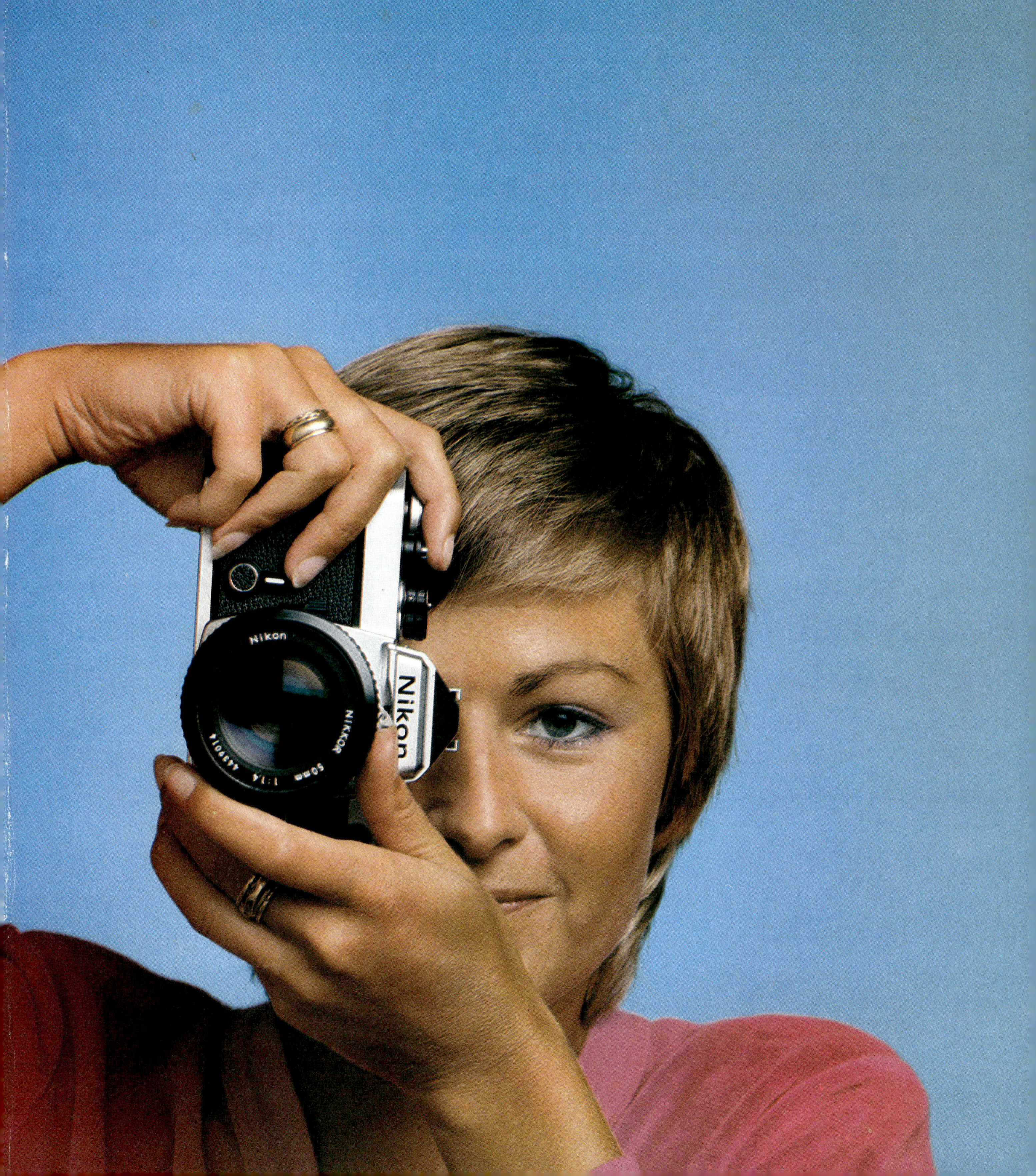

1000
500
250
125
60
30
15
8
4
2
1
2
4
8
16

Michael Busselle

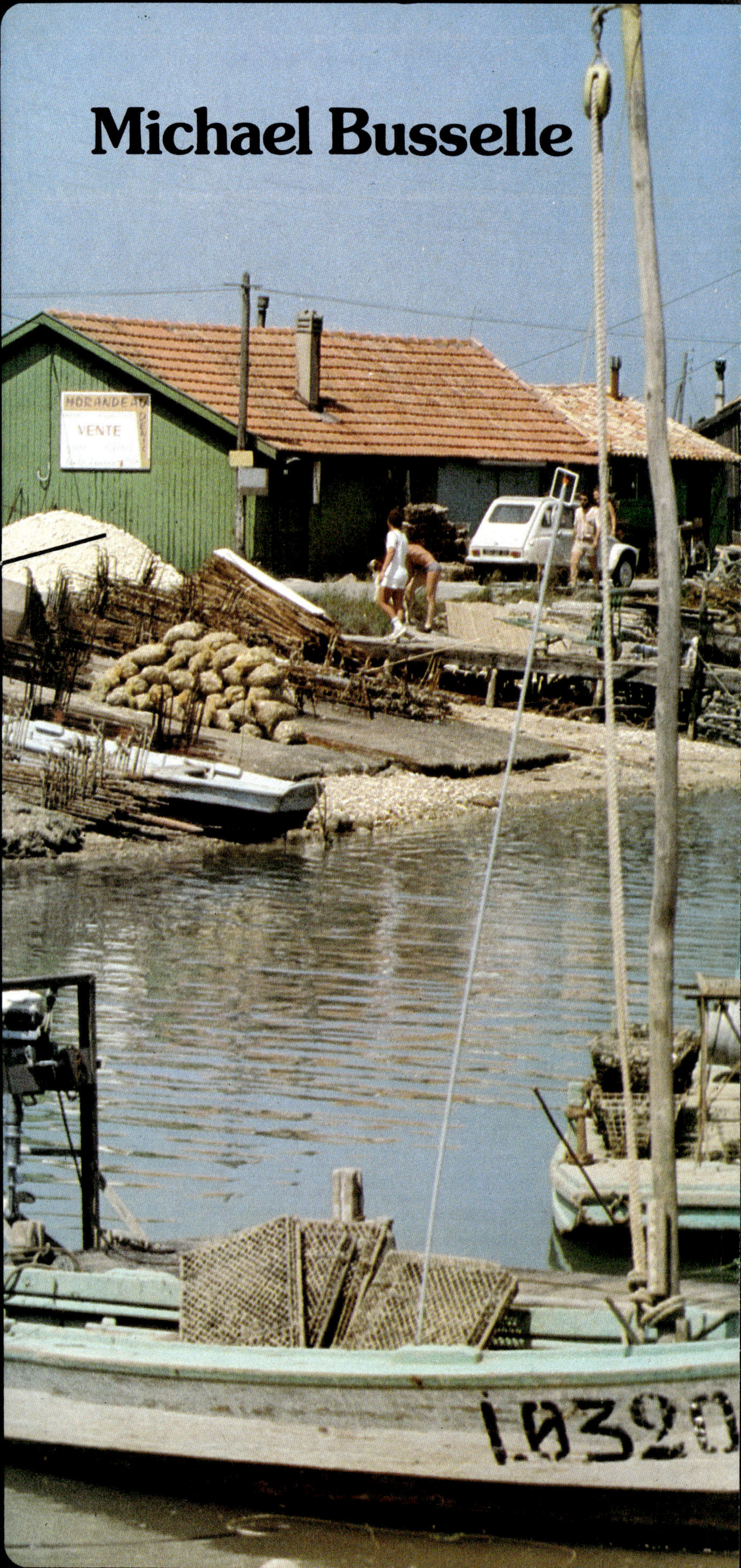

HOW TO TAKE BETTER PICTURES

Crescent Books New York

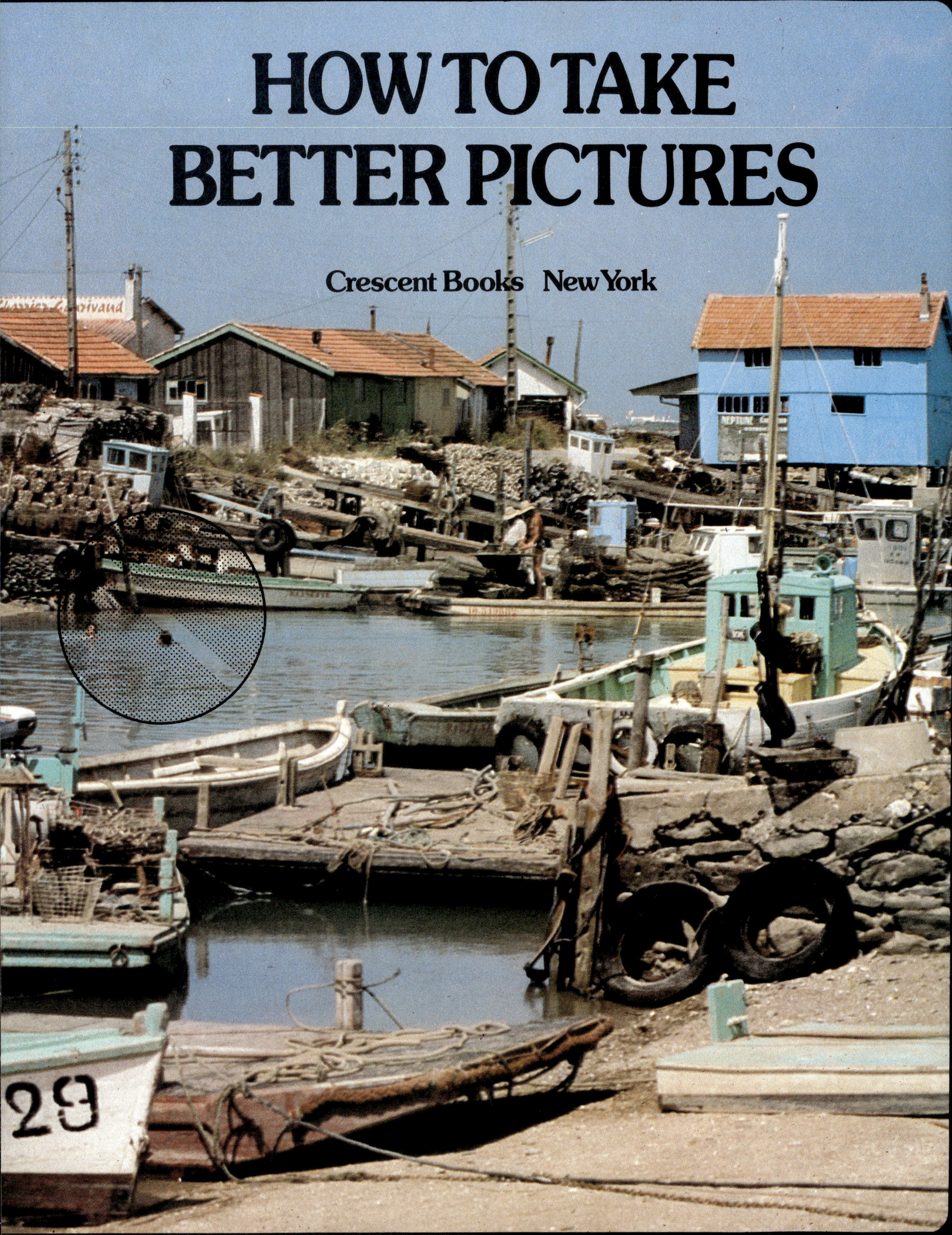

4 5·6 8

Contents

Copyright © 1981 by Michael Busselle

First English edition published in 1981 by
Artus Publishing Company Ltd
91 Clapham High Street
London SW4 7TA

This edition is published by Crescent Books,
a division of Crown Publishers, Inc

Printed in the United States of America

a b c d e f g

Library of Congress Cataloging in Publication Data

Busselle, Michael

How to take better pictures
1. Photography—Handbooks, manuals, etc. 1. Title.
TR146.B96 770'.28 80–19316
ISBN 0–517–326272

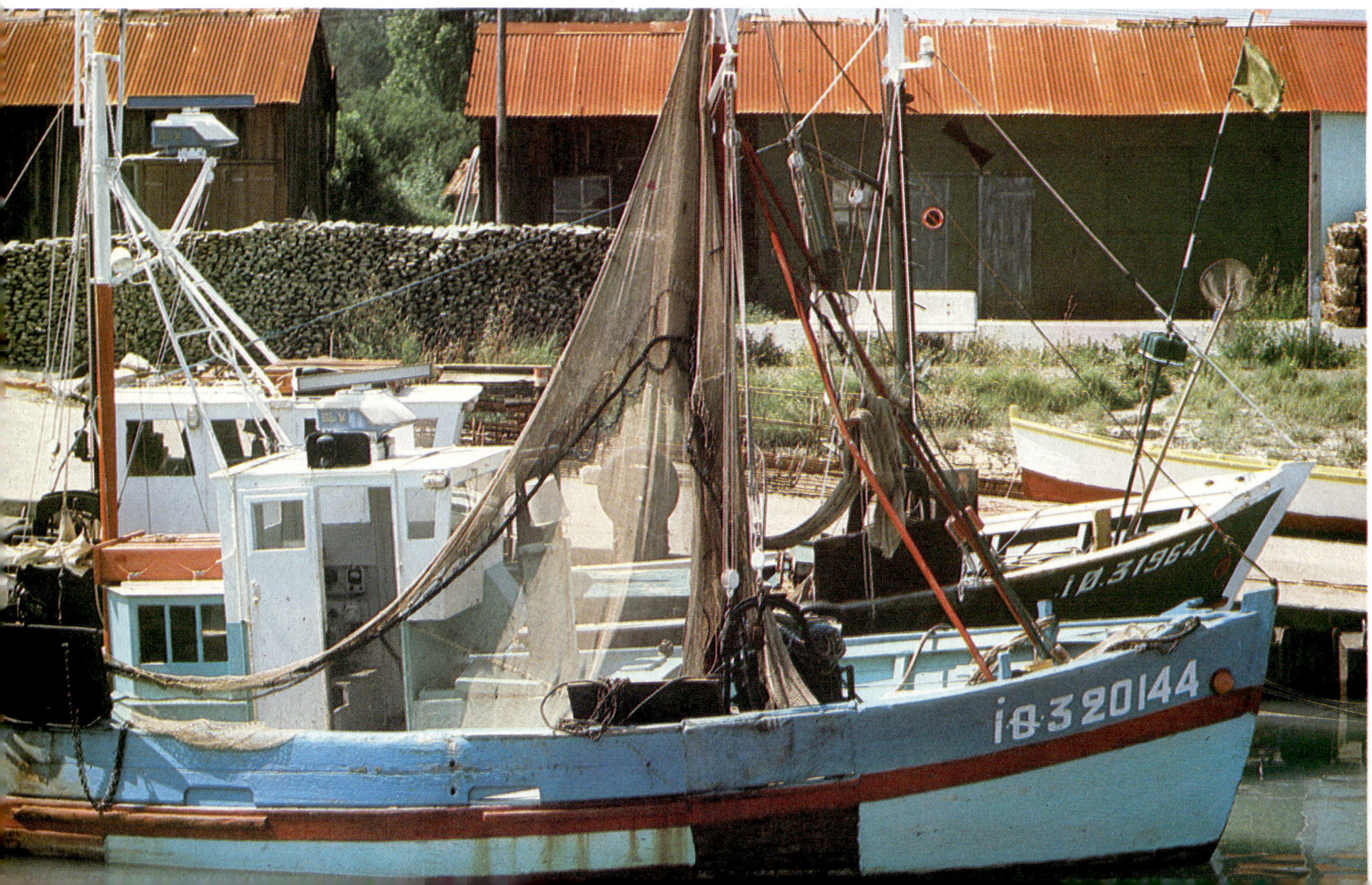

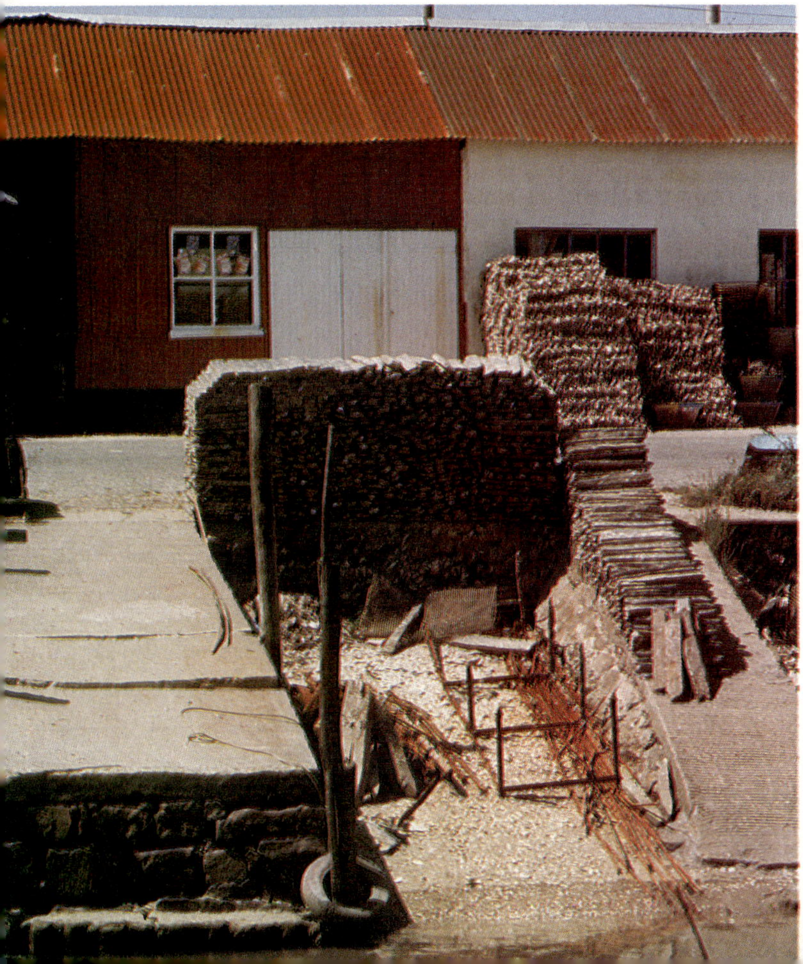

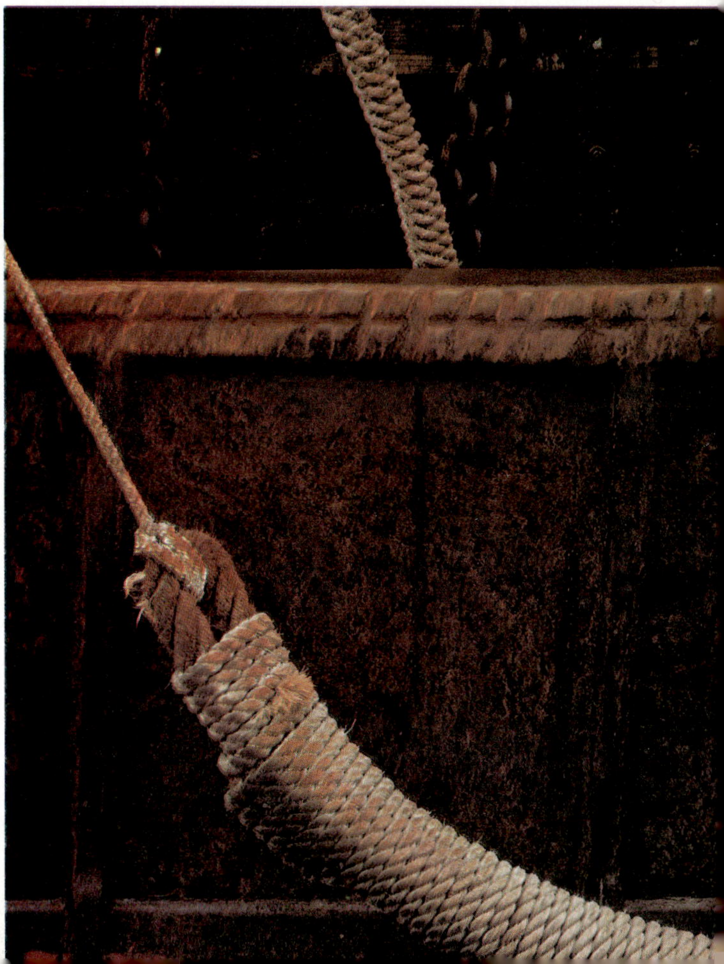

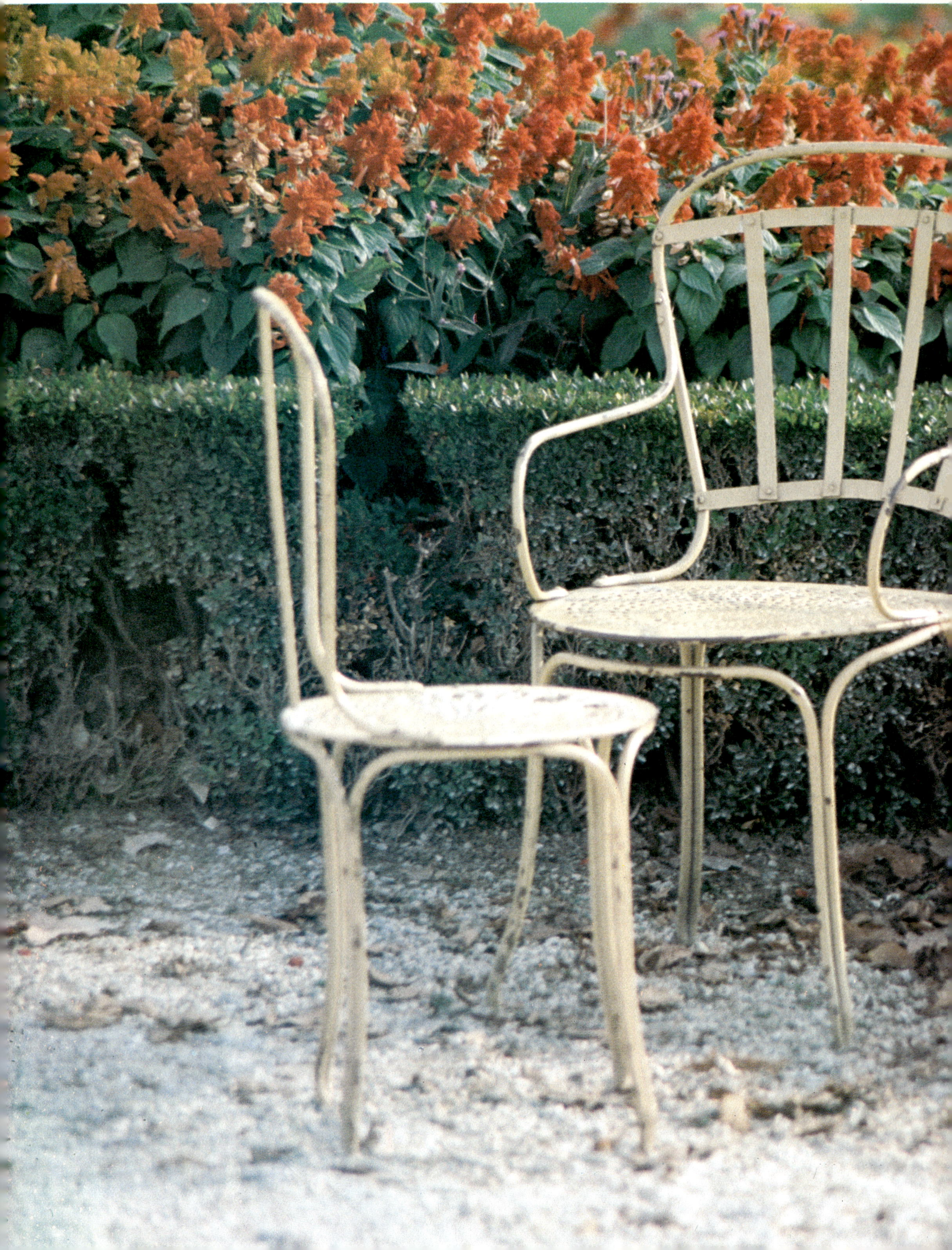

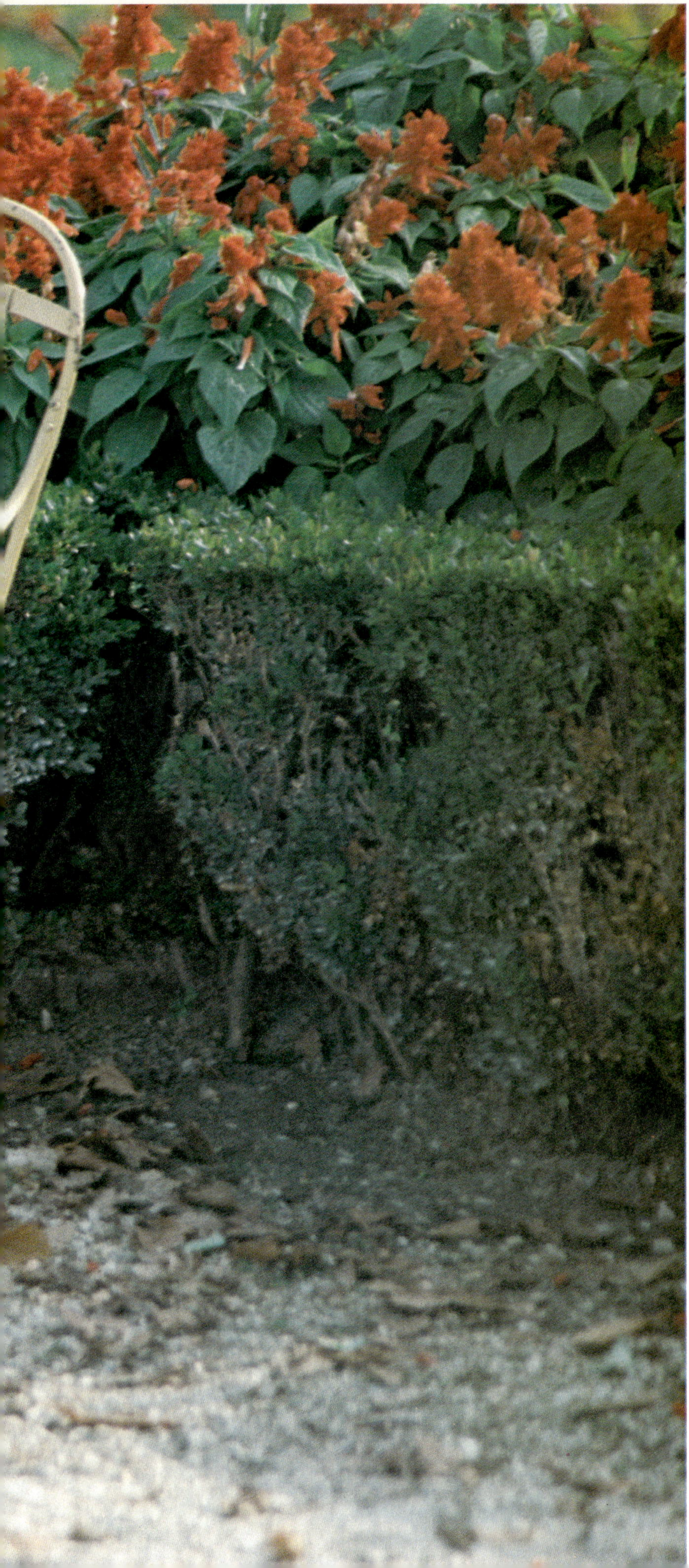

SEEING LIKE A CAMERA

How often do you consider with some dismay your latest set of photographs? It is a frequent reaction. Somehow the scenes pictured do not look quite like the scenes as you remember them. Is this the result of using an inadequate camera or just that your memory was perhaps a little rose coloured? The truth is that your eyes are automatically guided to the most interesting aspect of each scene, filtering out the unwanted and distracting elements. Unfortunately a camera is not like that: it sees and records exactly what is there. The essence of good photography is to train your eyes to see like a camera and then understand how to guide and control the camera in order to record what you want to see. A very good measure of your photographic skills is the frequency with which you are able to produce a picture which accurately records the impression you wished to convey at the time it was taken. This is much more simple than it sounds. There are no special or difficult skills to acquire in taking good pictures. All you need is to be observant, to see clearly and objectively the things you want to photograph and to learn the basic commonsense methods of aiming and controlling the camera.

The camera viewfinder is the photographer's frame. It is entirely under his control. What he chooses to include and what is left out is the single most important decision that a photographer makes when shooting a picture. A great deal can be learned about taking good photographs simply by looking through the viewfinder and watching what happens when the angle and position of the camera are altered. Soon the photographer will be able to identify the most important elements of a picture and see which aspects of the surrounding scene or the background will create a distraction, and then aim the camera so that its viewfinder contains only the objects he wishes to be included.

'A photographer's eye' is an expression used to describe this way of seeing things, and an experienced photographer will see in this way without the aid of a camera by learning to apply to his eyesight the same restrictions and objectivity that the camera imposes on a scene. Once you have taught yourself to see like this everything else will fall into place. Whether you have a simple cartridge-loading camera or an elaborate single lens reflex the process of taking good pictures will become infinitely more simple and the technical aspects of photography will be much easier to understand and control.

Exploring the subject

If you were to ask ten photographers each to take one picture of the same subject you would be surprised at the vast differences that would be seen between the resulting photographs. The most basic subject can be seen and photographed in many different ways. Don't be content to take a picture from the spot where you happen to be without even considering the other possibilities that the subject may offer. One of the real pleasures of photography is in exploring the many possibilities of the subject.

With most subjects the camera's position is the only adjustable factor, and this can have a dramatic effect on the quality of the picture. Resist the temptation to take the photograph straight away. Walk around the subject a little, see how it looks from six paces to the left or a dozen to the right, even try looking at it from the opposite side or with the camera held near the ground. It isn't even necessary to make exposures, but you can learn a great deal by seeing how much the picture can be changed, and more than likely improved, by careful exploration. Often by doing this you become more aware of the reasons you have for wanting to take the picture in the first place and this is an important step in improving the quality of your photographs. Many photographers, even experienced ones, see a subject that inspires them without initially being fully aware of what it is in particular that has prompted their reaction. Quite often you will find you want to take several pictures, not just one. When you try to include too many elements in your picture the resulting image can be disappointingly confused.

It is important to look for the changing relationships between the elements in your viewfinder when moving the camera to left and right or higher and lower, and also the effect on perspective – the change in the apparent size of objects as you move further away or closer towards them. If you find a scene which contains a foreground subject with some other elements in the middle distance – a girl, a tree and a distant hill for instance – you can see how the picture changes by moving the camera around.

As you move closer to the girl she will become much larger in proportion to the tree and the far hill, and as you move further back she will become smaller in relation to them. When you move the camera to the right the tree will also move further to the right of the girl, and vice versa. It can easily be seen that relatively small changes in the camera position can produce changes larger in the composition of the picture. In addition to the changes which it can bring about in the relative positions of the picture's components, the camera viewpoint can alter the effect of lighting, especially on a sunny day when there are bright highlights and strong shadows.

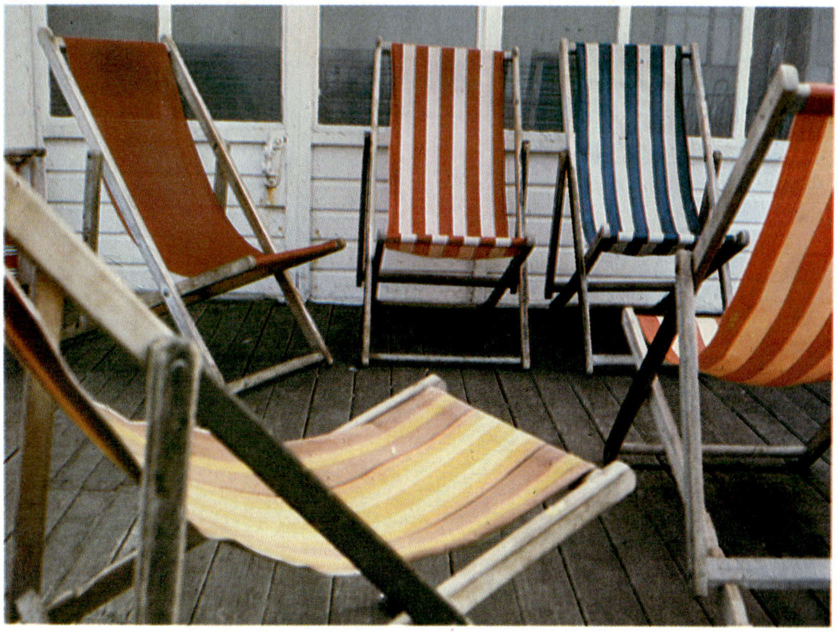

Above: Even something as simple as a group of deck-chairs shows how, by moving the camera from one side to another, higher and lower, further away and closer, the composition and effect of a picture can be greatly changed. None of these photographs required a movement of more than a few feet. The same lens and exposure were used for each of them; the only thing that changed was the camera viewpoint.

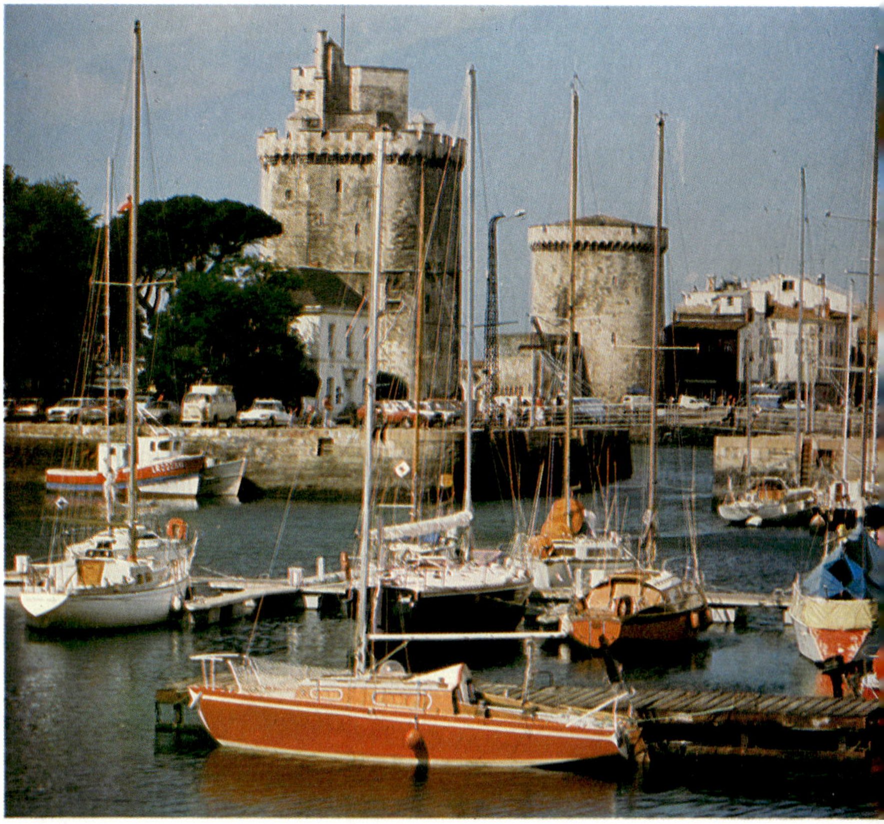

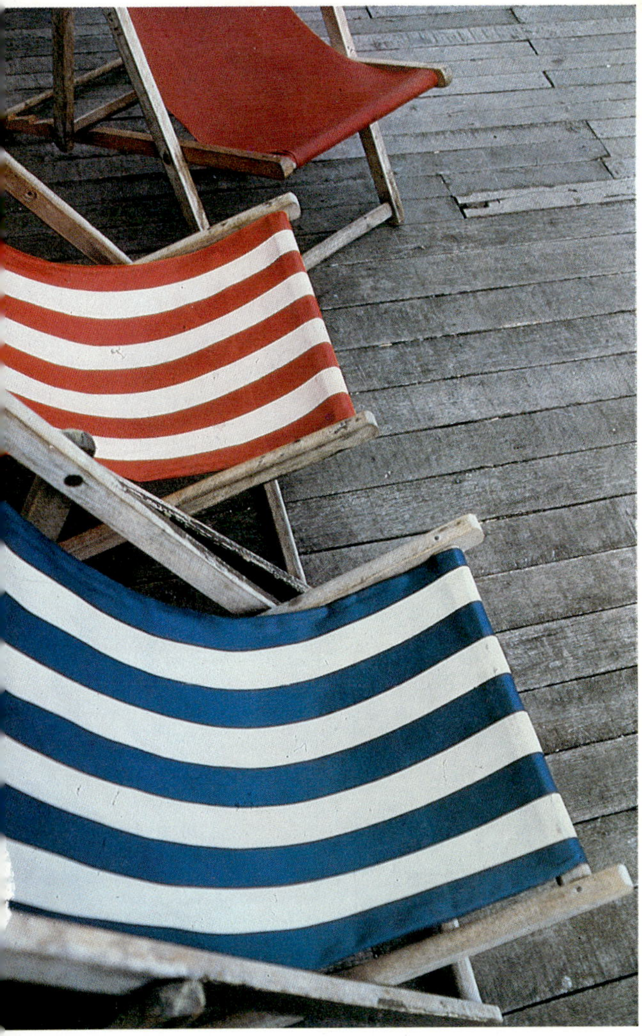

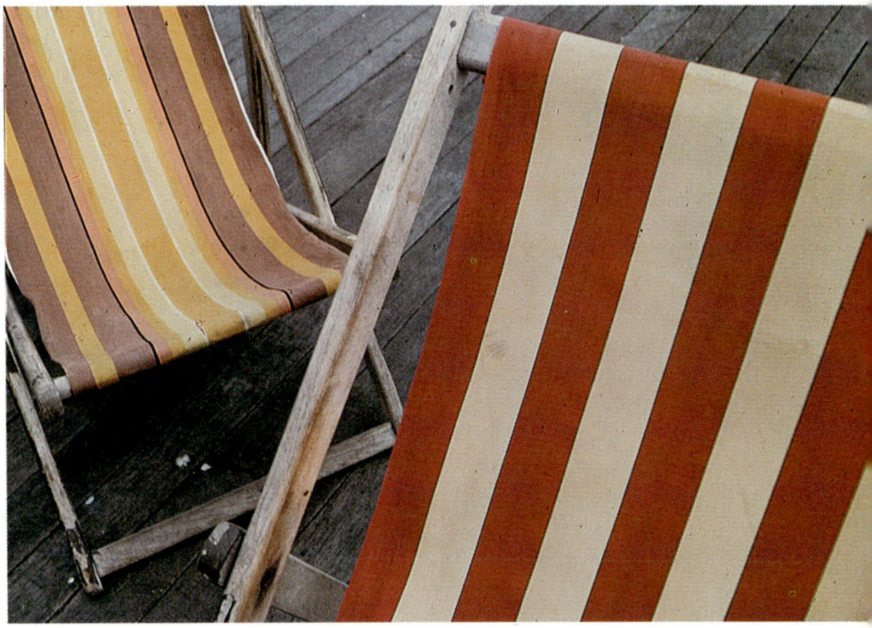

Below: Two views of La Rochelle demonstrate how, by walking a couple of hundred yards, pictures that are quite different in composition and colour quality can be produced. Although they were taken within a few minutes of each other, using the same lens, you could be forgiven for not realizing that they show the same place.

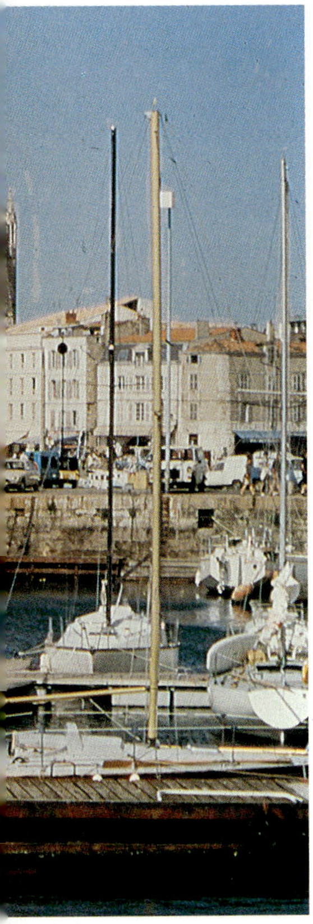

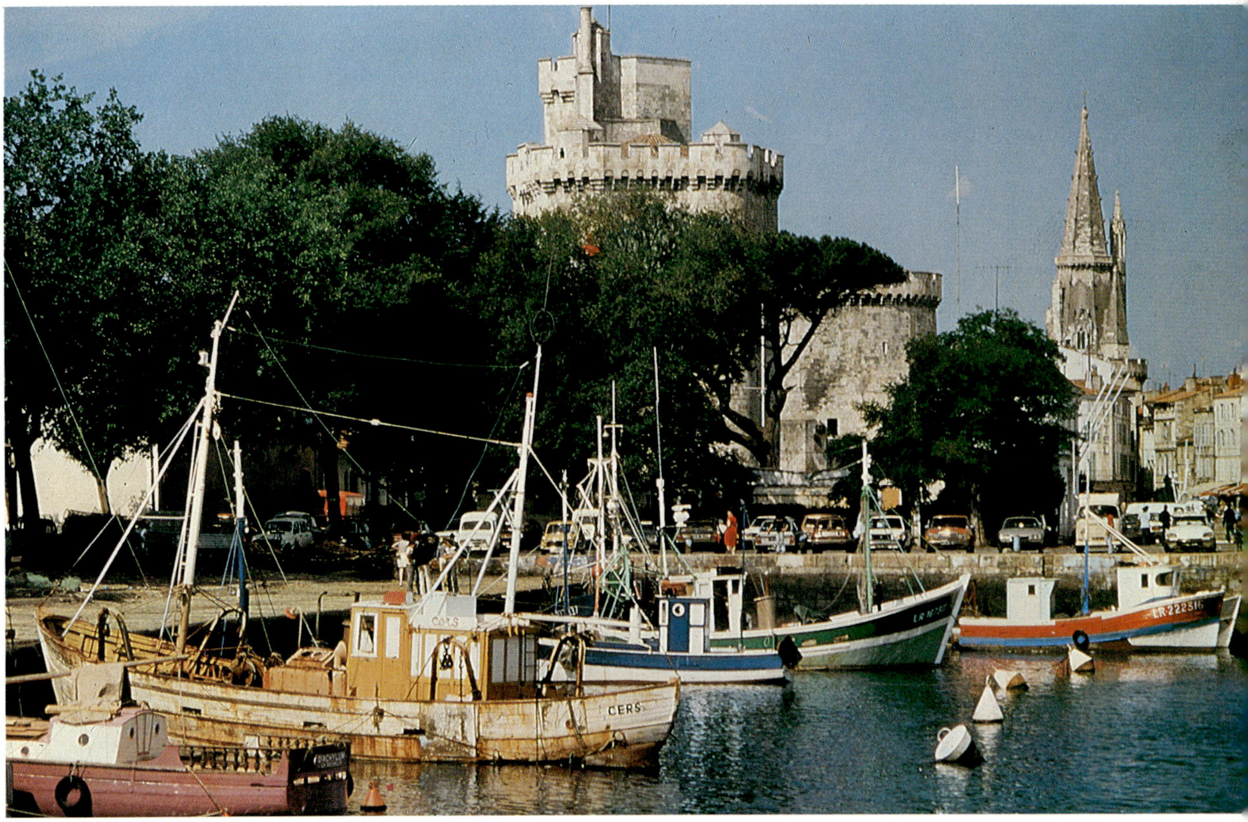

Framing the picture

Most successful photographs have one single predominant centre of interest. It may be as obvious as an individual face or something quite subtle like a particular tree in a landscape picture. Usually there is one significant element to which everything else in the frame plays a supporting role and to which the viewer's eye is naturally drawn. It is the way in which this centre of interest is placed within the frame of the picture and the way other aspects of the scene relate to it that largely determine the effect of a photograph.

Many unsuccessful pictures are the result of failure to isolate the subject and frame the picture correctly. Sometimes the centre of interest is not easily recognizable because there is more than one and the viewer's attention is divided and confused. Often the other elements in the picture compete for attention rather than help to accentuate the main point of interest. The way in which the picture is framed is the first and most important way of achieving the desired emphasis. Perhaps the most obvious way of making sure that something is the main centre of interest is to frame the picture so tightly that almost everything else is excluded and the main subject *is* the picture. It is certainly true that close-up and tightly framed pictures do have an immediate impact and it is also true that many poor pictures are a result of the camera not being close enough to the subject. But there are many occasions when it is possible to create more interest and impact in a photograph by including other details, providing it is done in such a way that they enhance the main subject and contribute to the mood and effect of the picture.

The decision as to how the picture should be framed and where within the frame the subject should be placed is the essence of composition. Framing the picture in such a way that the subject is placed in the centre is rarely the best solution. A picture which has the main point of interest in the centre is often static and too symmetrical for a natural effect. The picture will be enhanced if the subject is positioned rather to one side and a little above or below the exact centre of the picture. In a landscape, for example, it is preferable for the horizon line to be placed approximately one third of the distance from the top or bottom of the frame rather than

The single tree is the predominant element in this landscape picture, partly because it is silhouetted against the skyline but mainly because it has been positioned at the strongest point in the frame, rather than in the centre. The simple colour scheme also helps to emphasize the tree.

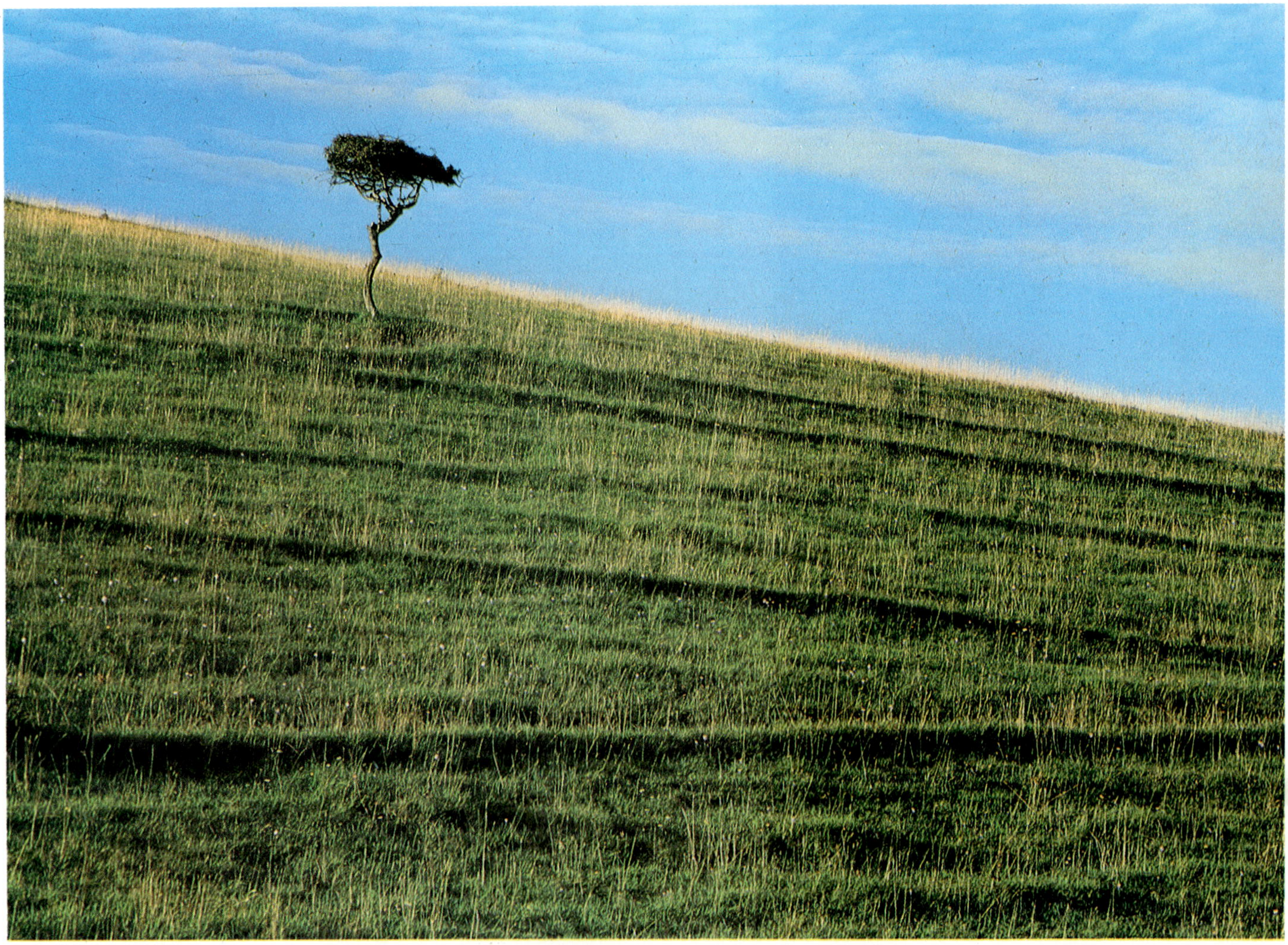

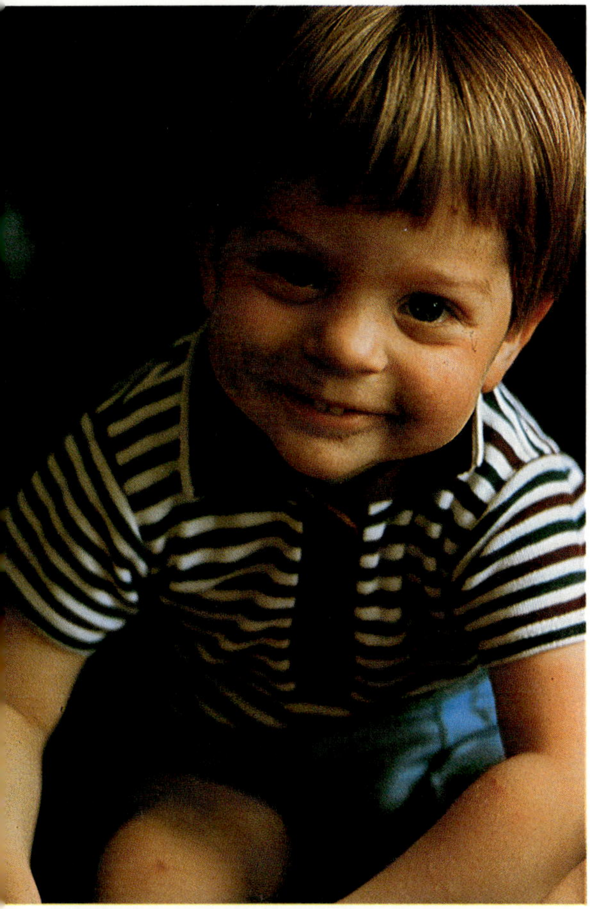

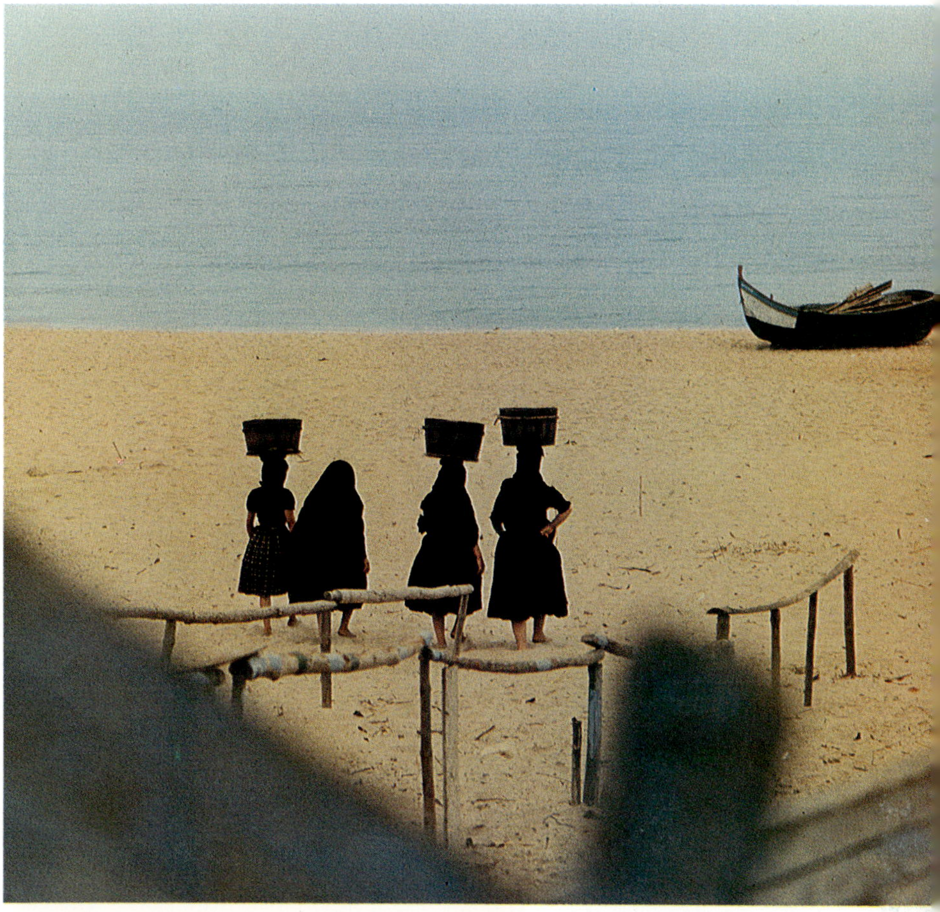

through the middle. As with all rules there are exceptions and sometimes a picture will benefit from being given a more symmetrical treatment, but the most important thing is that it should be done in a considered way. Once you begin to think about the arrangement of your picture it is quite surprising how quickly you will develop a good sense of composition.

Even when the subject occupies only a small part of the overall picture it is still possible for it to have as much impact as in a close-up, provided it is in some way slightly isolated or separated from the rest of the image. This can be achieved in a number of ways. The most basic method is by contrast: a dark-toned subject – a man in a black suit for instance – will immediately attract attention if the surroundings are of a predominantly light tone, even if he is quite small in the picture; and, of course, in colour the same effect can be achieved by using contrasting colours. This contrast can also be achieved by lighting. If, for example, your subject is in bright sunlight, you can manoeuvre your camera so that an area of background shadow is positioned directly behind it. In addition, it is often possible to focus sharply on the main point of interest and allow the background to remain out of focus; this can be particularly effective when you need to come closer in to a subject. Whatever method is chosen it is important that before the exposure is made you simply ask yourself – is my subject in the best position in the frame and does it stand out well from its surroundings?

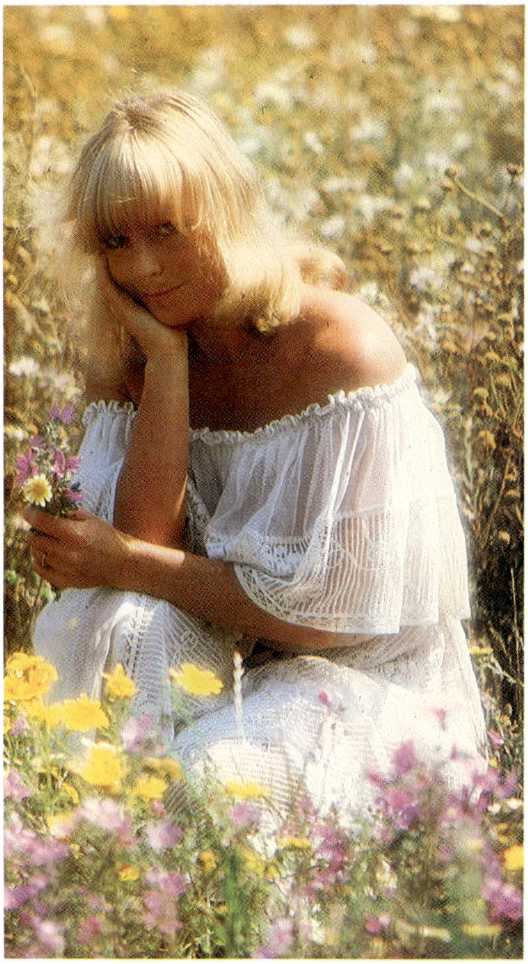

Above left: A very tightly framed portrait of a child, concentrating on his face, has ensured that no distracting elements are included.

Above right: The four ladies are the most prominent focal point, boldly silhouetted against the pale background. The out-of-focus foreground and a single boat add further interest to the picture.

The girl has been separated from what could have been a confusing and distracting background by shooting it out of focus and using a wide aperture and a long-focus lens.

Light and the subject

Below left: The soft light created by shooting in open shade has drawn out the bright colours on which this picture depends. Bright sunlight and strong shadows would have dulled this effect, bleaching the colours.

Below right: Shooting into the light shows the child partially in silhouette, emphasizing the shape of his body and isolating him from the background.

Light is vital to photography for a great many reasons other than that of simply providing the image on the film.

When you are choosing a film or calculating an exposure it is the quantity of light – its brightness – that is important. But the effect of a picture and its mood are dependent on the *quality* of the lighting. It is very important therefore to be aware of, and to understand, the changing relationship between the light and your subject. To most photographers light means daylight and even studio photographers base most of their techniques on the qualities of daylight. If you understand daylight, you can then apply that knowledge to any other type of lighting. In the early days of photography bright, unobscured sunlight was a virtual necessity for many pictures, not because of its quality, but simply because the first films and cameras needed bright light to provide enough exposure. Modern films and cameras make it possible to take pictures in almost any light that is bright enough to see by, and photographers today can afford to be as much concerned with the way it affects their subject as with how it affects the film.

Bright sunlight can still be an effective way of lighting a picture but it does have drawbacks: it creates bright highlights and dense shadows which are difficult to record satisfactorily on film. The bright highlights can easily become bleached out and the shadows can become black voids with no detail. A good way of shooting in sunlight is to ensure, by moving either your camera or the subject, that the picture is composed primarily of highlight or shadow and expose accordingly. A scene which is mostly in shadow, for instance, given the correct exposure, will provide a far more pleasing picture than one where there is an equal mixture of light and dark tones – neither of which is likely to be exposed correctly. A method of shooting in bright sunlight which can be effective with some subjects is to photograph towards the light so that it is behind the subject. As far as the camera is concerned your subject is now in the shade, so it is important to give extra exposure. Two stops extra is usually enough and if you have a simple camera you can use the 'cloud' setting. It is also important to ensure that the camera lens is shielded from the direct light of the sun – a lens hood can help with this – as otherwise 'flare' will be caused, where reflections inside the camera lens form a pale, weak image on the print.

Bright sunlight can be very effective when taking landscape pictures, particularly early or late in the day when the shadows are longer. The shadows provide bold textures in fields and woods, giving the picture extra bite and more detail. But often sunlight is softened by the presence of a little cloud or haze so that the

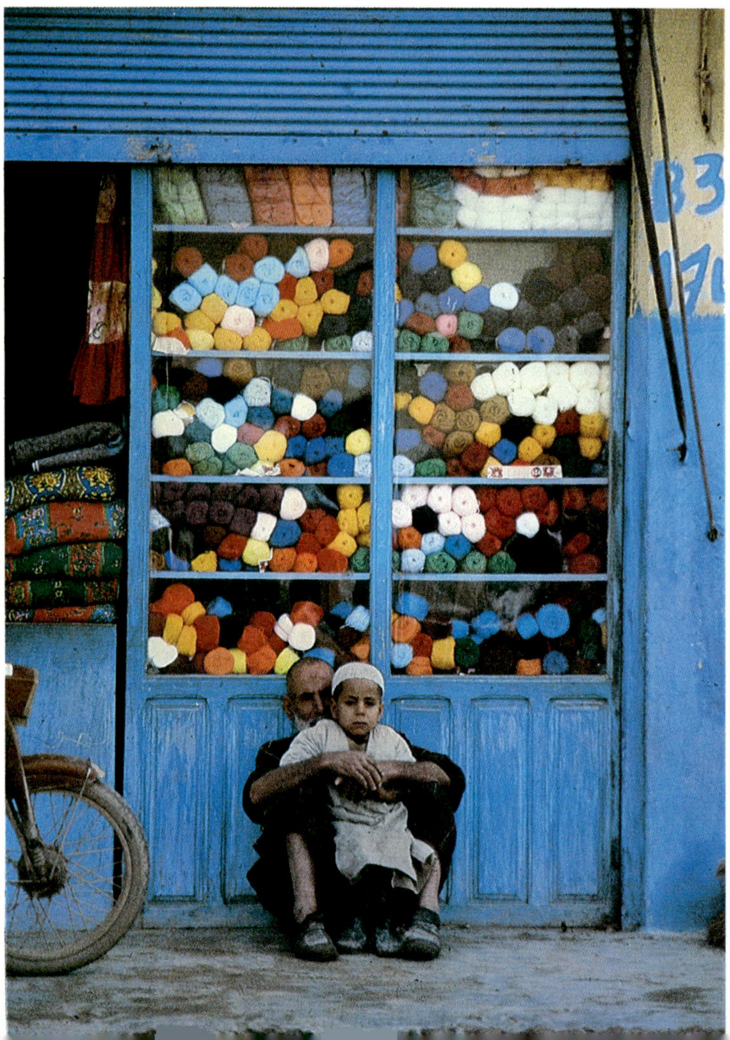

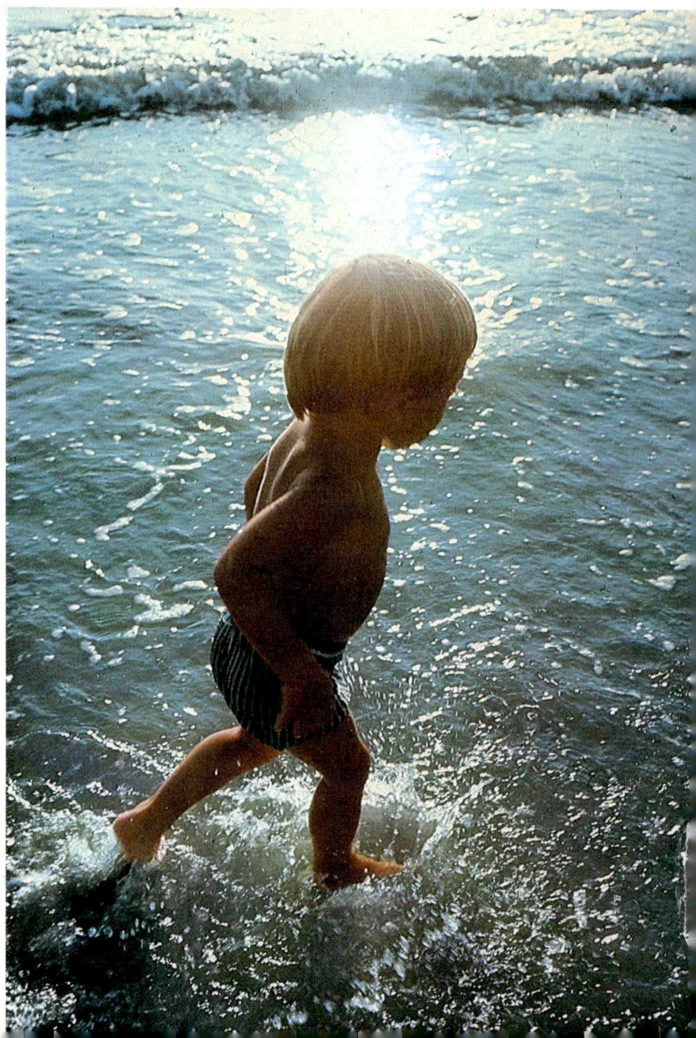

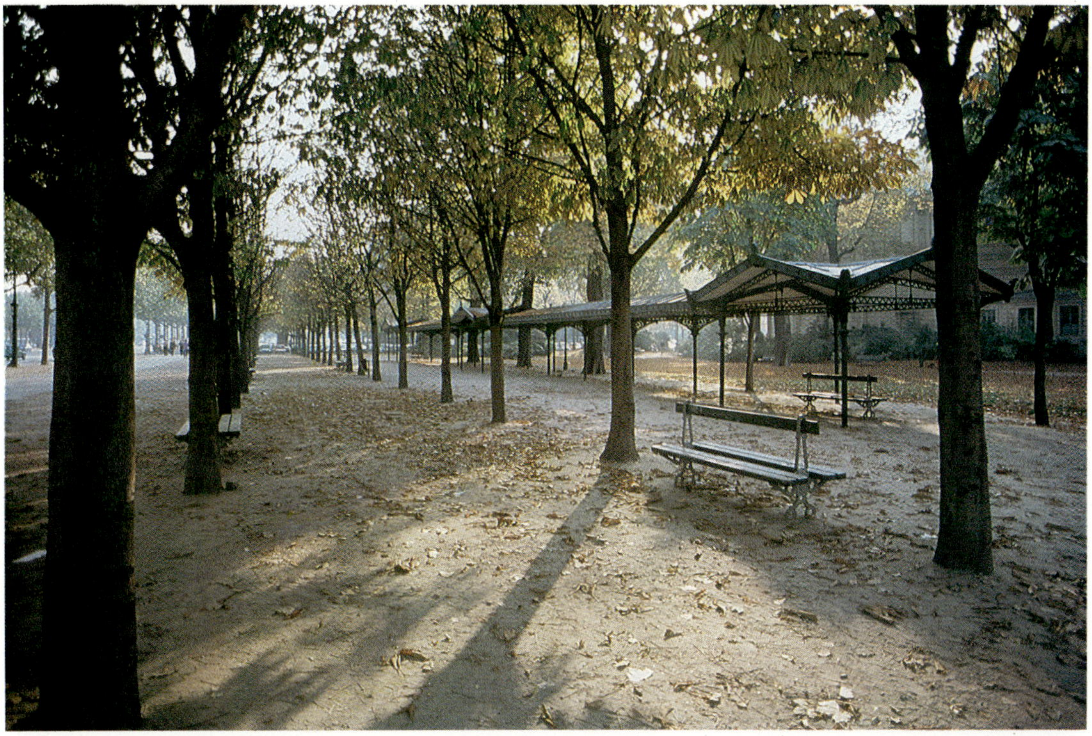

Photographed early in the day, autumn sunlight filtering through the trees and producing long shadows has given a mellow quality to this picture, establishing its mood.

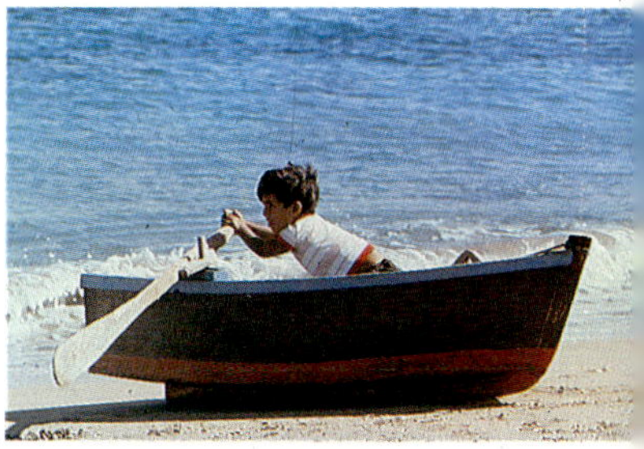

Above: Harsh midday sunlight has been softened by the reflective quality of sand. An 81A filter (see p. 34) prevented the problem of a blue cast which can occur in these conditions.

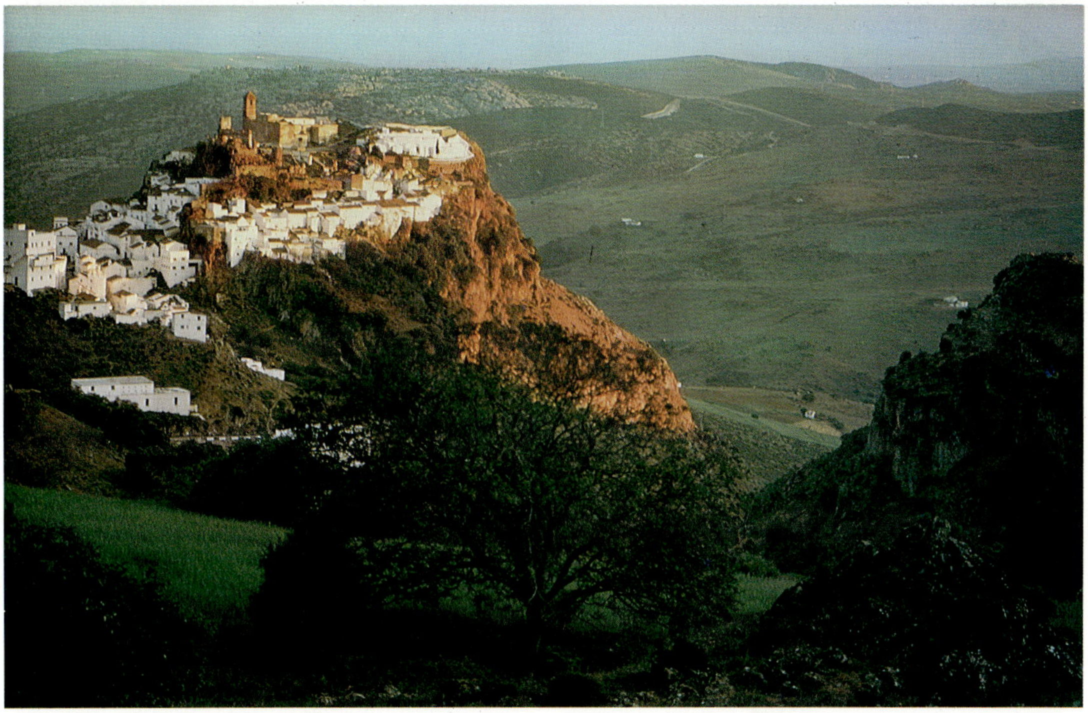

Left: Evening sunlight has created deep shadows and bright highlights on this Spanish hilltop village. The warm cast of the light has added colour to the red rock, drawing it out from the surrounding landscape.

shadows are less dense and have a softer edge. Also light-toned surroundings such as a sandy beach or a white wall reflect light back into the shadows, breaking up the density, and this can be far more pleasing, especially when photographing people.

When taking colour pictures it is important to realize that the colour of daylight can vary considerably. Daylight colour film is manufactured to give 'correct' colour results when the sun is high in the sky, and early morning or late afternoon light will produce a much warmer, more yellow quality. This can be quite attractive in most pictures, but if it is too strong – as when shooting a portrait, where the skin would look sallow – a slightly bluish filter will tone it down a little.

A cloudy day can produce a result which is a little colder, or bluer, than normal and in this case it may be preferable to use a slightly yellowish filter to add a little warmth to the picture. Skin tones in particular can look less attractive when a blue cast is present and it is better to use a filter if in doubt. Even on a clear sunny day it is possible to produce a blue cast if your subject is in the shade, as light is being reflected by the blue sky.

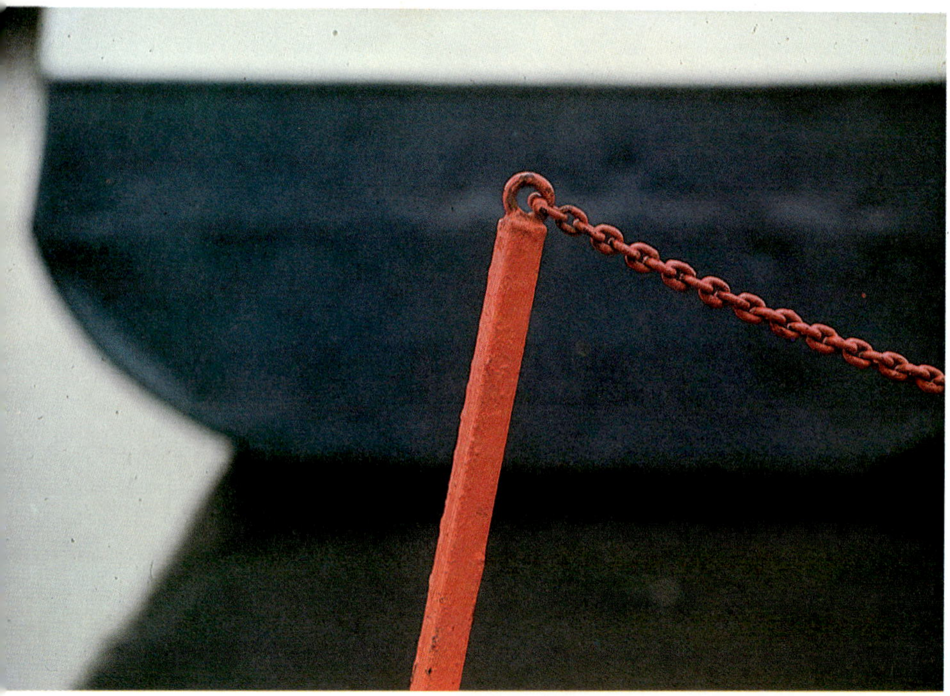

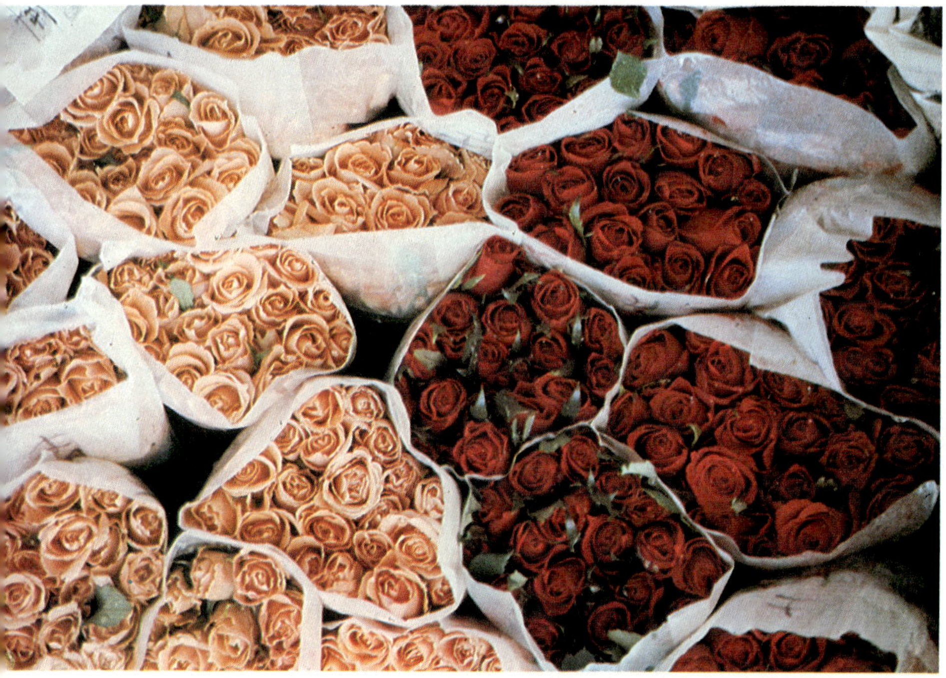

Top: A bold colour contrast produced by a bright red chain against a blue boat.

Above: Careful framing, excluding other colours, makes a harmonious composition of these pink and red roses.

Right: The monochromatic quality of this picture stresses the shape and texture of a weatherworn boat.

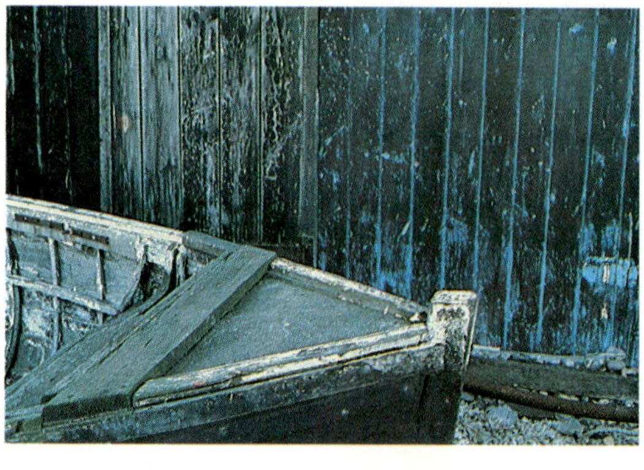

Most photographers are inspired by a colourful scene in which there is a kaleidoscopic range of different hues. But just as it is a mistake to respond too quickly and not think carefully about the subject and the composition, it can be even more disappointing if you do not give equal consideration to the colours in your picture. Too many colours scattered indiscriminately throughout your picture will result in a confusing and haphazard image even if you have arranged the subject itself carefully. A picture which has a simple and thoughtfully composed colour scheme will always be more pleasing and effective than a multi-coloured jumble.

There are two basic methods of using colour effectively in a photograph. One way is to ensure that there is a single predominant colour which contrasts quite boldly with its surroundings, and the other is to frame the picture in such a way that each of the colours present harmonizes with the others to give an even and unified overall quality. Using a single contrasting colour is a method which usually produces a picture of more immediate impact, while the harmonizing of colours gives a quieter, more mellow effect.

In colour photography it is easiest to consider the colours in terms of their primary and secondary roles. The primary colours are red, green and blue and each of these has a secondary colour which is in direct contrast with it. Opposite red is bluish-green which is called cyan, opposite green is a bluish-red called magenta, while the direct contrast to blue is yellow. In practice a contrast exists between any two colours that are fairly wide apart on the colour spectrum which, like a rainbow, ranges from red through orange and yellow to green then blue and finally indigo and violet. Red, therefore, will form a strong contrast with green and blue and the strength of the contrast will depend on the depth of the colours. Full-bodied, saturated colours will provide a more powerful contrast than pastel hues. In addition any colour will form an effective contrast with a neutral tone such as black, grey or even white. Because the effect of the single, contrasting colour is so strong its effect in terms of composition must be carefully judged. In normal circumstances the main point of interest of a scene should also be the colour which will attract the strongest attention. It is important, too, to avoid having these contrasting colours in the background of the picture as they will appear as a fussy and distracting detail, leading the eye away from the main subject.

With most subjects, the only control the photographer has over the colours is by careful framing and selection of the picture area. With a portrait it is possible to ask your model to wear clothes of a particular colour and to position them against a background of the colour you require; but with other types of picture the colours must be controlled by the careful choice of camera viewpoint and by excluding unwanted colours from the surrounding area.

Creating a picture with harmonizing colours requires almost the opposite technique. The effect of colour harmony occurs when all the colours in the picture are from a similar area of the spectrum. For example, the autumn colours in a woodland scene – orange, yellow and brown – will automatically harmonize with each other, as will the green fields and blue skies of a summer landscape. Even colours which are not so close together will tend to harmonize providing the change from one hue to another is gradual.

Also colours that are *not* fully saturated – pastel or darker tones – will tend to harmonize more easily. A harmonized colour scheme works well with subjects that have a bold composition with well defined shapes and possibly strong shadows, where the presence of bright, contrasting colours would add an additional and possibly confusing element.

In general terms a good colour photograph should aim to have immediately identifiable colour quality whether it be a subtle blend of harmonizing hues or a single bold, contrasting colour.

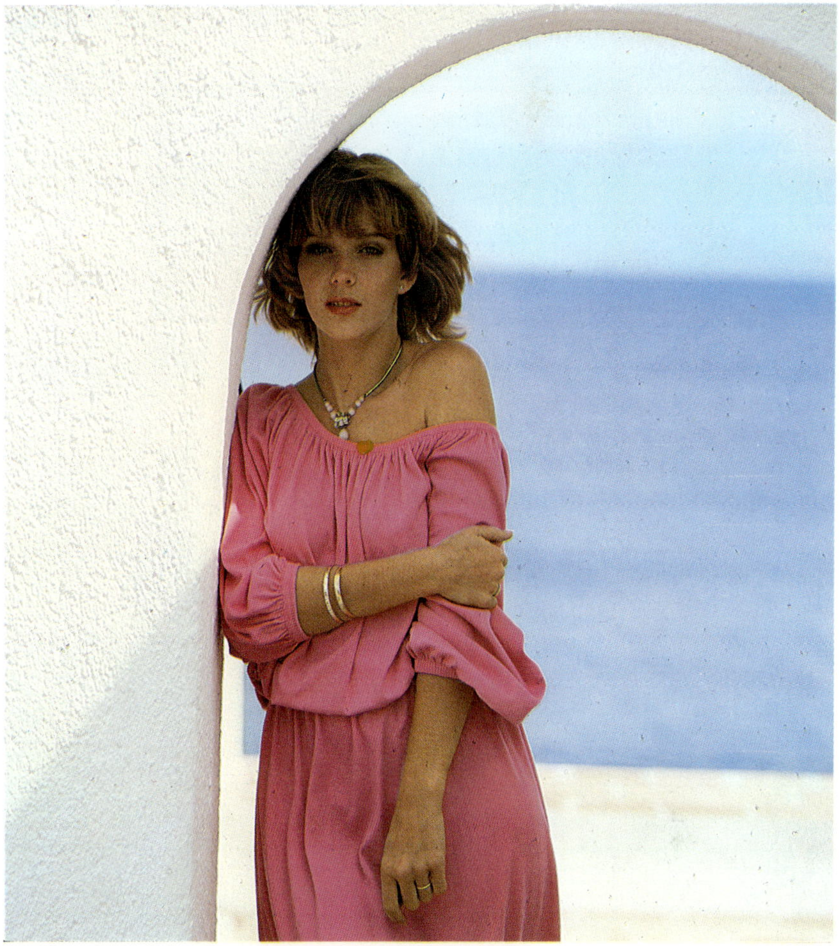

Above: The girl's bright pink dress was deliberately chosen to create a bold colour contrast with the white and blue background.

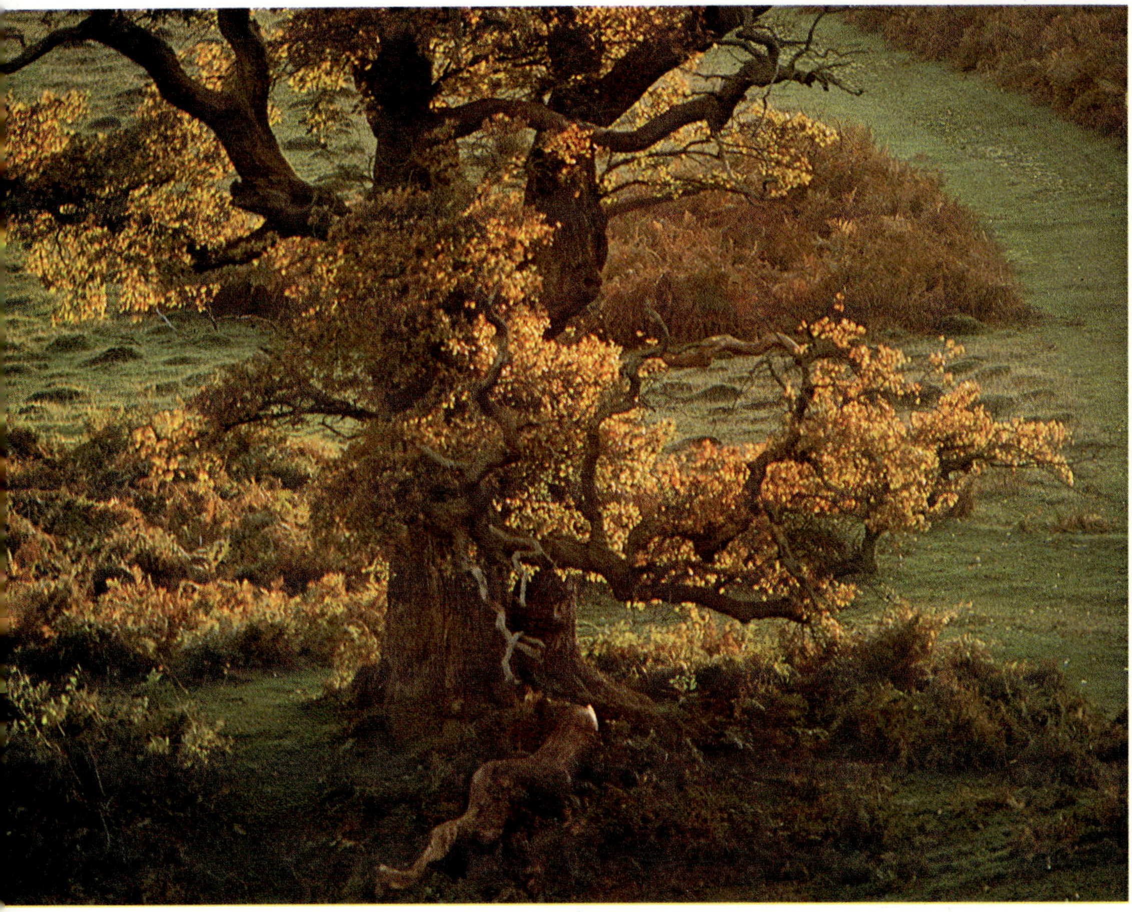

Although backlighting has produced quite strong contrasts in this autumn scene, the natural harmony of the green, yellow and brown has prevented the picture from becoming confusing.

The pictorial elements

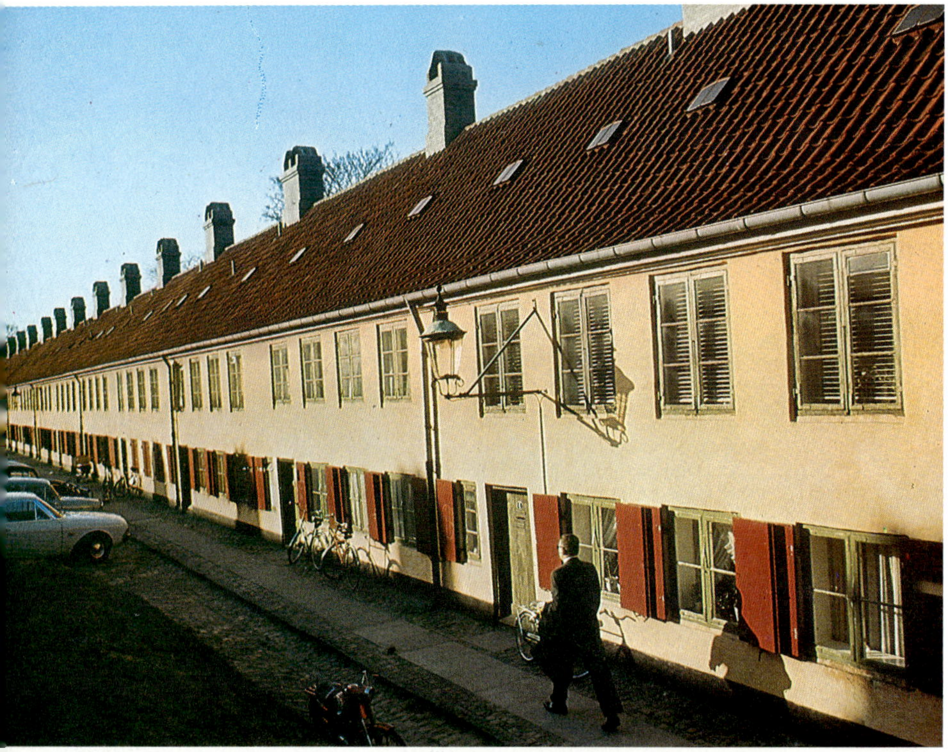

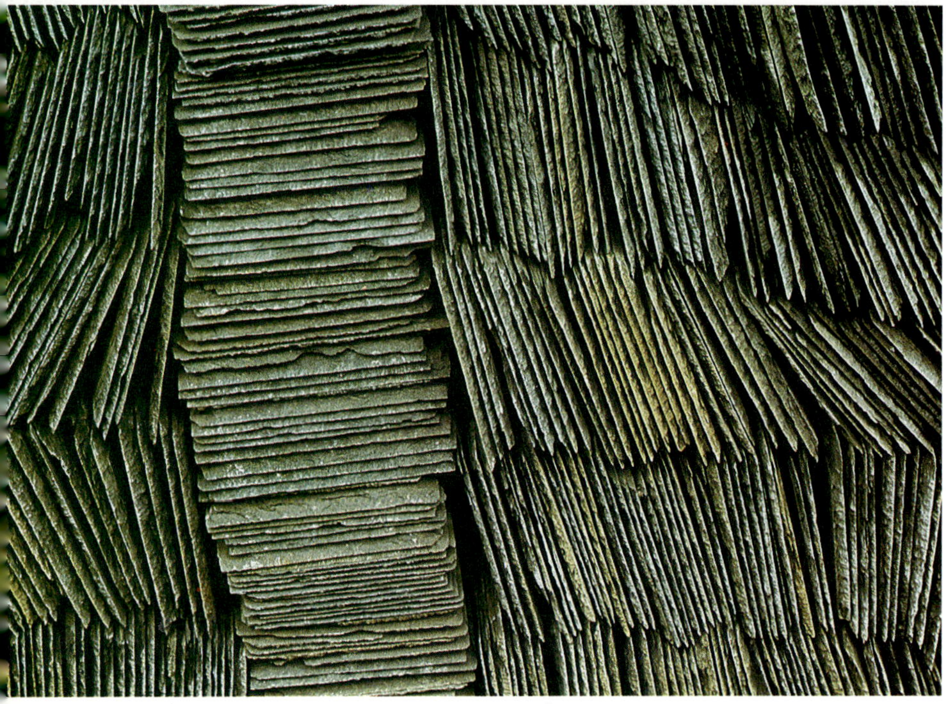

Top: Camera viewpoint and a wide-angle lens accentuate strong lines of perspective.

Above: By careful framing and composition a natural pattern has been achieved, underlined by the monochromatic quality of the tiles.

Photography is in fact a grand illusion. When it is skilfully applied an impression of reality can be created on a flat piece of paper or film – a phenomenon nowadays taken for granted. It does this by providing the viewer of the picture with a variety of visual reminders of what the real scene was like. A feeling of solidity and depth can be achieved by lighting which provides a subtle range of tones on a solid object.

Texture is another important element to consider when creating an illusion of reality. The photographic process can record such fine detail that photographic reproductions of textures are often used in manufacturing processes as substitutes for the real thing – such as printed laminates that simulate wood.

The illusion of depth and distance can also give an effective three-dimensional quality to a two-dimensional picture if the photographer uses or exaggerates the existing perspective. If you look along a row of houses, you will see that the farthest house appears to be only a fraction of the size of the nearest house.

Patterns can provide a powerful visual effect in a photograph, and the repetition of a number of similar shapes in a picture can be almost mesmerizing.

Another element of interest in a photograph is when the subject itself has a bold or interesting outline. This shape can be accentuated by ensuring that there is a bold tonal or colour contrast between the subject and the background; even a pure silhouette can be effective if the shape of the subject is sufficiently interesting and is used as part of the overall composition.

It is important to remember that while each of these pictorial elements can provide a strong additional quality to a picture, it is rarely that one alone will produce anything more than a superficial impact. They are of more value when used in conjunction with each other and as part of the picture rather than being the sole reason for it.

Being aware that onc or more of these elements exists in a potential photograph helps you to decide how best to approach the subject. For example, in a portrait of an old man with an interesting lined face, the texture of his skin might persuade you to photograph him from an angle where the lighting accentuates it; or, alternatively, a young child with a pleasing profile could make you want a picture where the shape of your subject's head can be seen clearly in a silhouette. When you are exploring the various ways in which your subject might be photographed, also consider the way in which any of these qualities may be accentuated to give extra impact in your picture. In a landscape shot it may be preferable to choose a camera position which allows you to include some foreground details in order to give a stronger impression of

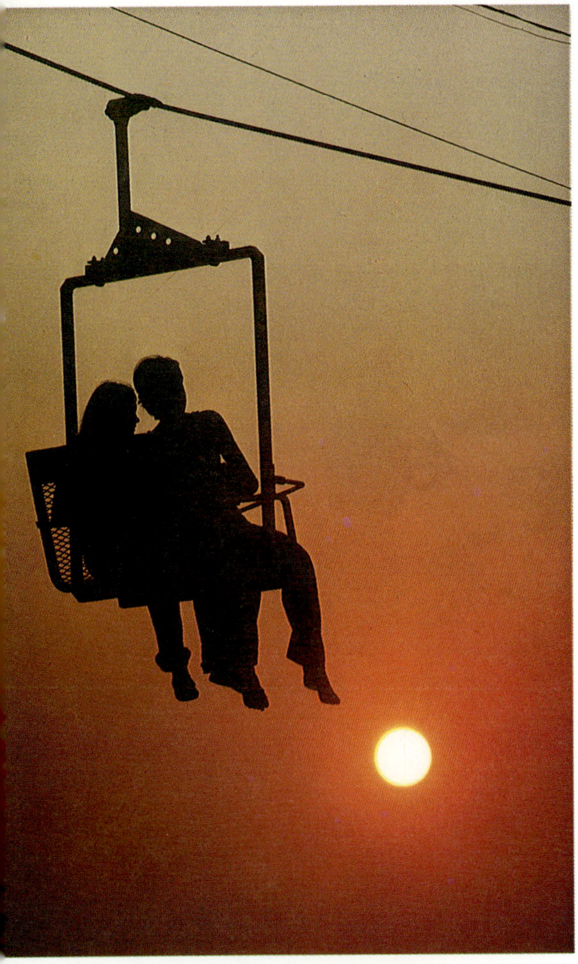

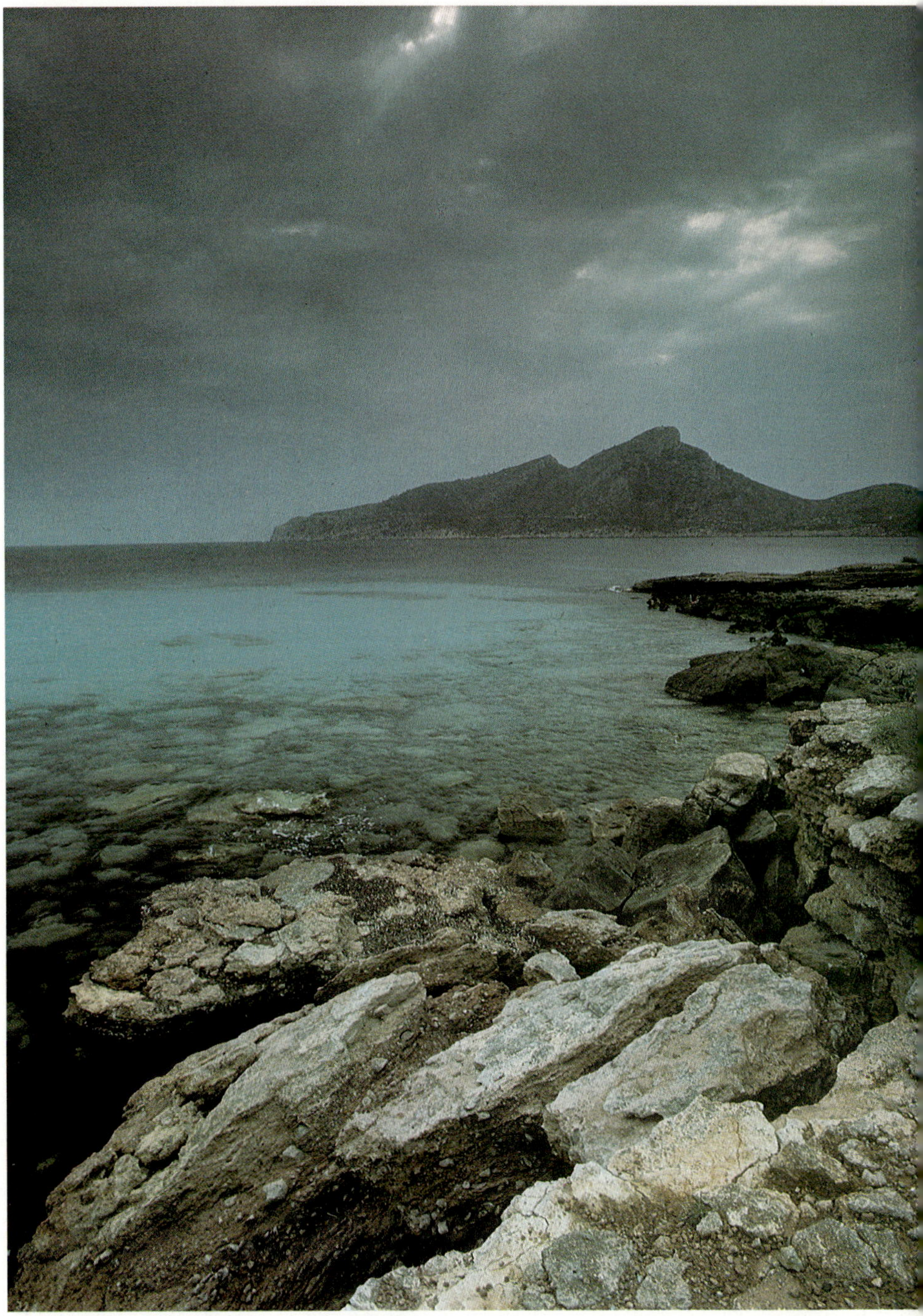

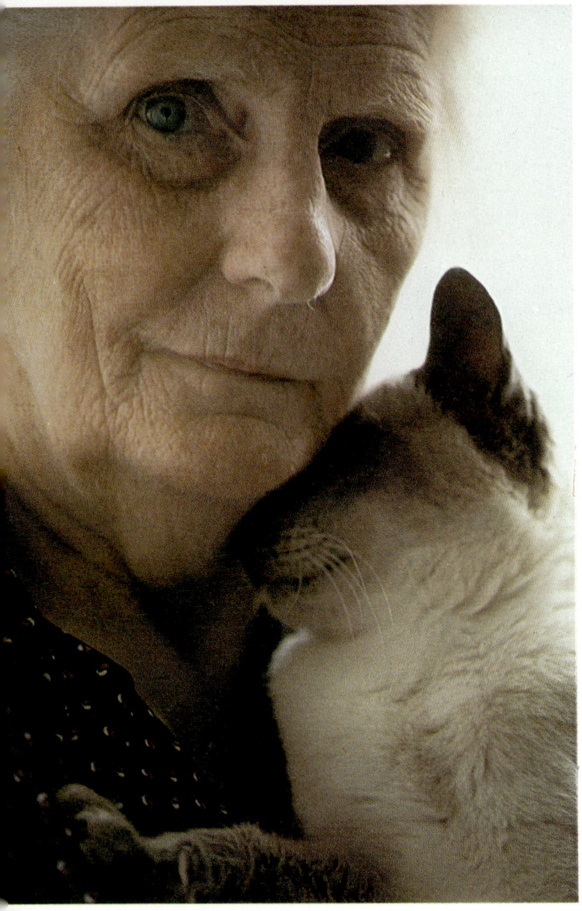

Above left: The shape of this couple, silhouetted in a chair-lift, has become the main point of interest in the picture, the sun contributing mood.

Above: The inclusion of close foreground details has produced an impression of depth in this seascape. A wide-angle lens has helped this effect.

Left: Strong side lighting has brought out the skin texture in this portrait of a lady with her cat.

both depth and distance to the picture.

It is very instructive to look at some good photographs in books or magazines and see which of these qualities has contributed to them. Try to work out what the photographer has done in order to make the most of them. It is even more useful to look specifically for pictures which feature each element and combine them in a pleasing composition. It may be easier to spend one afternoon looking for pattern pictures, another looking for shots showing texture, and so on. These pictorial elements are very much a part of the photographer's stock-in-trade, and it is vital to good photography to understand how to use them.

This diagram shows the function of a camera in its simplest form. The lens gathers the light rays reflected from the subject and projects them on to the film where it is seen inverted and reversed left to right. The lens has a focusing mount which enables it to produce a sharp image of the subject over a range of distances. It has a variable aperture to control the amount of light passing through it and a shutter to control the length of time the image is allowed to play on the film.

Cameras are often thought of as rather complex, even magical, contraptions and most people make little attempt to understand how they work. Indeed, modern cameras can be so highly automated and easy to operate that you don't need more than a basic knowledge. But a camera is a fairly simple instrument and, as with most tools, the more you understand how it works the easier it is to achieve the best results, to appreciate why things sometimes go wrong, and to know what to do about them next time.

No matter how expensive or complicated they may appear the camera functions are the same whatever type you use. The camera has a light-tight box with a place for the film at one end and a lens at the other. There is a variable opening to control the amount of light which passes through the lens, and a shutter which governs the length of time the light is allowed to play on the film. In all but the simplest cameras you can change the focus of the lens to create an equally sharp image of either close or distant objects. Finally, there is a viewfinder through which you look to aim the camera and frame the picture.

The lens governs the basic quality of the image. On an inexpensive, simple camera, such as a pocket cartridge-loading 110, the lens is usually made of plastic and permanently set at a focusing distance of around fifteen feet. A photograph taken from about seven feet to infinity will be recorded acceptably well on the film providing the picture is not enlarged too much. For instance, a 3 × 4 inch EN print will in most cases show adequate detail from a 110 size negative. 'Acceptable' is the operative word; the more critical you become and the larger you wish to make your prints, the more the inadequacies of a cheap lens will become apparent. For example, a medium-price, glass lens on a 35 mm camera which can be focused to a precise distance can easily produce prints to the larger sizes of 15 × 12 inches or 16 × 20 inches with fine detail sharply reproduced.

The aperture is simply a device which enables the size of the lens opening to be adjusted according to the brightness of the light. A simple camera may have only two settings – 'cloudy' and 'sunny' – but more advanced cameras have a number of settings marked in 'f' numbers, such as f2.8, f4, f5.6, f8 and so on. Whatever camera, lens or film you are using, these numbers are constant – f 8, for example, always passes the same amount of light. Each f number allows through twice as much light as the number above, and half as much as that below – f 8 passes half as much light as f 5.6 and twice as much as f 11. As the f number increases the size of the aperture decreases.

Shutter speeds are measured in seconds and fractions of a second. On the camera, 1/125 of a second, for example, is usually shown as 125. On a simple camera, the shutter is often limited to

The basic camera

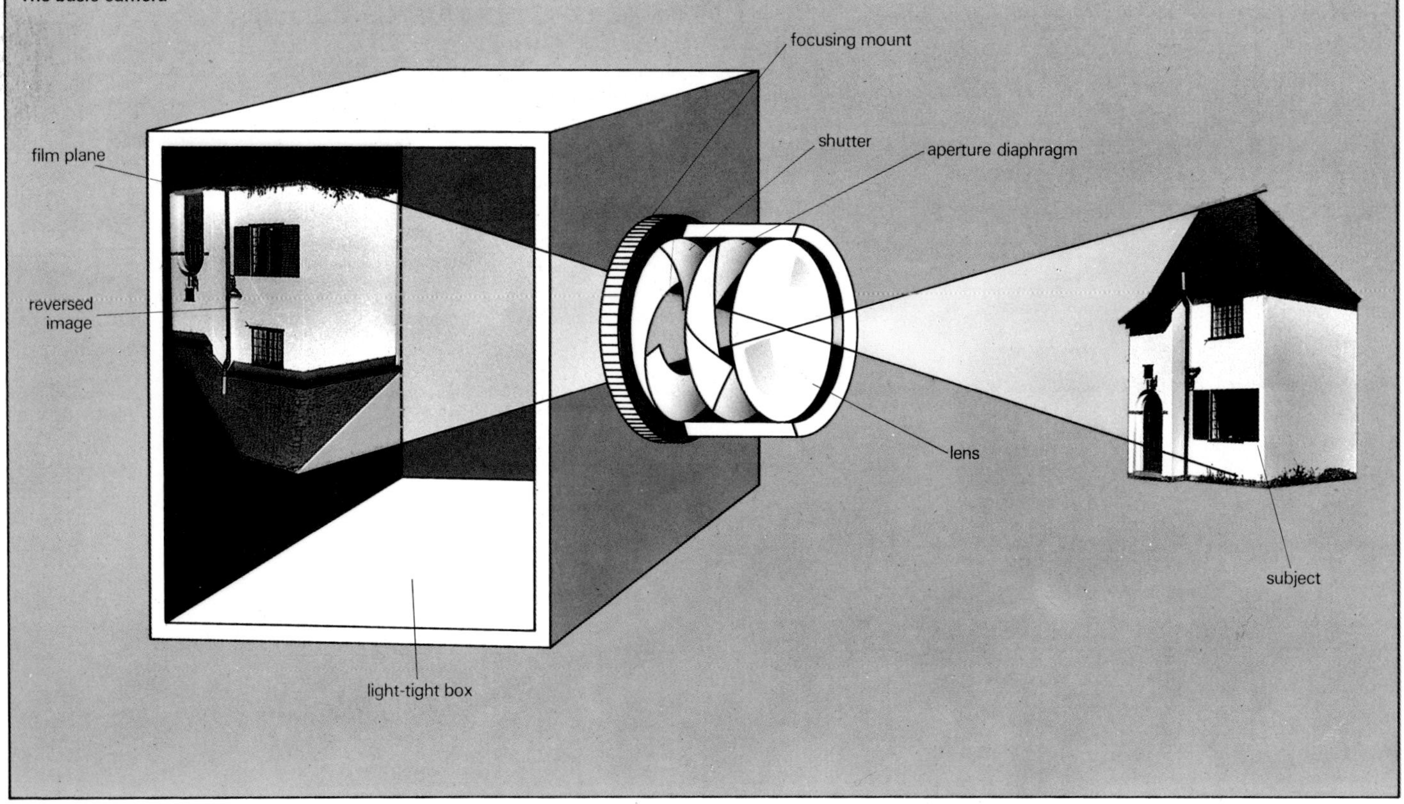

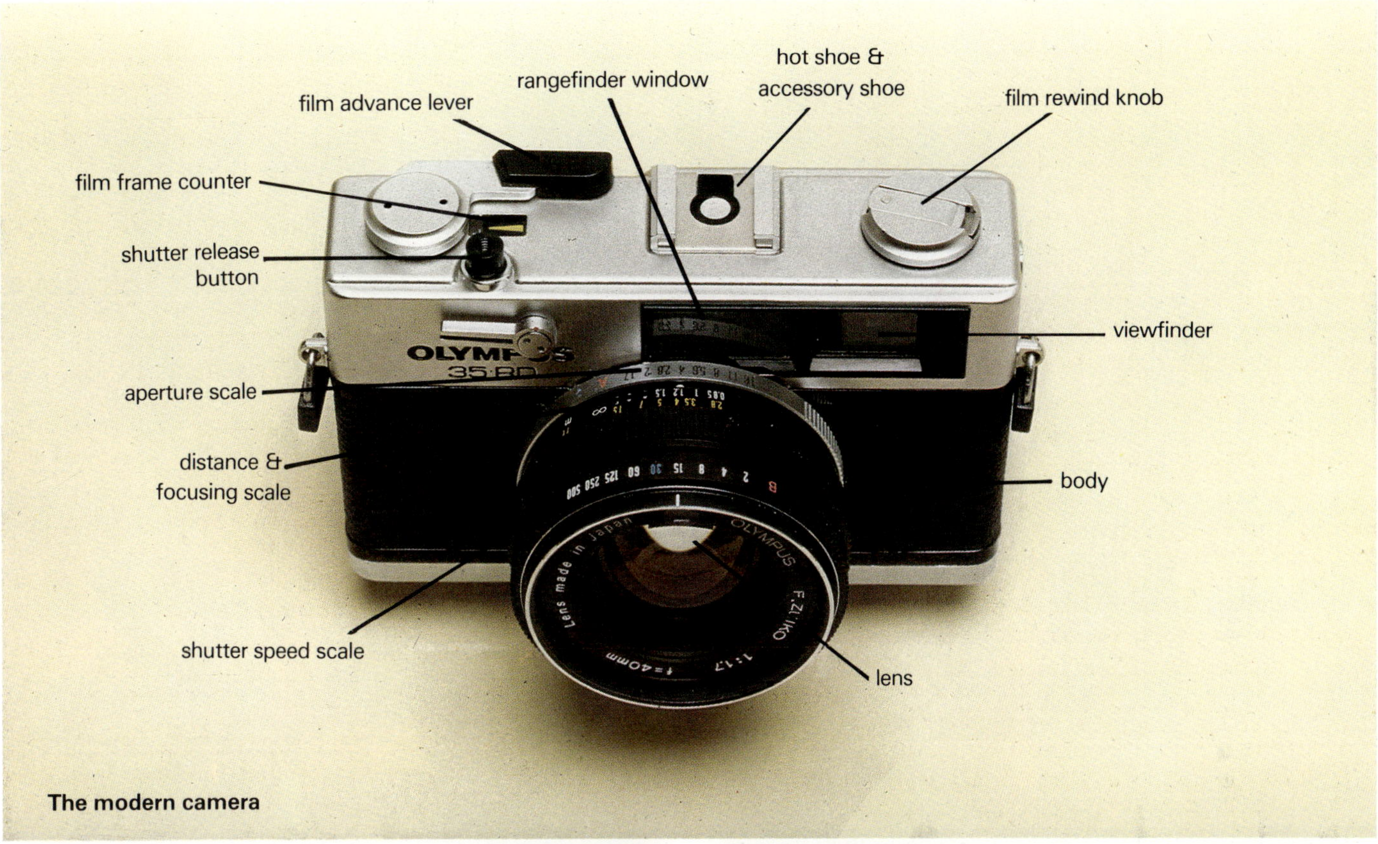

The modern camera

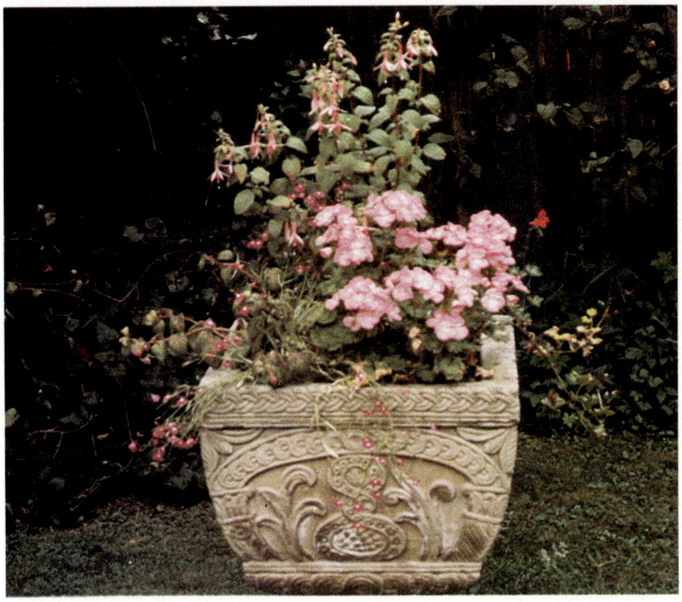

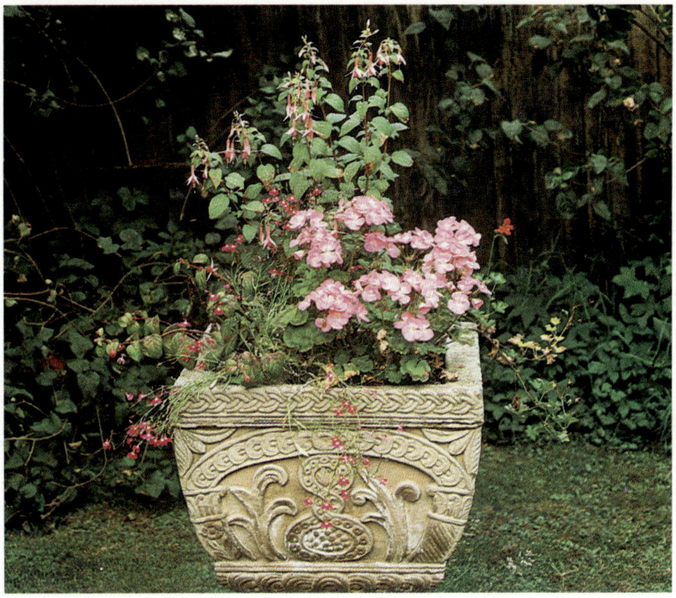

Above left and right: These two pictures are details from a 110 mm and a 35 mm transparency, both enlarged to 30 cm across. A smaller degree of enlargement, such as an EN print, would show much less difference in quality.

one or two speeds – 1/60 second and 1/125 second are common. Even with just a cloudy and sunny aperture setting and two shutter speeds good pictures can be given the right exposure under a variety of normal conditions. But obviously a wider range of settings enables an accurate exposure to be given across a much wider range of lighting conditions.

The viewfinder shows you the subject that you are photographing. On a simple camera it often gives only an approximate indication of the view which the lens itself 'sees'. Usually more is included on the film than you actually see through the viewfinder. If you then make an extra allowance when framing the picture you will find that the subject appears somewhat smaller in your picture than you expected. With this type of camera it is worth taking a test picture. Make an accurate note of the exact limit of the scene through the viewfinder and then compare it with the negative. Once you know how much extra the viewfinder is allowing you will be able to frame your pictures more accurately with confidence.

Different types of camera

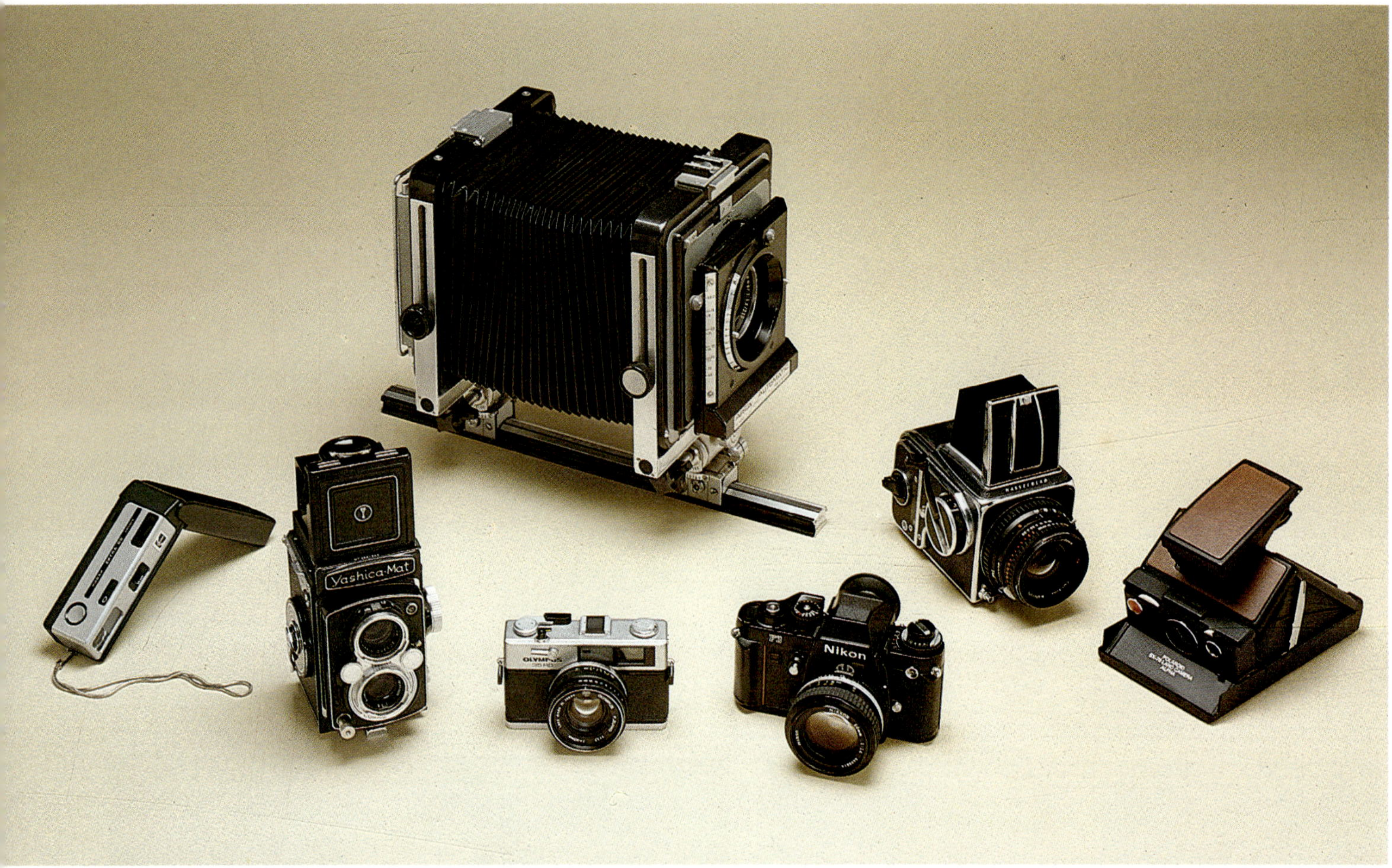

This photograph shows some of the different camera types. *Left to right:* simple 110 cartridge-loading, fixed-focus camera; twin lens reflex, roll-film camera; 5 × 4 inch monorail studio camera; 35 mm range-finder/view-finder camera; 35 mm single lens reflex camera; roll-film single lens reflex camera; instant-picture single lens reflex camera.

The major differences between camera types are between the viewing and focusing systems and the size of film which those systems accept. Also, some cameras are designed to accept lenses of various focal lengths and others have a fixed lens.

The viewfinder camera. This type of camera design includes the simple and inexpensive instamatic or cartridge-loading camera. The main feature of this viewing system is that you frame the picture through an optical system that is quite separate from the lens. For most pictures this is quite satisfactory, but because it is situated a little way away, it does give a slightly different view from the one that the lens sees. You will have to allow for this when taking close-up pictures – less than five feet or so. A further disadvantage is that the scene will appear quite sharp overall in the viewfinder whereas the camera lens will record sharply only the object upon which it is focused. In addition it is not possible to see the effects of any lens attachments which might be used when looking through the viewfinder. These cameras take most types and sizes of film from the small 110 cartridge to 120 roll film, and also instant-picture film. The more expensive varieties are equipped with automatic rangefinder focusing, which avoids having to judge the focusing distance, and automatic exposure systems. Some, like the Leica, are designed to accept interchangeable lenses.

Most *twin lens reflex* cameras are of a rather more bulky design and accept only roll film. With this camera the viewing and focusing is provided by a separate but matched lens

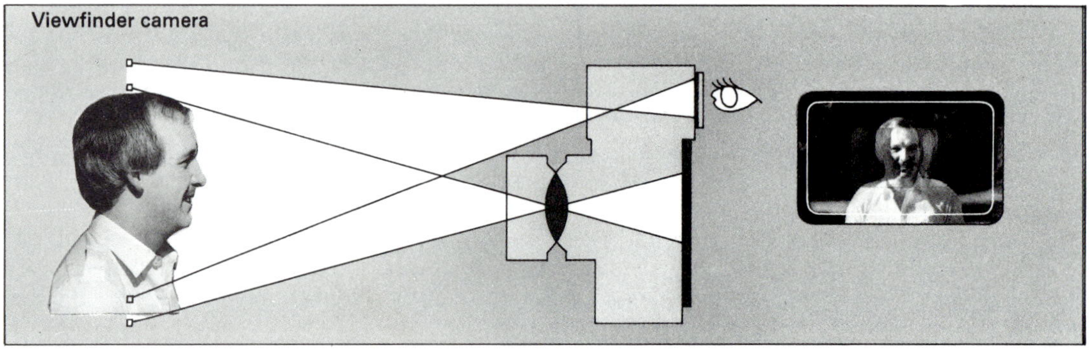

Twin-lens reflex (TLR)

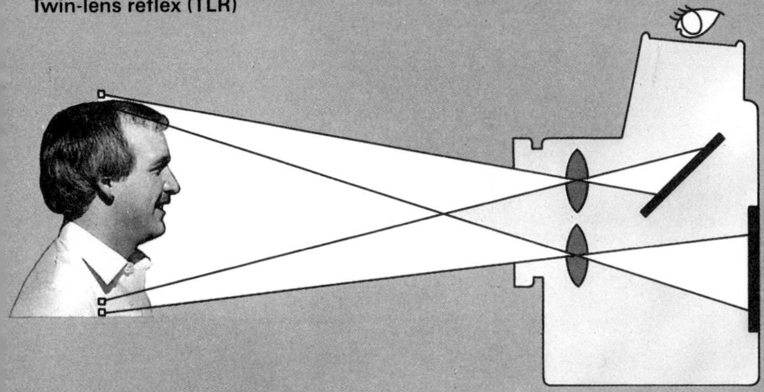

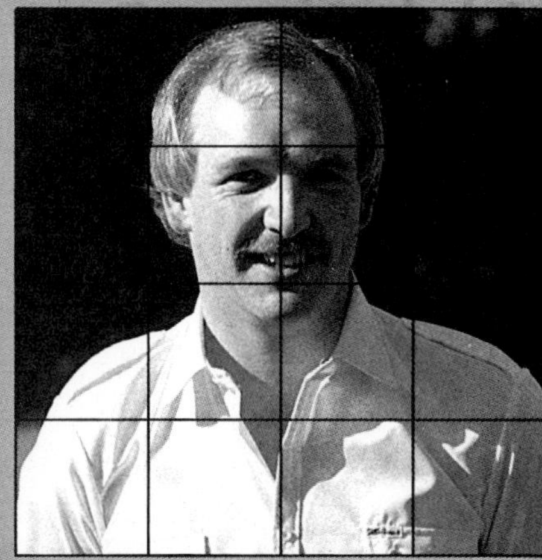

Single-lens reflex (SLR)

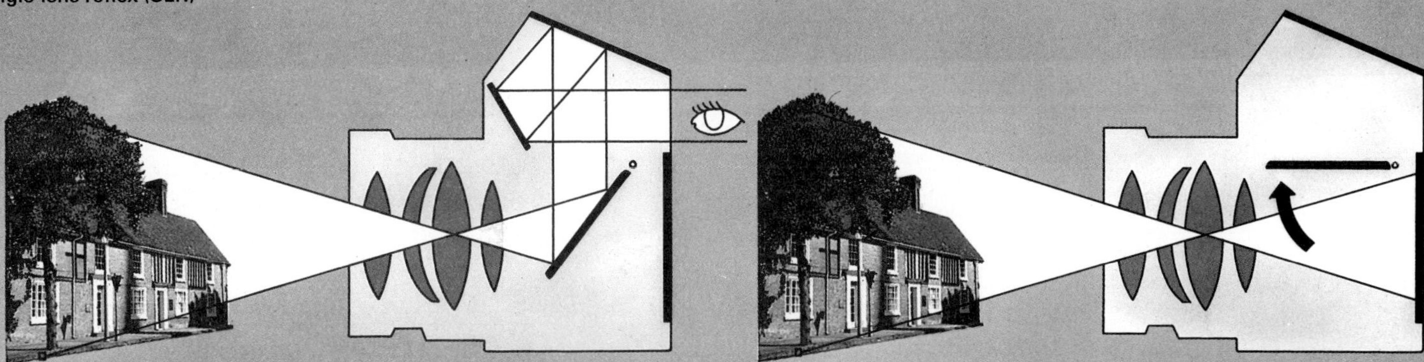

viewing with mirror down

exposure with mirror up

mounted above the taking lens. This projects an image via a mirror on to a ground-glass screen on the top of the camera. It is possible to focus very accurately with this type of camera and one can see the effect of the sharp and unsharp areas of the image on the screen, but it is still a slightly different view from that projected by the camera lens and the image is reversed left to right, which can be a little disconcerting.

The single lens reflex (or SLR) provides the system which is undoubtedly the most accurate and convenient method of viewing and focusing. By use of a mirror and a prism, an image is diverted from the camera lens itself up into the viewfinder where a view of the scene is shown exactly as it will appear on the film – even the effect of attachments on the lens can be seen. When the shutter is released the mirror flicks up out of the way to allow the image on to the film. With most cameras it returns automatically, and with normal shutter speeds of 1/30 second or longer one experiences only a 'blink' of interrupted viewing. Versions of this type of camera use most film sizes from 110 cartridge to 120 roll film and instant-picture film, but the widest variety are designed to use 35 mm cassettes. You can change the lens on most 35 mm single lens reflex cameras and there is a wide range of lenses, from extreme wide-angle to long-focus and telephoto. In addition they can easily be fitted with close-up attachments and some can even be fitted to microscopes and telescopes. The majority of these cameras are now fitted with integrated exposure meters which measure the light after it has passed through the camera lens, and there are many fully automatic versions where one has only to set the aperture and the camera will automatically select the correct shutter speed, called aperture priority. It is also possible to have cameras which are shutter priority and some offer a choice between the two. Other features which are rapidly becoming commonplace include electric winders, which enable the film to be automatically advanced after the shutter has fired, and motor drives which offer the advantage of shooting continuously at high speed.

Choosing a camera. In general, the difference between cameras of equivalent price will be in the method and convenience of use rather than the quality of results. If you want a camera to photograph your family and take pictures on holidays then a viewfinder camera with a fixed lens will be perfectly adequate. If you think you will eventually want to use wide-angle or long-focus lenses then it would obviously be wise to choose a camera with an interchangeable facility even if you do not make immediate use of it. If close-up photography is of particular interest to you then a single lens reflex would be a positive advantage, although it is not impossible with other types of camera.

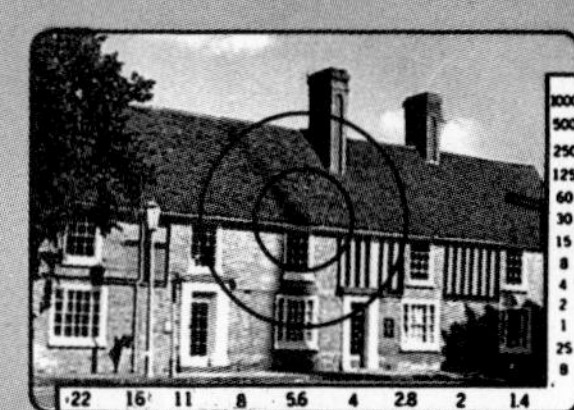

Opposite and above: The three diagrams show the ways in which the viewfinders of the different camera types see the object. With the exception of the single lens reflex the view is slightly different from that seen by the camera lens itself.

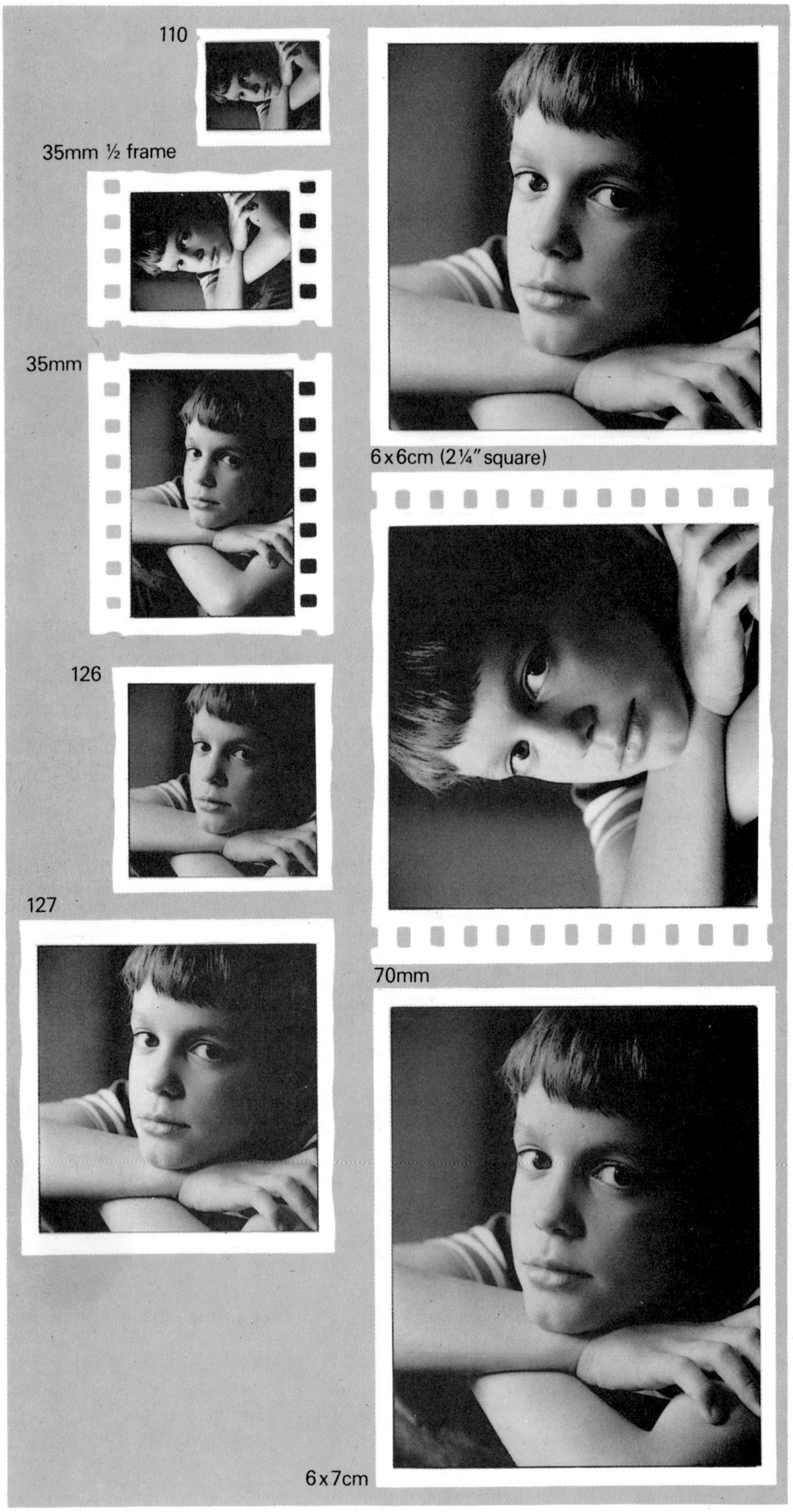

This diagram shows the relative sizes of the most widely used film formats.

All types of film work on the same principle. They are coated with a light-sensitive emulsion, which after development turns dark in proportion to the amount of light it has received. A bright area in the scene photographed will therefore record as a dark area on the negative film. When this is printed on to a similar emulsion on a paper base, the dark tone in the negative will revert back to the original bright area it was in reality. With colour transparency film the negative is destroyed during the processing. The same applies to instant-picture film: it is only when you use black-and-white film or colour-negative film that you have a separate negative which is retained for further use.

Film types. The choice of film depends on film size and method of loading, black-and-white or colour, negative or reversal, and finally speed or sensitivity. When it is magnified it is possible to see the grains from which the emulsion is formed. These grains are larger with the faster, more sensitive films. Consequently the clearest and sharpest results are obtained with a large format negative (or transparency) which does not have to be enlarged so much, or a slow film which has a finer grain to start with. These differences will not be very noticeable with small size prints such as EN prints (3 × 4 inches) but if you have prints of 10 × 8 inches or larger the difference in quality will begin to show.

There are currently two methods of measuring film speeds. The first is ASA and the second is DIN. A doubling of the ASA number indicates a doubling of the film speed. For example, a 100 ASA film is twice the speed of a 50 ASA film. The DIN system indicates a doubling of the film speed in multiples of three. For example, a film of 21 DIN is twice the speed of 18 DIN. A new system is being introduced called ISO which combines both ASA and DIN film speeds. For example, the film speed will, in the future, be marked ISO 100/21, which will be twice the speed of ISO 50/18. A film of ISO 25/15 is the slowest in both colour and black-and-white with the exception of specialist scientific film. This is half the speed and would need twice as much exposure to produce the same effect as a film of ISO 50/18. A medium-speed film is considered to be ISO 100/21. This would require an exposure of only a quarter (two f stops less) of that required for the slow ISO 25/15 film.

A fast film is one which has an ISO rating of 400/27 or more. This requires only one-sixteenth of the exposure of ISO 25/15 film or five f stops less. If the ISO 25/15 film were exposed at f2.8 you could use f11 with the same shutter speed but with ISO 400/27 film and achieve the same result.

It is possible to obtain even faster ISO ratings by 'push' processing (using special developers)

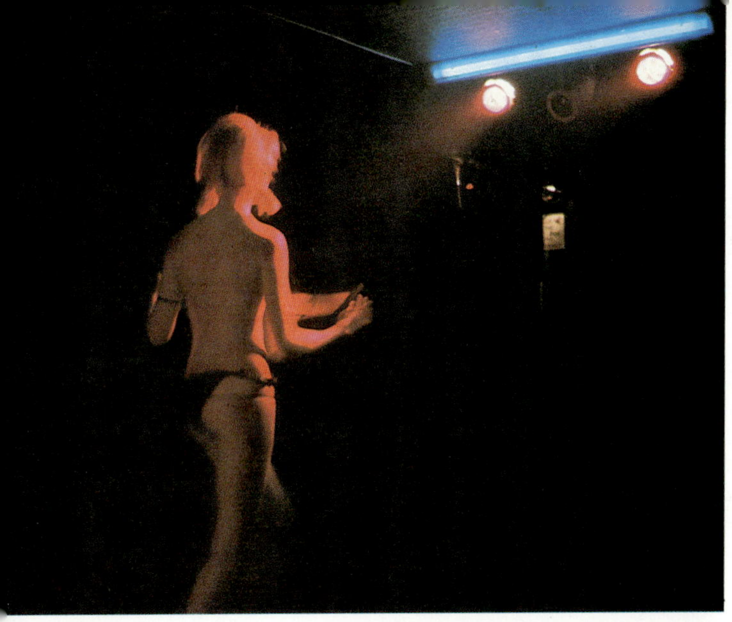

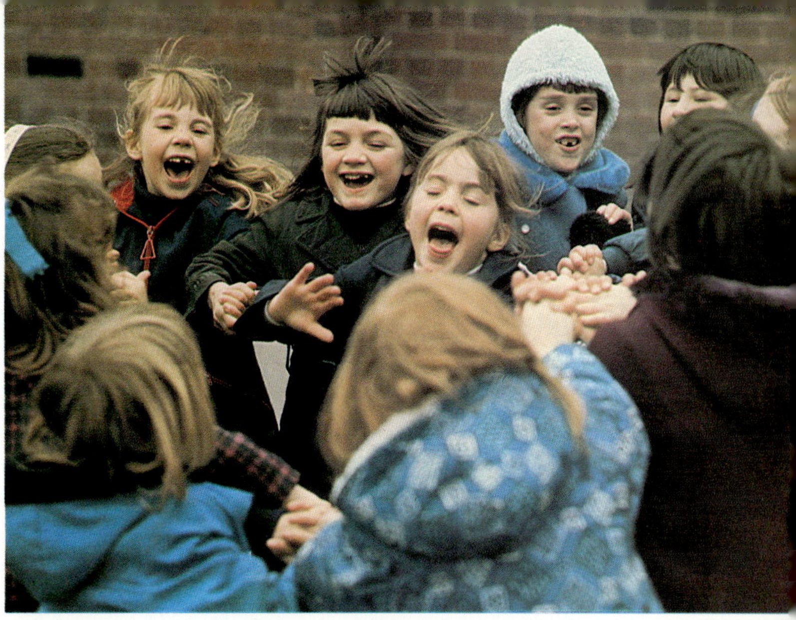

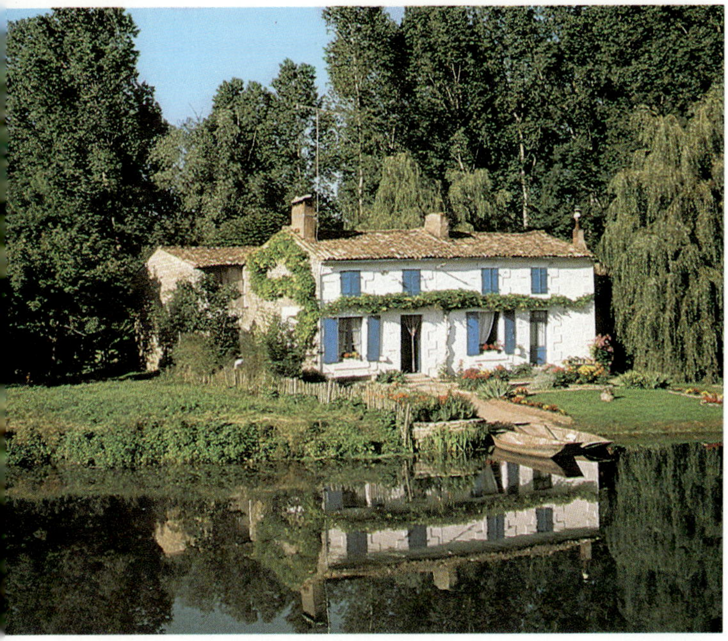

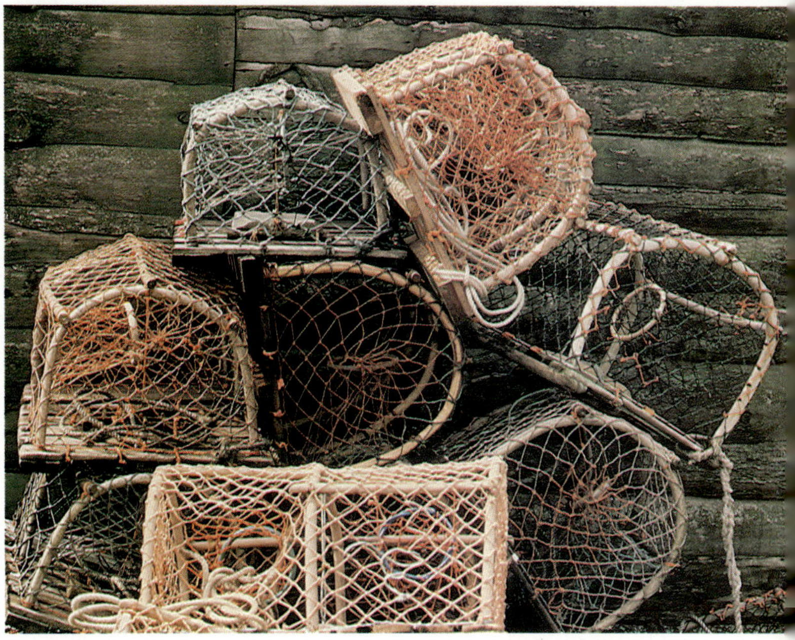

but there is a considerable increase in the size of the grain and a corresponding loss of quality particularly when enlarged. If you are taking pictures in poor light conditions then most processing laboratories will provide speed-increasing processing if asked. Medium-speed film is usually the best choice for most normal lighting conditions and for most subjects. The slower films are best used when fine detail needs to be recorded, or big enlargements are required. The fast films are best suited for poor lighting conditions or when a fast shutter speed is needed, as in sport or action photography.

Colour films. The choice between colour transparencies and colour negatives is really dependent on the kind of pictures you require. If you only want colour prints then a negative film is the best choice. As these films have a wider exposure tolerance they are a good choice for use in the more simple cameras with their limited choice of shutter speed and aperture. Colour transparency film is, however, essential if you want to project slides or sell to magazines, as prints are not usually acceptable. It is, of course, possible to make prints from colour transparencies. In addition to choosing between negative and transparency films it is also necessary, when shooting indoors, to use a transparency film which is specially balanced for using with artificial lighting, such as tungsten or photoflood. Film for use in normal daylight will produce a pronounced orange colour cast if used in artificial lighting conditions. It is also important to realize that the colour rendition of films varies considerably from one type to another. You may well prefer the results that one particular film gives you. For this reason it can be well worthwhile to experiment with a variety of films until you have found one that suits you best.

Top left: Ultra-fast film is necessary in poor lighting conditions and when using very fast shutter speeds. *Top right:* Fast film is ideal for recording subject movement. *Above left:* Medium speed film is best for good lighting conditions. *Above right:* Slow film should be used when fine detail and texture are important in the picture.

Exposure

Correct exposure is vital if consistent results are to be obtained. This is dependent on four factors: the speed of the film being used; the amount of light being reflected from the subject; the shutter speed; and the aperture or f stop. It is easiest to understand if you standardize on two of them and allow only two factors to vary. The film speed is easy to establish as it is marked on the packet and is always constant. For most subjects it is quite convenient to fix on a shutter speed of say 1/125 second. All you need to do then is to vary the aperture in order to compensate for the change in brightness of the subject: this can be measured by an exposure meter. This is in fact how most automatic cameras work: by setting the film speed and the aperture. The built-in light meter then automatically controls the shutter speed to maintain a constant level of light reaching the film as the subject brightness changes.

The diagram demonstrates how an exposure meter reads the strength of the light reflected from a subject. The reading represents an average of the lightest and darkest parts of the subject.

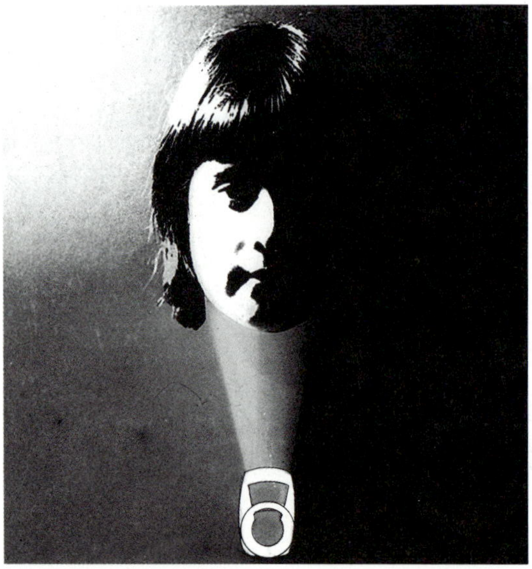

Below: This picture shows the effect on the film when more or less than the correct exposure is given.

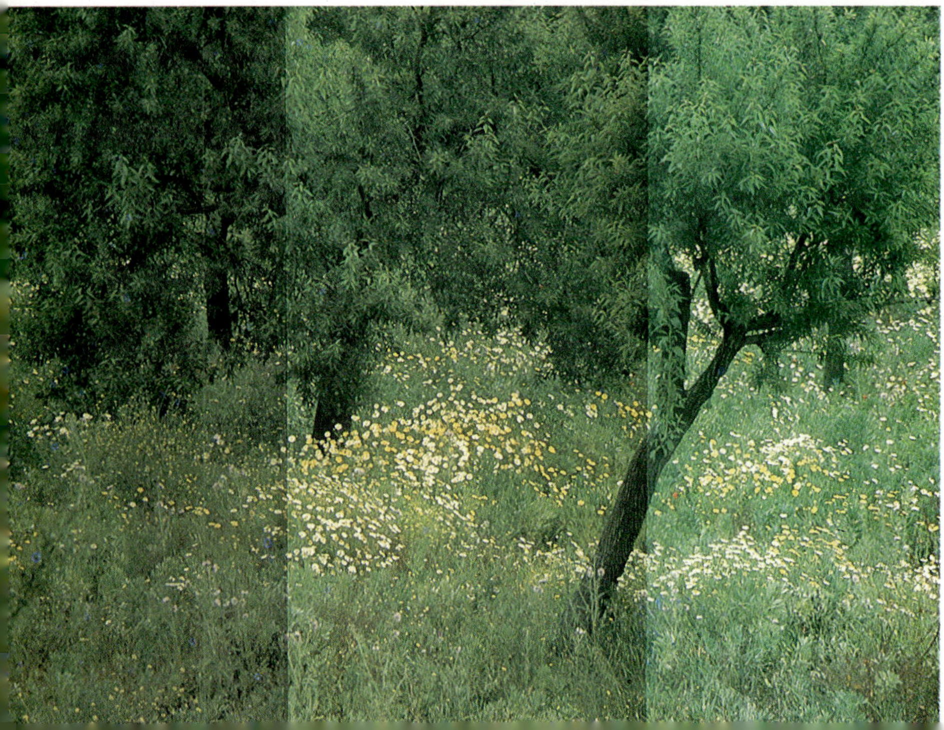

A 'correct' exposure is one where enough exposure has been given to record detail in both the shadow areas and in the highlight areas. This is only possible when the two extremes of the brightness range are within the tolerance of the film – if not, it is necessary to sacrifice one to the benefit of the other. The problem with an exposure meter is that it assumes that the brightness range is acceptable to the film and also that there is an equal distribution of tones – highlights, midtones, and shadows – throughout the scene. It is important therefore, that before you take your exposure reading you look at the scene you are about to photograph and decide which is the most important area to record correctly, thus providing the meter with the average tones it needs to give an accurate reading. If there is a large amount of very bright highlight in the picture – sky in a landscape picture for instance – the exposure meter will be misled and indicate less exposure than is needed. The result will be shadows that are too dark and without detail while highlights will be muddy and grey. If, on the other hand, dark tones are in more abundance than normal – a picture of someone wearing a dark suit and standing in a dark doorway for example – the meter will indicate more exposure than is really necessary. The shadows will be recorded too light and weak and the highlight details will be bleached out.

The most common pitfalls are to allow too much sky in the area being read, or to include too-bright highlights by shooting against the light or including street lights in a night scene. Such situations will always result in under-exposure unless an allowance is made. It is also important to be aware of how exposure affects the quality of the picture. Often the effect you want to achieve may well be a result of giving rather more or less than the 'correct' exposure. It can be very helpful sometimes to 'bracket' exposures, which means making several exposures of the same subject – one at the calculated setting, and the others a stop or half a stop more and less than indicated.

The owners of fully automatic cameras can still 'bracket' their exposures by simply setting the film speed dial to a higher or lower number than the actual film speed. If, for instance, you are using ISO 100/21 film and you set the dial to ISO 50/18 the camera will give a one stop extra exposure. If you set it to ISO 200/24 it will result in one stop less exposure. Exposure is one of the most important ways of controlling the quality of your pictures, and bracketing will help you to judge the effects you can create.

Exposure meters. Most exposure meters, whether built into the camera or separate, work on a similar principle: they measure the light which is being reflected from the subject. Some hand meters have an incident light attachment which measures the light falling on the subject. A separate meter is useful when you use a tripod frequently as it enables close-up readings to be taken from the subject without having to move the camera. And of course if the meter goes wrong you don't have to lose your camera to the repair shop as well.

The through-the-lens meters which are fitted to most single lens reflex cameras have the advantage that they are centre-weighted. This means that the meter is biased to read more from the central part of the frame where the main subject is usually placed, which reduces the possibility of misleading readings from skies etc. With an automatic camera it is sensible to check the settings that the camera has selected and not just use it blindly.

In most situations, with a little experience, exposure is largely a matter of common sense. You will gain this experience quickly if you make a mental note of exposures in normal situations, and your meter will be less likely to mislead you.

The exposure meter

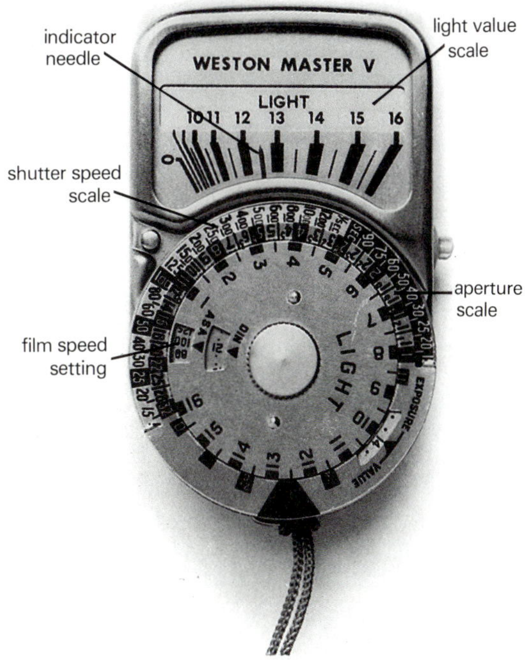

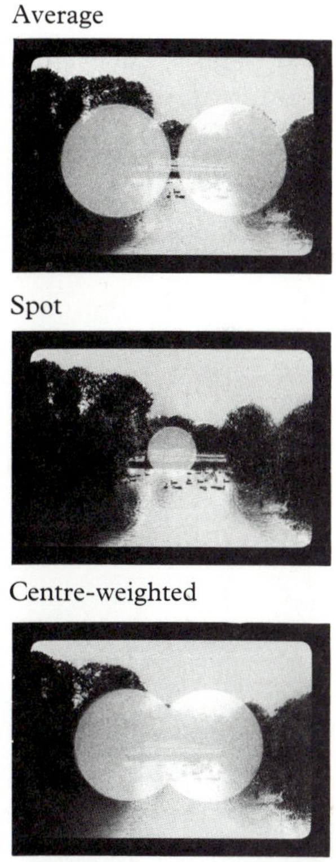

Above: A modern, hand-held exposure meter. The reading is set off against a scale and transferred to the camera settings.

Right: Three different types of through-the-lens metering. The average meter gives equal bias to the whole scene. The spot meter reads only from the small area at which the spot is aimed. The centre-weighted meter gives emphasis to the centre of the image but takes the rest of the scene into account.

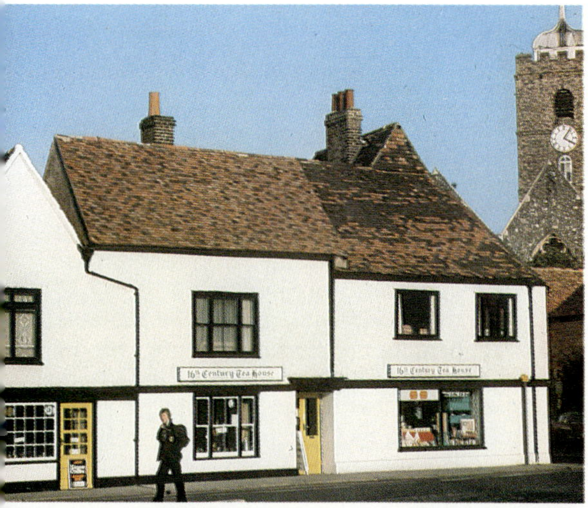

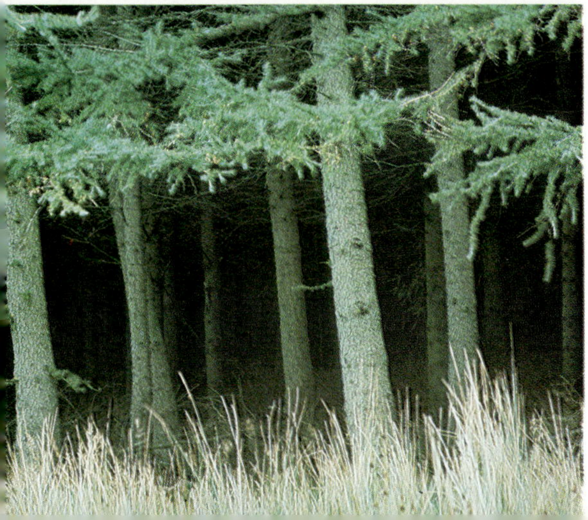

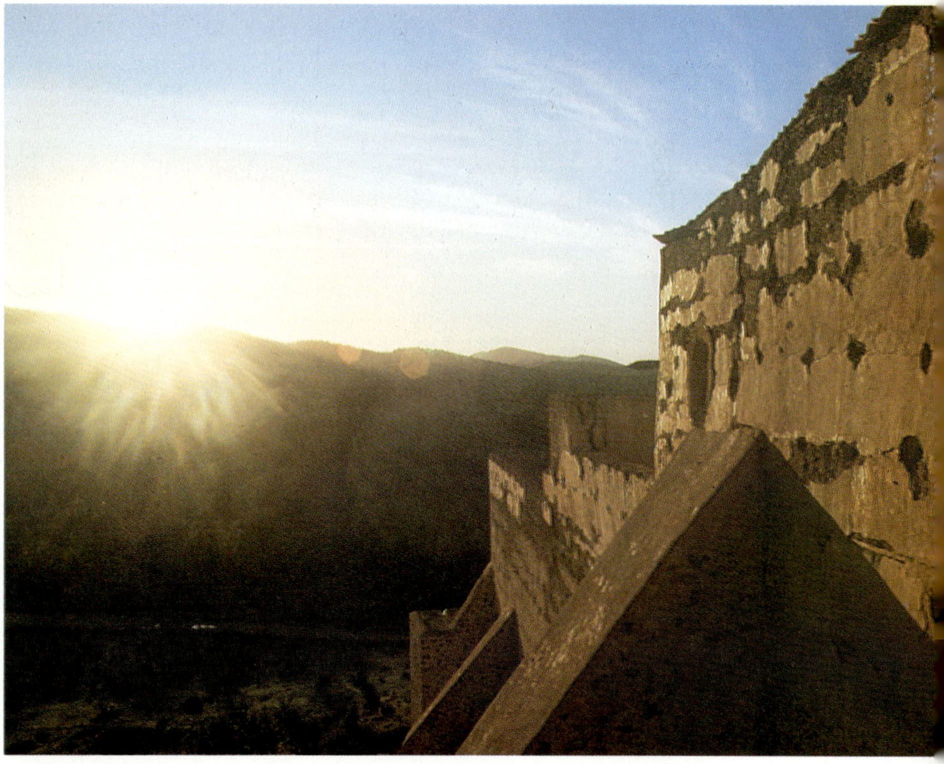

Above left: More than average light tones will cause the meter to indicate less than the correct exposure. *Left:* Predominantly dark tones will cause the meter to indicate more exposure than is required. *Above:* Shooting into the light will cause the meter to indicate less than the correct exposure.

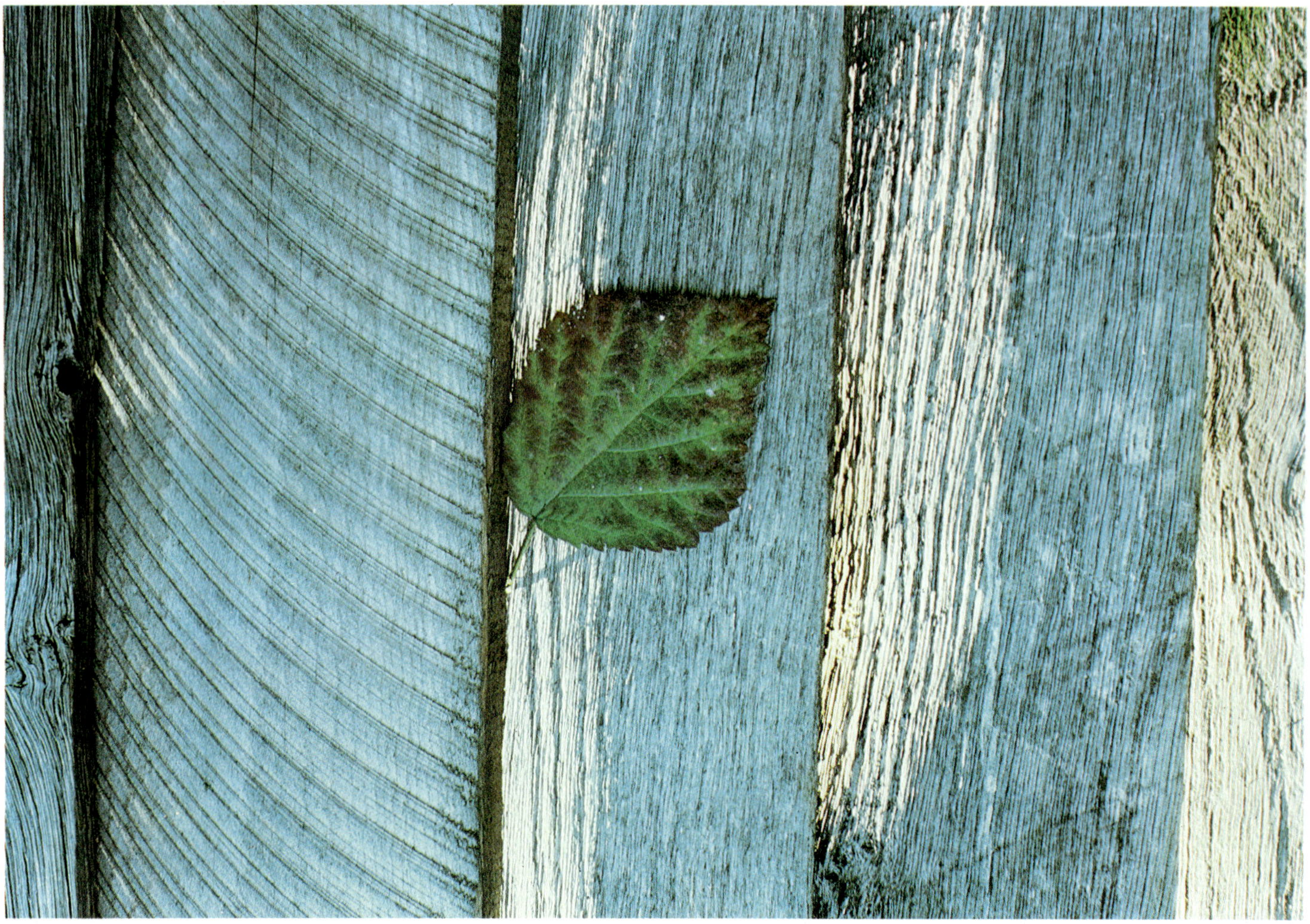

A sharp image requires a firmly supported camera to eliminate camera shake, a fast enough shutter speed to freeze subject movement, a small enough aperture to ensure adequate depth of field and, of course, accurate focusing. The picture above was taken with a camera mounted on a tripod at a minimum aperture of f16. A slow, fine-grained film was used to ensure maximum detail.

The technique of taking a sharp picture is just as important as the technique of getting the exposure right. Although it is by no means difficult, it does require some special considerations. There are four main reasons for *not* producing a sharp result. The most common is camera shake, the result of the camera not being held firmly or the shutter release being operated in a stabbing motion. Many simple cameras have a shutter speed which is fixed at around 1/60 second; this may seem very brief but it is very easy indeed to produce the effects of camera shake with this period, if the camera is not held properly and the shutter not released in a smooth squeezing movement. Even when shutter speeds of 1/125 second or 1/250 second are used this problem can still be experienced if the camera is handled carelessly. It is well worthwhile practising, particularly with a new and unfamiliar camera, and watching in a mirror what happens when you press the shutter.

It is important to find a way of holding the camera and releasing the shutter that suits your hands. The small, light cameras such as the cartridge-loading variety can be particularly difficult to hold steady, and, of course, the problem is compounded by the fact that the resulting small negatives have to be enlarged so much more. Whenever you find it necessary to use a shutter speed of less than about 1/30 second it is advisable to find some extra support. A tripod provides the ideal solution, but if you do not have one it is possible to get considerable benefit by bracing the camera against a tree, or the back of a chair.

Subject movement is another problem where the camera, although held steady, has not had a brief enough shutter speed setting to arrest the movement of the subject. With a simple camera it may have to be accepted that there is a limit to the degree of movement which can be recorded sharply on such cameras, although techniques like panning and careful timing can help to minimize the problem.

Inaccurate focusing is a third possible cause of an unsharp image, particularly when you use a camera where the distance of the subject has to be judged. This needs to be done quite carefully, especially with the closer focusing settings, say twelve feet and less. If your camera does not have a range finder or a focusing screen it can be helpful to frame, say, a head and shoulder

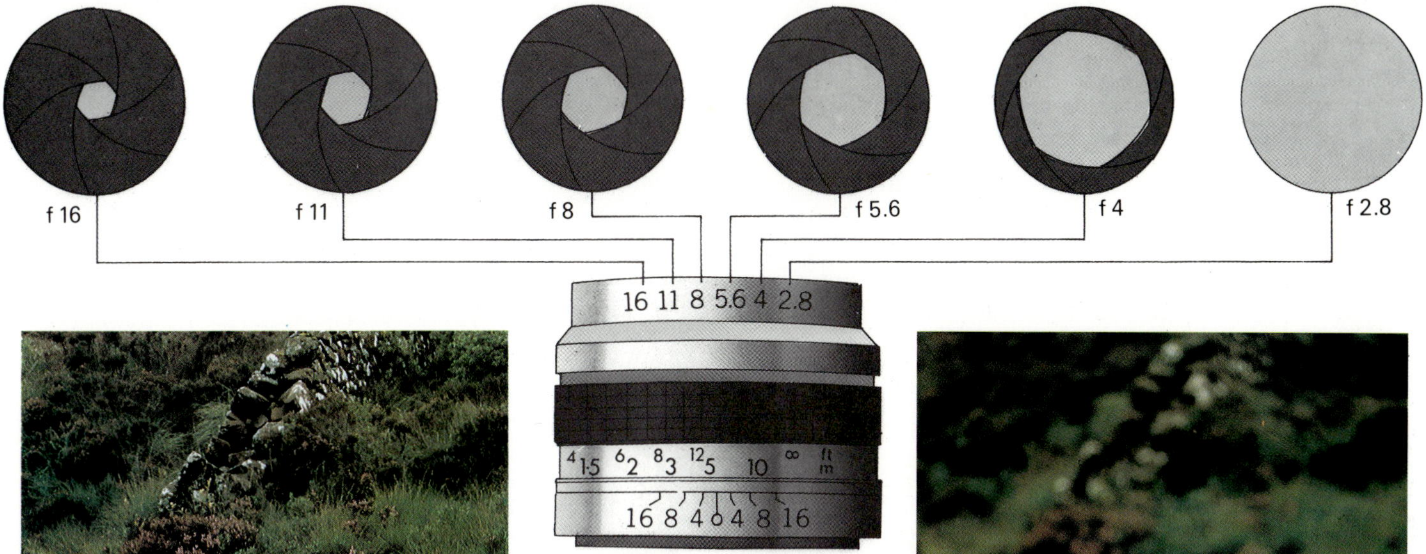

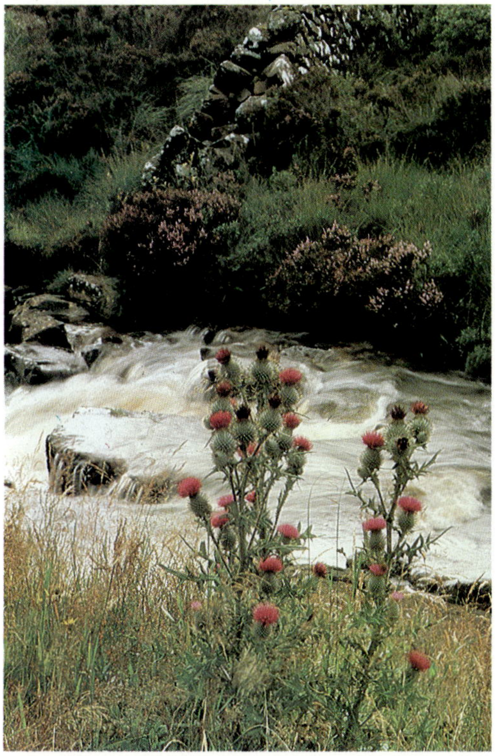

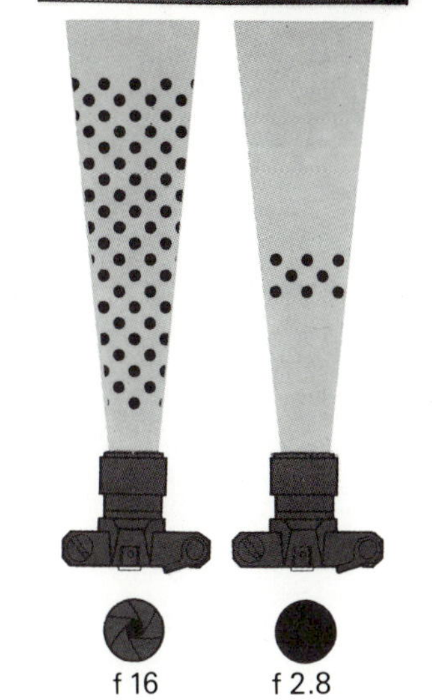

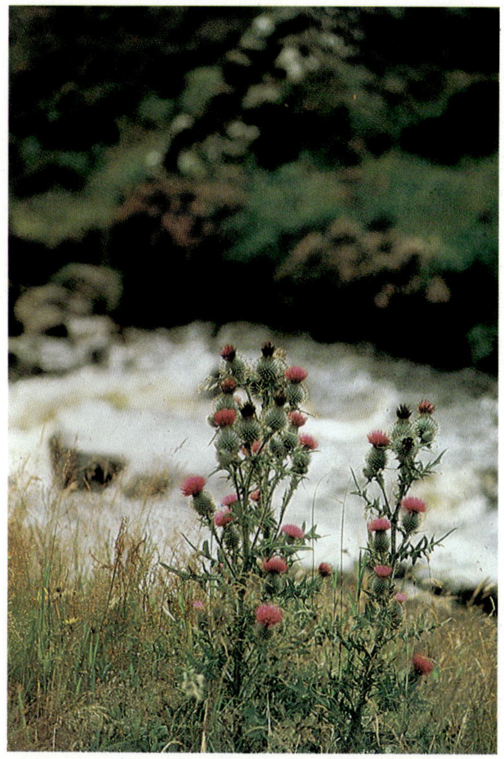

portrait carefully in your viewfinder and then measure the distance you are from your subject. If you do the same with a full-length picture you will be able to make a quite accurate estimate with similar pictures in the future.

The closer the camera is to the subject the more accurate the focusing needs to be, as the depth of field becomes more limited. When you focus your lens at a particular distance the amount of the picture that is completely sharp extends only a little way each side of the subject focused upon. The further the subject or scene extends beyond this point the more unsharp the image becomes, and as the point of focus becomes closer to the camera so the depth of field also becomes narrower. This band of sharp focus can be greatly extended by using a small aperture, and most lenses have a scale engraved on the focusing mount indicating the depth of field either side of a particular focusing distance at each of the aperture settings. The depth of field extends somewhat further behind the point of focus than in front, so it is best to focus at a point slightly closer to the camera rather than the centre of the area you want recorded sharply.

It is important to take care of your lenses and not allow them to become dusty or smeared as this also will affect their ability to record a sharp image. Any cleaning should be carried out very gently, using a blower brush to remove any surface dust or grit, and if the lens is a little bit smeary a very light polish with a lens tissue or a selvyt cloth is the best remedy.

The two photographs above illustrate the degree of depth of field achieved by shooting at f16 (*left*) and f2.8 (*right*), with the lens focused at the same point in both cases.

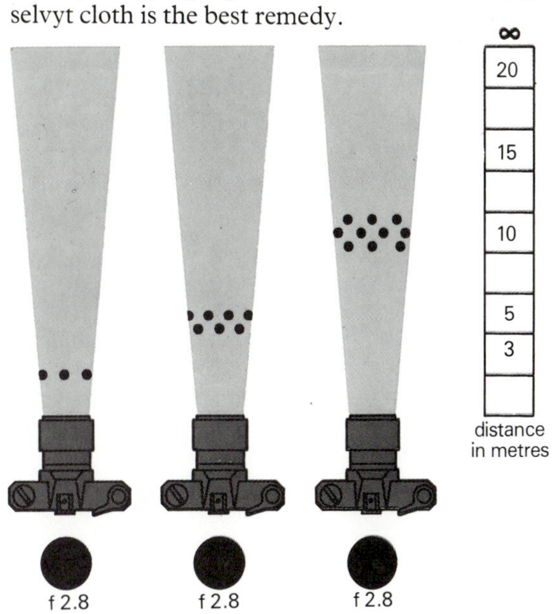

The depth of field increases when the lens is focused at progressively greater distances with a constant aperture setting.

Photographing movement

The fact that many cameras today are fitted with shutters that can make an exposure of 1/1000 second or even less means that it is possible to take pictures of movement and action showing details which cannot be seen by the naked eye. Even cameras with slower minimum shutter speeds can record quite rapid movements providing a few precautions are taken. If you want completely to freeze the action of someone or something moving very quickly – at a horse race for example – the obvious solution is to use the fastest shutter speed you have. An exposure of 1/1000 second will stop the motion of all but the swiftest actions. If, however, you do not have such a fast shutter speed setting on your camera, or if the light level will not allow such a short exposure to be given, then your chances of success can be improved by using a few simple techniques.

Below: A fast shutter speed of 1/1000 second was used to freeze the movement of the galloping horses. The lower picture shows the effect produced by panning the camera and using a slow shutter speed, 1/30 second.

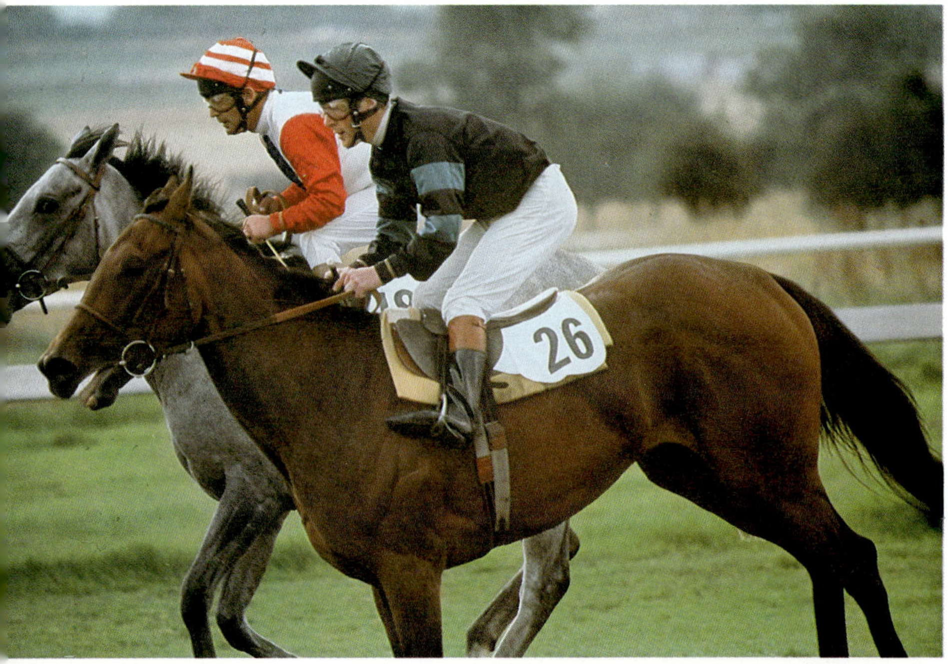

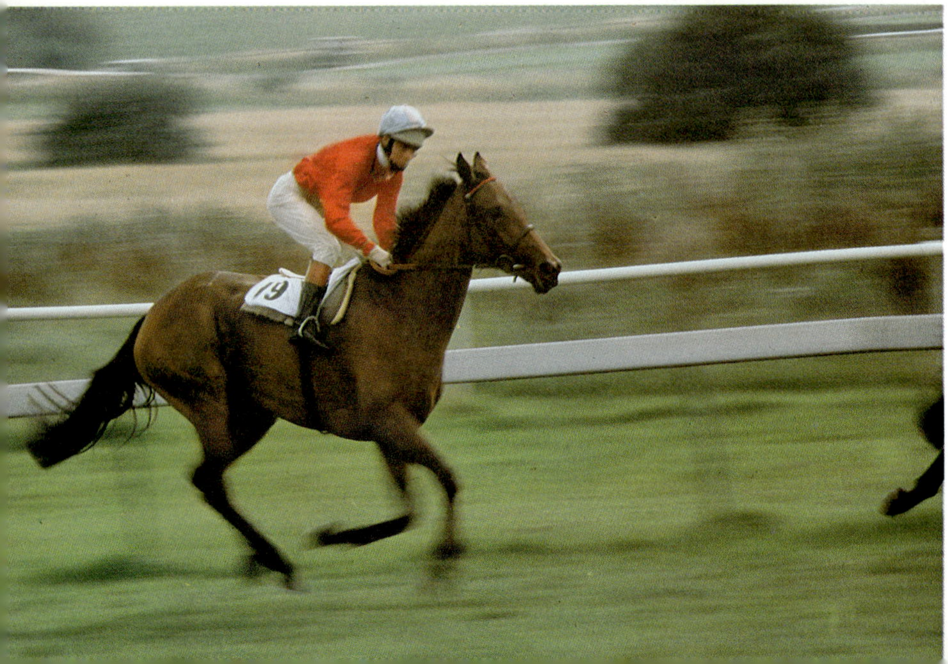

A subject travelling directly across the camera's field of vision will need a considerably faster shutter speed to freeze it than would the same thing moving at the same speed towards the camera. Even something which is moving quite quickly towards the camera, a sprinter for instance, could be recorded reasonably sharply at a shutter speed of 1/250 second or in some circumstances slower still. When you want to photograph a person or an object that is moving across the camera's view the movement can be minimized by panning the camera. This involves swinging the camera in a smooth action to keep pace with the subject and releasing the shutter at a point where the subject is being held steady in the viewfinder. With something like a racing car this can result in a totally sharp image of the vehicle, except for the wheels, at relatively slow shutter speeds; and with a subject like a running man it should be possible to record his head and torso quite sharply, though his limbs and the background may be slightly blurred.

Another technique which can be useful when photographing a moving subject with a relatively slow shutter speed is to judge the moment of exposure to coincide with a period when the movement is at a minimum. For example, a horse going over a fence reaches a point at the apex of the jump where it is travelling much more slowly than at the approach, and with subjects like motor racing it can help considerably to choose a steep bend at which to take your pictures, when the speed of the cars is much less than when on the straight part of the track. This 'peak of the action' moment is possible with many subjects and it often provides the most dramatic point at which to shoot. With a little practice it is possible to anticipate it quite accurately.

Although these techniques help to give a sharp frozen image of a moving subject, the *impression* of movement is often suggested more effectively by deliberately allowing a degree of blur to be produced in the picture. A good example of this, and one which is frequently used by sports photographers, is the technique of panning the camera combined with the use of a quite slow shutter speed. In motor racing pictures for example, it is quite possible to photograph a car which is moving at 150 mph at a shutter speed of 1/60 second or even less. Providing the panning is carried out smoothly and carefully the image of the car will be quite sharp, but the background will record as blurred streaks of tone or colour, giving a better impression of speed than a completely sharp, frozen picture. With objects which are static within themselves, although moving, such as a car, it is possible to get an almost completely sharp image in this way. But with a subject such as a racehorse where parts of its body are moving in different directions at

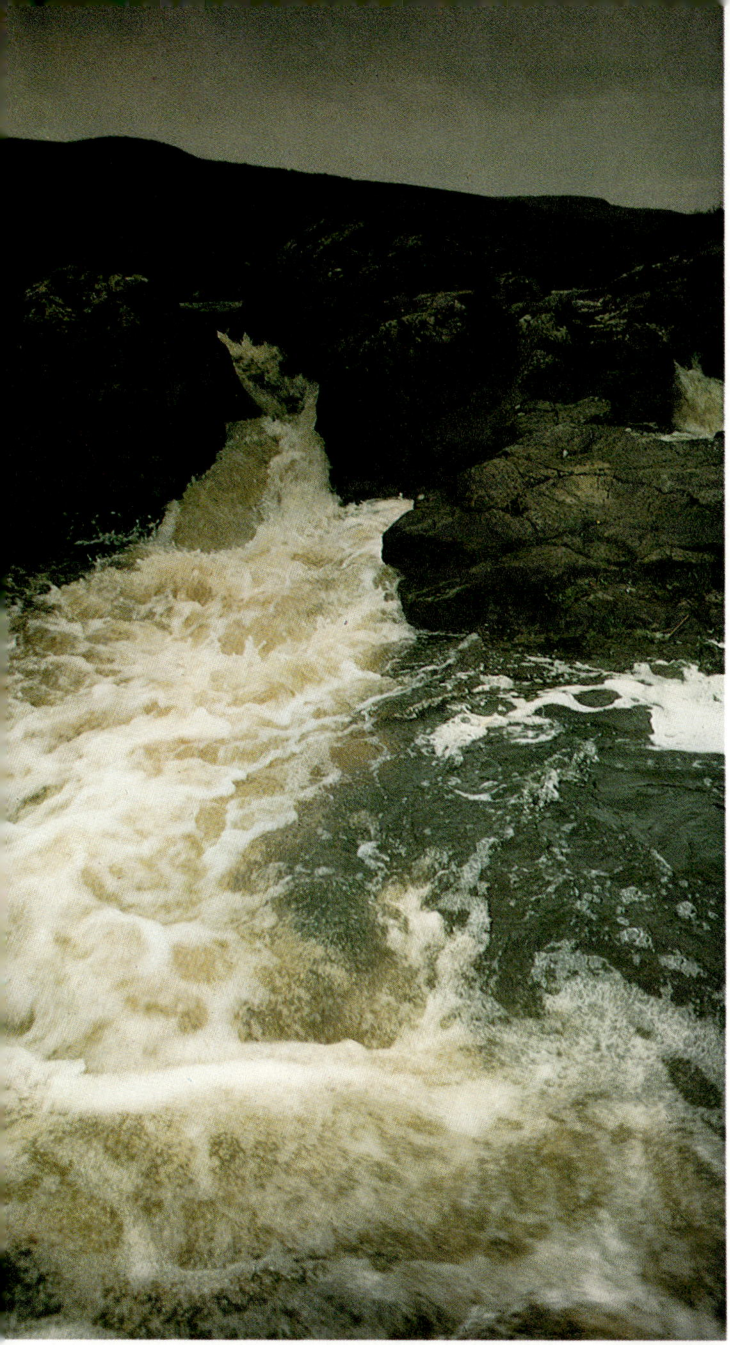

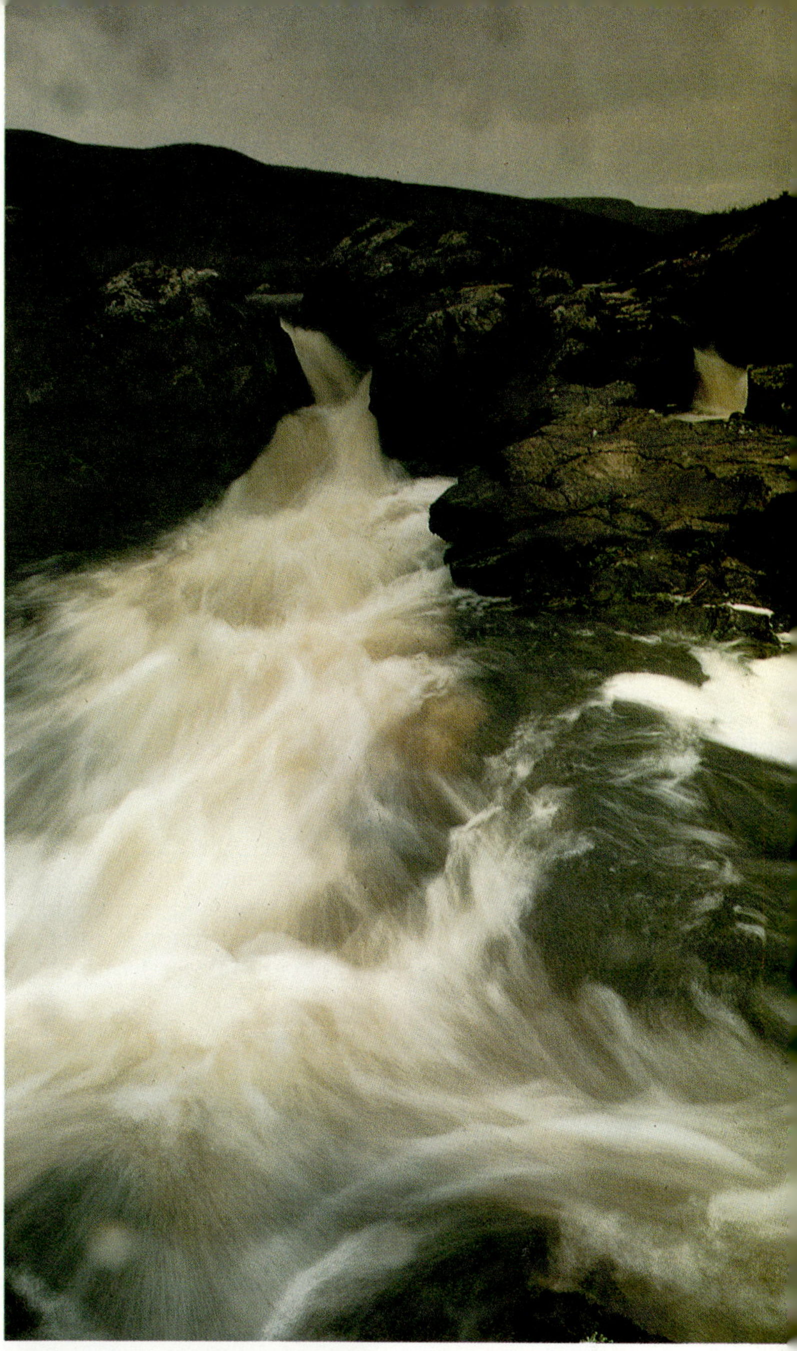

different speeds it can produce very effective, sometimes almost abstract pictures, with some parts of the subject quite sharp and others reduced to streaks and blurs. These effects are always stronger when there is a marked tonal or colour difference within the subject and its background. For example the faces in the crowd at a sports meeting often produce an effectively 'streaked' background with the panning technique.

Another way of using blurred movement effectively is to use a long exposure and have the camera static, allowing the moving part of the scene to be blurred but the remainder sharply recorded. Even exposures of one second or more can be used if the camera is mounted on a tripod, and subjects such as moving cars in a street scene at night, a waterfall, or waves breaking over rocks can produce quite unusual and often beautiful effects when treated in this way.

Above left: A fast shutter speed has frozen the movement of the water. *Above right:* Using a tripod an exposure of several seconds has given an entirely different effect.

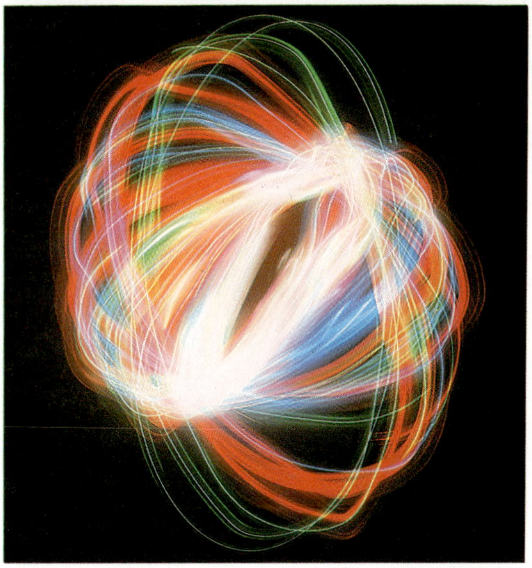

This picture was made by suspending a torch above the camera and allowing it to swing while the camera shutter was left open for a minute or so. The colour was introduced by different filters over the lens during this period.

Opposite: The four photographs show the results of using different flash techniques.

A small flash gun is probably the first major accessory that most photographers buy and it is a useful piece of equipment to own. Even the small penlight battery-powered units now have considerable power and many are fitted with sensors so that exposure calculations are not necessary. Exposure is, however, a simple matter. All that is necessary is to divide the distance of the flash from the subject into the flash guide number (which is printed on the flash gun) for a given film speed, and the result is the f stop number required. For instance if the guide number was eighty for ISO 100/21 film and you were ten feet from your subject then you would need to set your aperture at f 8.

The most common cause of disappointing flash pictures is that although the subject of the picture is quite well lit, the background can be lost in a black void. There are two basic ways of avoiding this. It must be appreciated that the strength of the flash diminishes the further it travels and if you have set your aperture correctly for your subject at, say, ten feet, this will not be the correct exposure for things at a greater distance. If, for instance, the background was ten feet behind your subject, the flash would only have a quarter of its power when it reached it, consequently the background would be two stops underexposed. One solution is to keep your subject quite close to the background and avoid very dark tones in the background. As a rule the distance of the subject from the camera should be at least three-quarters of the distance from the camera to background.

Using the flash gun at the camera position – in the flash shoe for instance – can produce a rather flat lighting with little modelling on people's faces. It is preferable to hold the flash gun somewhat away from the camera – two feet above and a little to one side is usually enough – in order to produce more three-dimensional lighting with more texture and detail.

Another method of using a small flash gun which will help to provide more pleasing lighting, at the same time eliminating the hard shadow that is thrown on to the background from the subject, is to bounce the light from a wall, or preferably the ceiling. This needs to be quite light in tone and when using colour film it should be fairly neutral – obviously white is best. Extra exposure must be given as the flash is travelling further and some light will be scattered away from the subject. In an average-size living room with, say, a ten-foot high white ceiling, about two stops extra will be about right. It is best to aim the flash at a point on the ceiling slightly closer to the camera than the subject, as otherwise the light on the subject's face will come too much from directly above and will cause heavy shadows in the eyes and under the chin.

Most novice photographers tend to think of flash as the sole source of light at night. It can also be very effective simply to supplement the existing light both indoors and out. Exposure is quite easy to calculate if you think of it as two separate pictures on one piece of film. First measure the existing light from the scene you are going to photograph; say that 1/60 seconds at f 8 is calculated, then measure the flash to subject distance and work out the correct exposure.

Let us assume that again f 8 is required. However, as the flash is only intended to supplement the existing light, slightly less than this would be better, say one stop. All you need to do is to set your aperture at f 11, adjust the shutter speed to 1/30 second to compensate for the smaller aperture, and you will have nicely balanced lighting. Once you have mastered the basic principle it is a simple matter to use this technique to create different effects. Giving the correct available light exposure and a little less than the correct flash exposure will produce a quite natural effect, but by reducing or increasing either of them you can make both the subject or the background lighter or darker at will. With colour pictures it can be interesting to experiment by using coloured acetates over the flash, the camera lens, or both: this can produce some quite bizarre results.

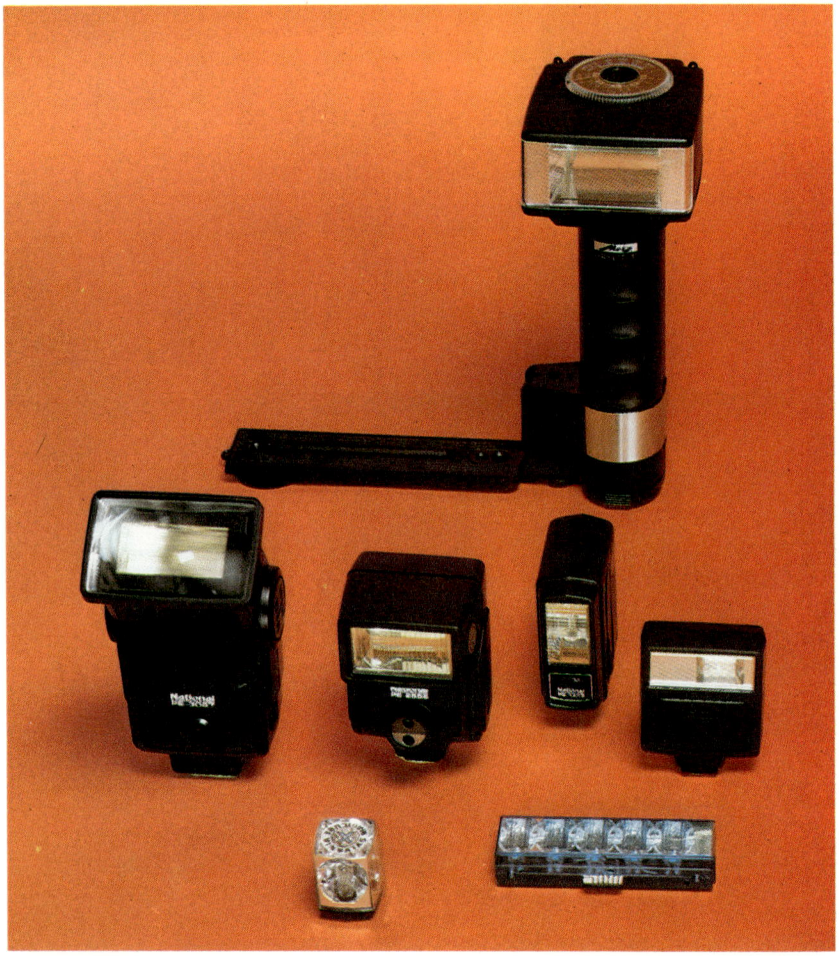

Below: A variety of widely used flash accessories. *Back:* A professional, high-power flash. *Centre left to right:* Swivel head gun (for bouncing); computer flash gun; two low-powered flash units. *Front:* Expendable flash cube and flash bar.

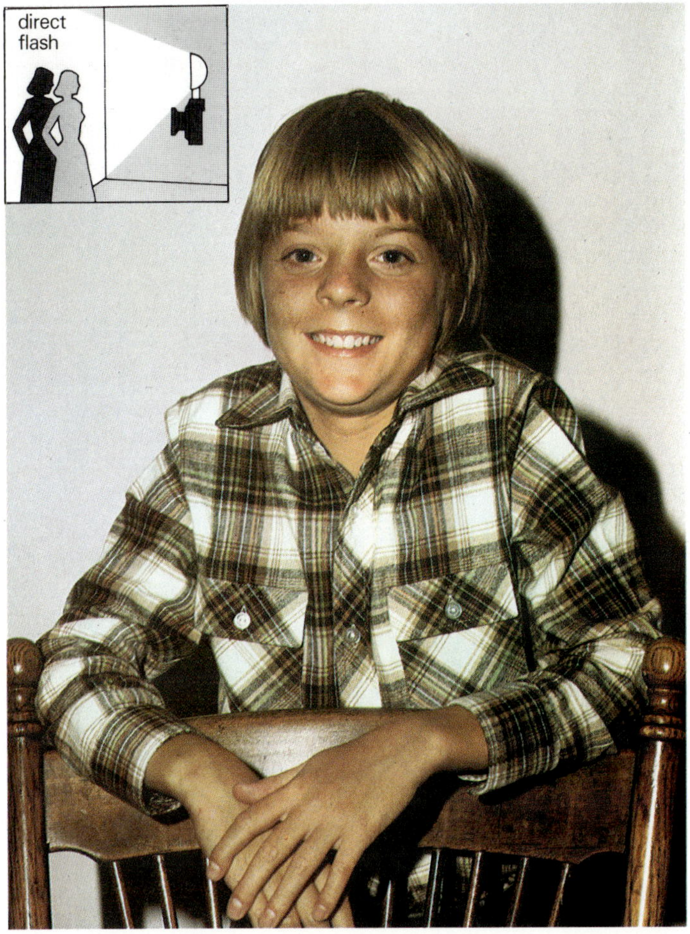
direct flash

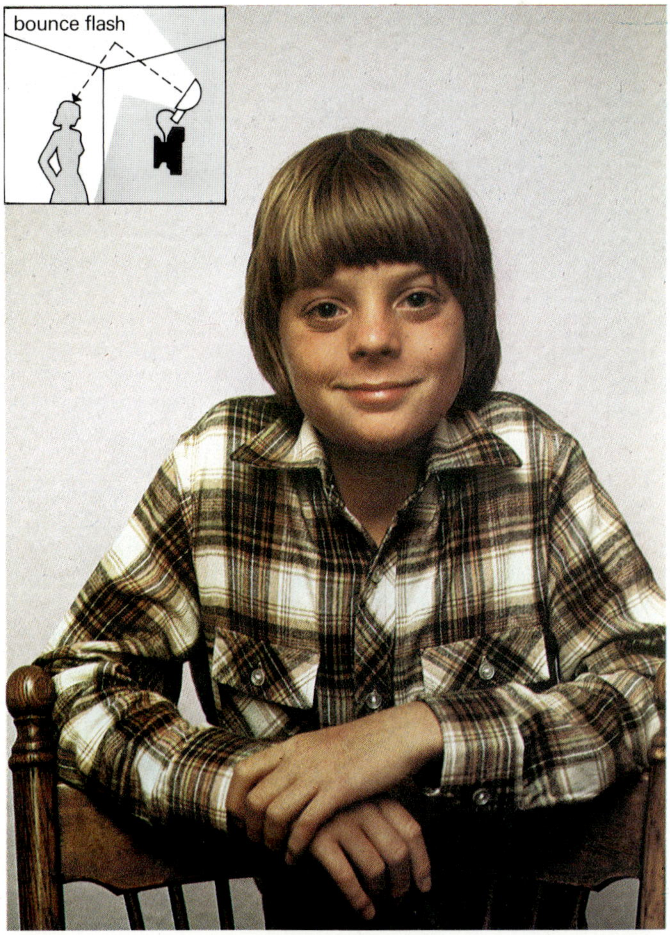
bounce flash

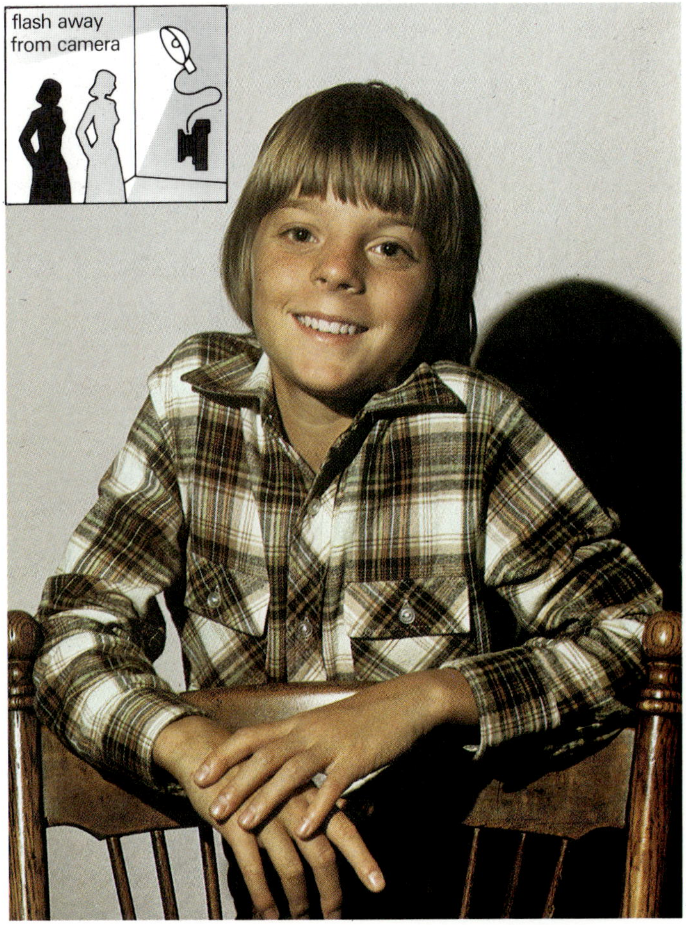
flash away from camera

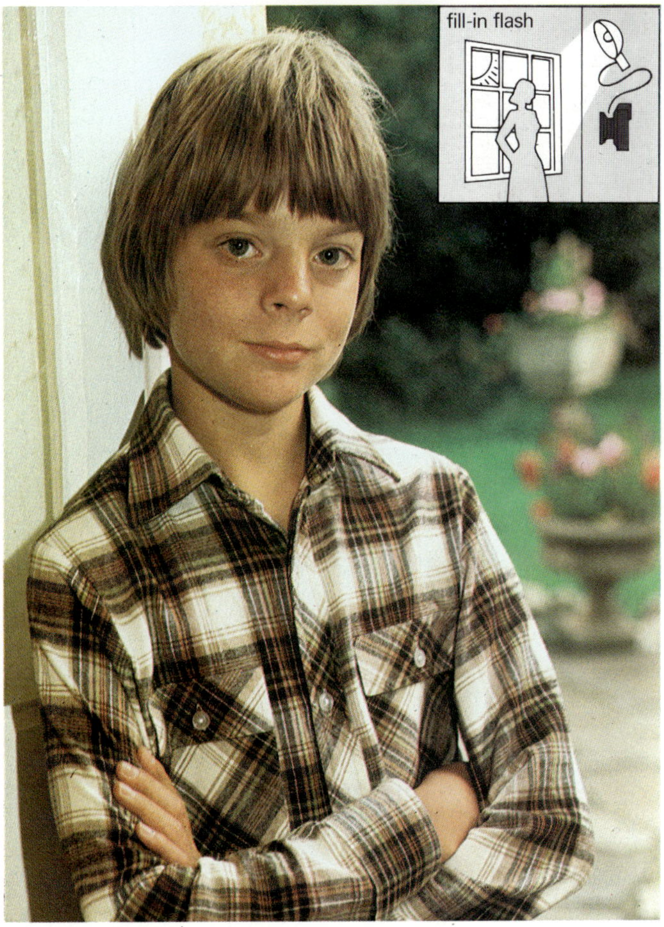
fill-in flash

Close-up equipment

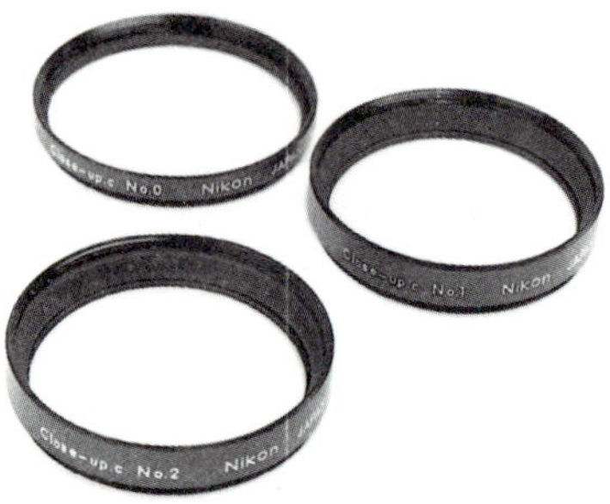

Above: Three close-up lenses of varying strengths.

Below: A set of extension tubes which can be used singly or in combination.

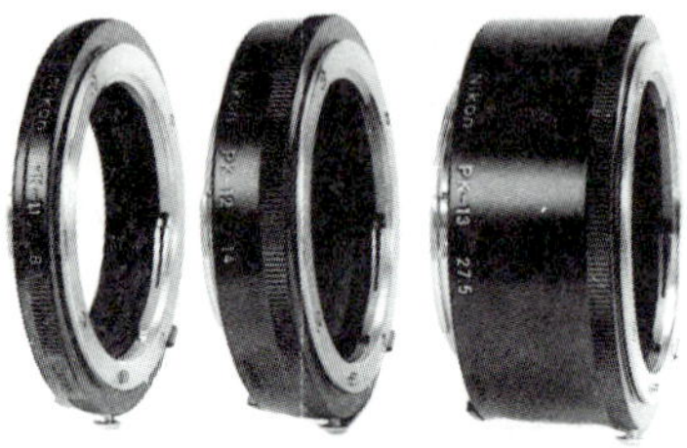

Below: This leaf was photographed with a close-up lens producing an image of approximately 1:3.

All but the most simple cameras are designed to focus at distances as close as three or four feet with a standard lens, but there are many types of picture where it is necessary to reduce the distance between the camera and subject. There is a variety of ways in which this can be achieved depending upon what type of camera you own and how much you are prepared to spend.

Close-up lenses. These are the most inexpensive attachments for extending the focusing range of a lens, and they can be used with most cameras that have a fixed lens, as well as those with interchangeable lenses. They are simply convex or positive lenses in a variety of strengths which are fitted into a filter mount and attached to the front of the camera lens. Depending on which strength of attachment is used and the focal length of the lens to which it is fitted it is possible to focus down to only a few inches. It is important when using these attachments to use as small an aperture as possible, as they will tend adversely to affect the performance of the camera lens, and a small aperture will minimize this effect.

It is important to remember, when using these attachments on a viewfinder camera, that the field of view shown in the viewfinder will become increasingly inaccurate the closer the camera is to the subject. It is possible to estimate the field of view actually covered by the camera by finding the true centre of the picture with the help of a straight edge (a thin piece of wood will do) running along the side of the lens axis into the picture. This will indicate where the centre of the picture area lies, and the view through the viewfinder can be adjusted accordingly.

A more convenient and satisfactory way of taking close-up pictures is with the help of extension tubes or a bellows unit. These can be fitted only to cameras with detachable lenses that have a built-in through-the-lens focusing system, such as a single lens reflex. Both of these accessories work on a similar principle, which is that they fit between the lens and the camera body and physically move it further away from the film, enabling it to focus at progressively closer distances. Extension tubes are usually sold in sets of three, each of a different length, and by combining them a range of different focusing distances can be used. The bellows are more controllable since they can simply be racked back and forth to achieve a continuously variable focusing distance.

A macro, or close-focusing lens is another convenient way of shooting close-ups for owners of single lens reflex cameras. It is a lens that can also be used for general purpose photography but has a greatly extended close-focusing range.

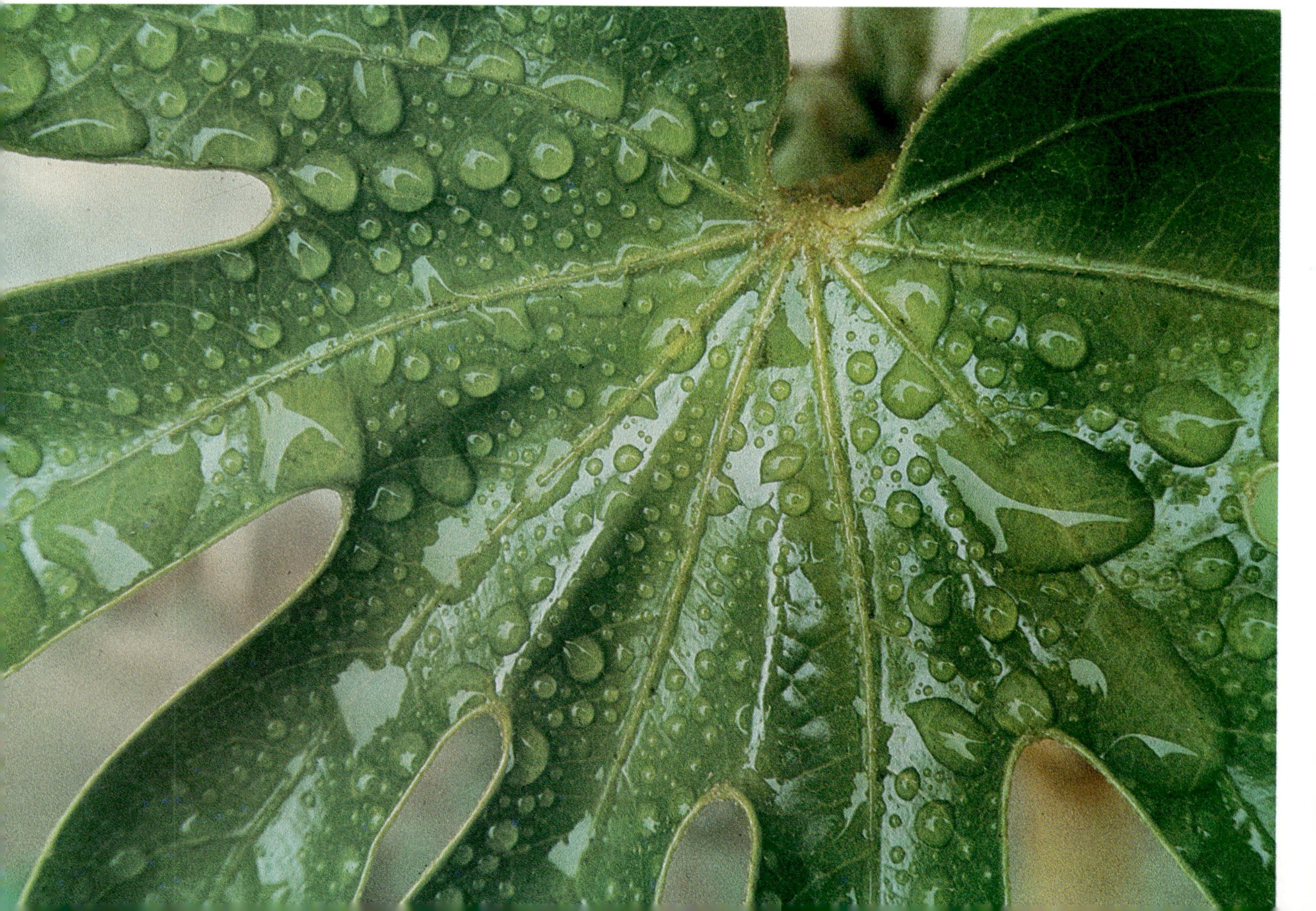

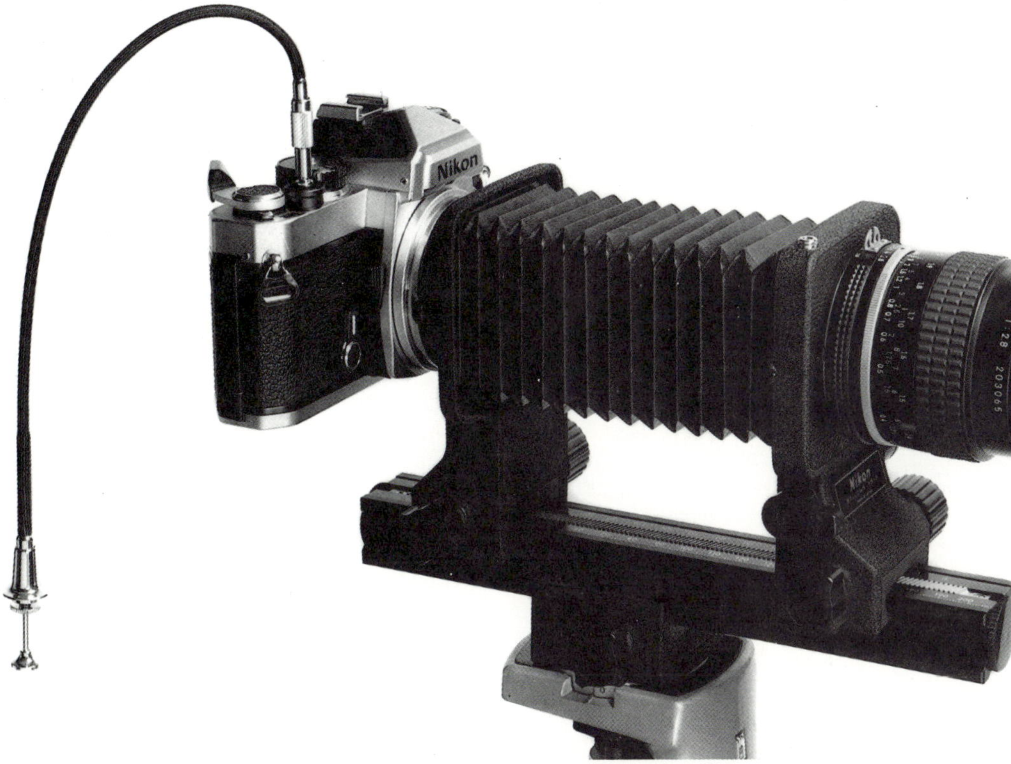

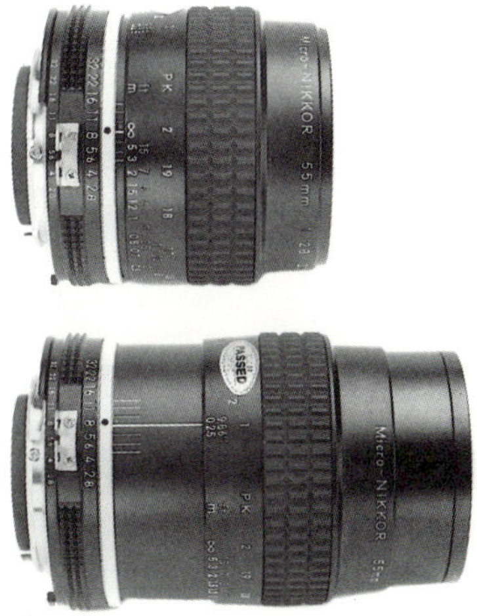

Left: A macro lens fitted to a bellows unit gives a variable close-focusing range. It is possibly the best combination of equipment for close-up photography.

Above: A macro lens at minimum and maximum extension. These are capable of focusing down to 1:2 ratio as illustrated above. When matched with a special extension tube they can focus down to 1:1.

Most lenses will focus down to about two feet, a macro lens will focus down to a couple of inches. A true macro lens will enable a larger than 1:1 image of the subject to be obtained on the film.

As soon as you start focusing at distances which are measured in inches rather than feet, the depth of field is drastically reduced and it is necessary to use the smallest aperture possible to ensure that your subject is sharp overall. If you are using natural light, then because of the small aperture quite long exposures will be needed and an invaluable accessory for close-up photography is a good, firm tripod with an adjustable head. This not only holds the camera steady on the longer exposures but also enables fine adjustments to be made to the camera position. At very close focusing distances the slightest movement of the camera will have a dramatic effect on both the focusing and the framing, and under these circumstances it is often easier to focus the image by moving the camera rather than using the focusing ring of the lens.

The exposure you give will also be affected when you are using extension tubes or bellows. Because the lens is being moved further away from the film, the light has also to travel further and extra exposure must be given to compensate. This can be calculated by measuring the distance the lens is at its new position from the film plane, squaring it and then dividing the number produced by the square of the focal length of the lens. Thus a 5 cm lens extended to 10 cm would need four times the exposure:

$$\frac{10^2}{5^2} = \frac{100}{25} = 4$$

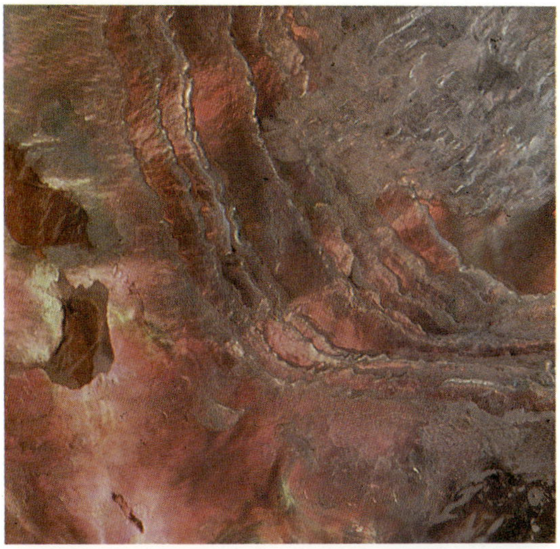

Left: Photo of an abalone shell taken with a macro lens at a ratio of 1:1.

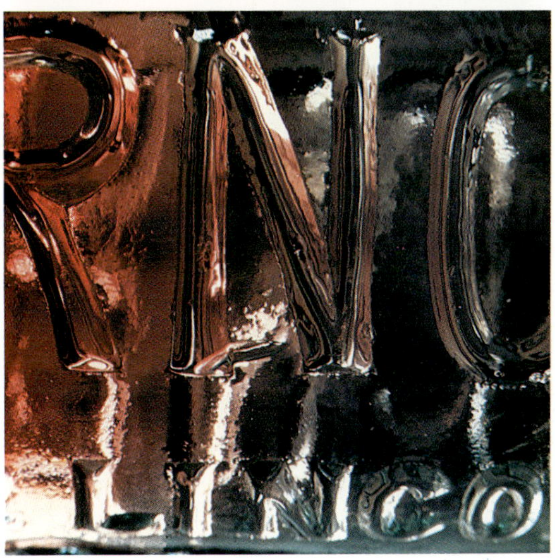

Below left: The base of this bottle was taken with a bellows unit at an approximate ratio of 2:1.

Exposure increase with lens extension in close-ups

Extension as %	With 50 mm lens	Exposure time
0%	50 mm	1 sec
10%	55 mm	1·2 sec
20%	60 mm	1·4 sec
30%	65 mm	1·7 sec
40%	70 mm	2 secs
50%	75 mm	2·3 secs
60%	80 mm	2·6 secs
70%	85 mm	2·9 secs
80%	90 mm	3·2 secs
90%	95 mm	3·6 secs
100%	100 mm	4 secs
110%	110 mm	4·8 secs
120%	120 mm	5·8 secs
130%	130 mm	6·8 secs
140%	140 mm	7·8 secs
150%	150 mm	9 secs

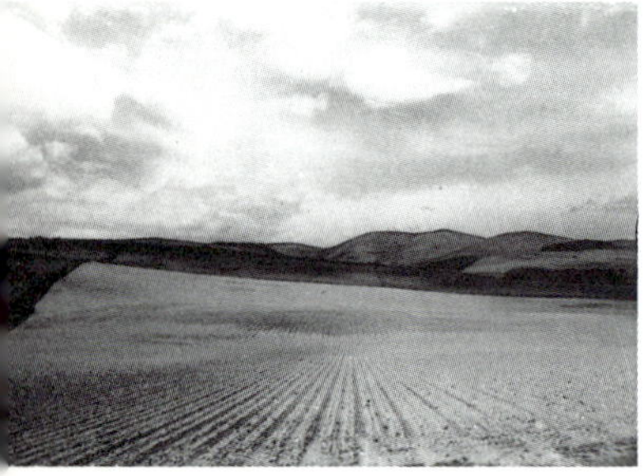

The above picture was taken without the use of a filter.

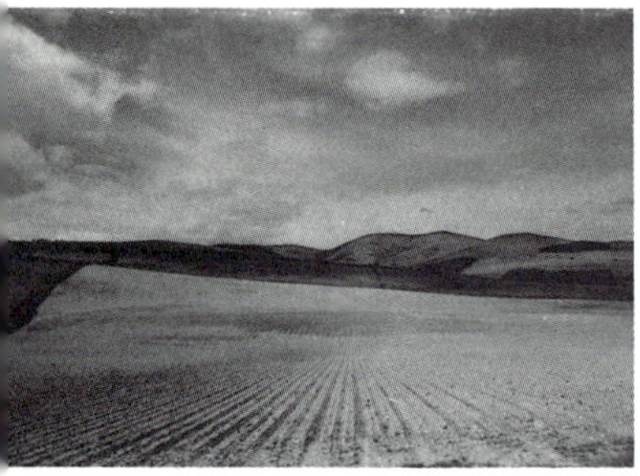

This picture was taken with a deep red filter which required a 3-stop increase in exposure to compensate.

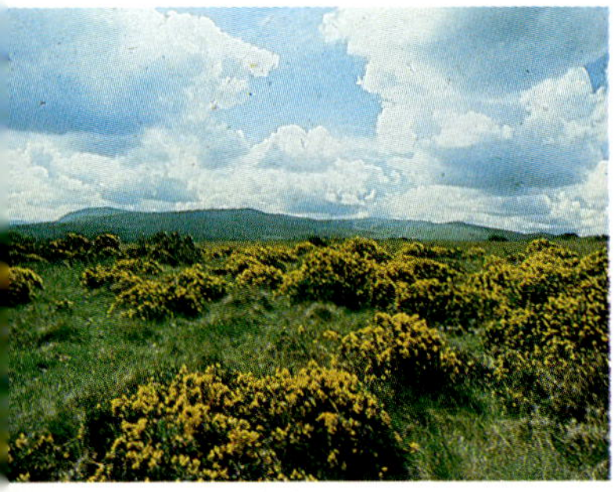

Above: No filter was used and the sky is overexposed and lacking in detail. *Right:* Slightly less exposure has been given and a polarizing filter has been used producing a far more dramatic result.

Black-and-white filters. Normal black-and-white films record colours in terms of the amount of light they reflect. For instance, a subject which consists of green, red and blue, each of equal brightness, would record on black-and-white film as a mixture of greys of a similar tone and may well look rather flat and uninteresting. Coloured filters can be used very effectively in black-and-white photography to alter the tonal balance and improve both the clarity and contrast of a photograph.

Each of the primary colours when used as a filter passes the light of its own colour quite freely but holds back some or all of the other two colours, depending on both the strength of the filter and the depth of the colours in the subject. A deep red filter, for example, would allow all the red in the scene to pass and would record them as a darker tone on the negative and subsequently lighter on the print. It would hold back the greens and the blues which would both record as much lighter tones on the negative and on the print would appear as very much darker tones than they would without the filter.

Filters for colour. The filters used for normal effects in colour photography are generally much weaker than those for black-and-white pictures since a filter of a deep-red, for example, would simply turn the picture into a purely red image. There are two basic types of filters for colour film: correction filters and effect filters.

Correction filters are designed to offset any differences between the colour quality of the light and the film in use. For example, if you wanted to take a picture in tungsten light but using daylight film, then without a filter the resulting picture would have a strong orange cast. By using a bluish correction filter the orange cast can be removed, giving a normal result. The opposite technique can be used when shooting in daylight with tungsten film. Both of these examples are quite strong filters and much weaker ones can be used to correct smaller changes in the colour quality of the light. A pale-straw colour filter, such as a Wratten 81A, can be used to remove the slight blue cast often produced when shooting on a cloudy day or in open shade when there is blue sky. A bluish filter such as a Wrattan 82A can be used to offset the warm cast created by evening sunlight. The effect of this type of filter is not intended to be noticed but there are occasions when you may want to create a particular colour effect, and there is a wide range of filters that can help to produce pictures with a more unusual quality. Colour burst filters, for example, can create rainbow-like streaks of light from bright highlights in a scene and graduated filters can be used to introduce a colour cast into only one-half of a picture, the sky in a landscape for example, leaving the rest of the image unaffected. One of the most useful filters which, although not having an unnatural effect,

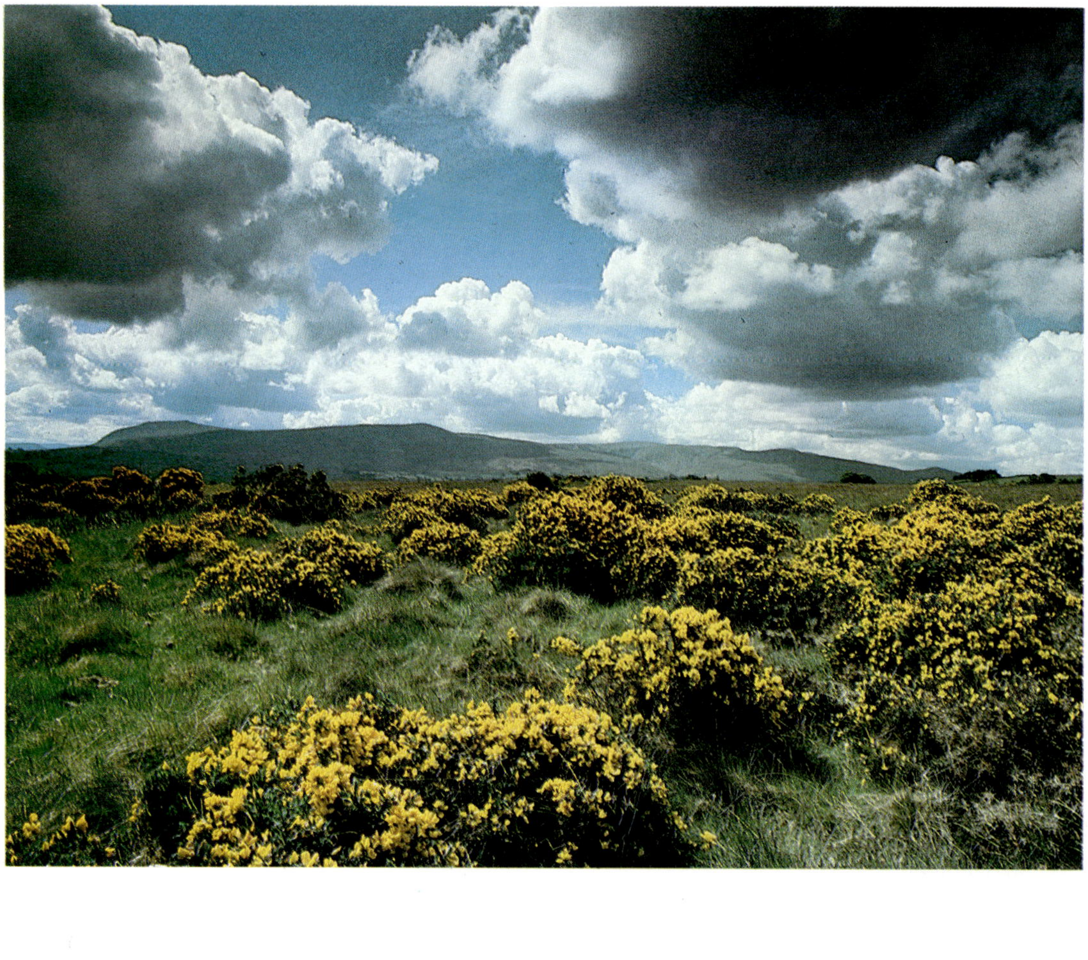

can produce pictures with much stronger colours and more impact, is the polarizing filter. It is neutral grey in colour and requires about one-and-a-half to two stops more exposure. It has the effect of reducing the amount of light which is reflected off the subject, resulting in pictures with much richer and deeper colours. It has to be rotated in its mount to obtain the strongest effect. It is particularly useful with subjects like landscape pictures. Blue skies are much deeper, with white clouds standing out in sharp relief, and, by reducing the light which is being reflected off foliage, strength is added to the colours of trees and fields. Also, when used at the seaside it can make the sea look much more colourful and translucent.

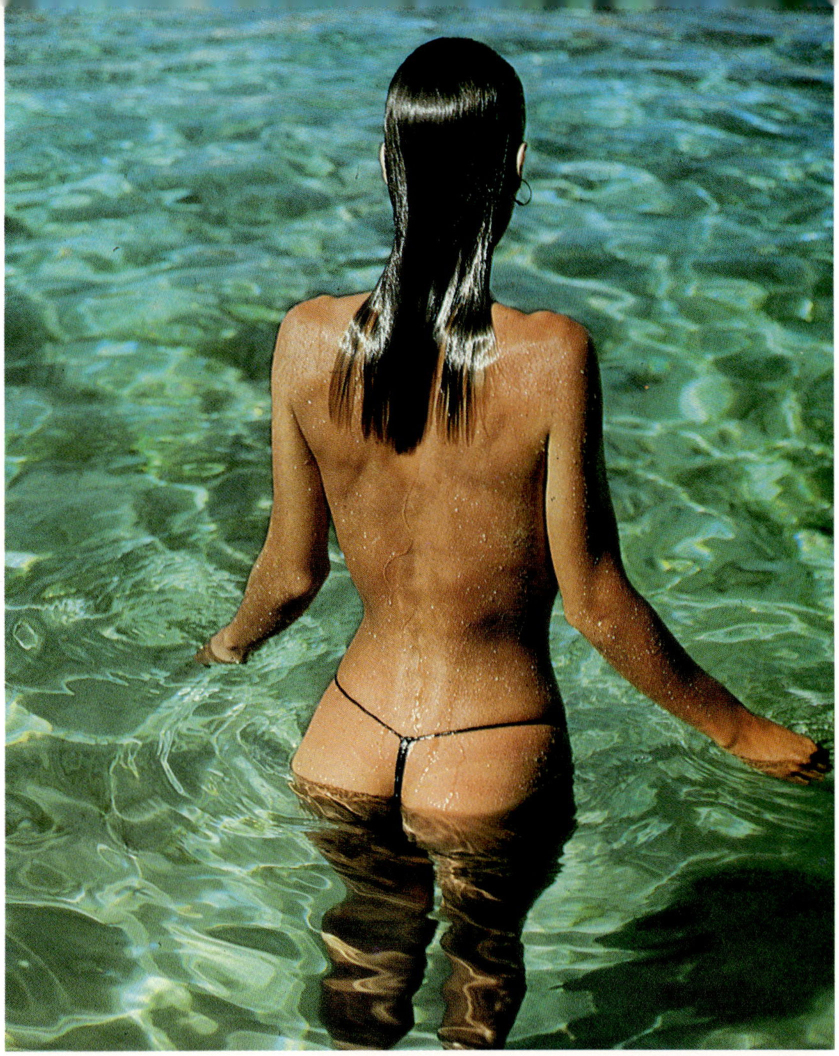

Right: This shows the effect of a polarizing filter on water, emphasizing its colour and translucence.

Below: A starburst filter was used to obtain this effect. These come in a variety of configurations; this one produces sixteen rays.

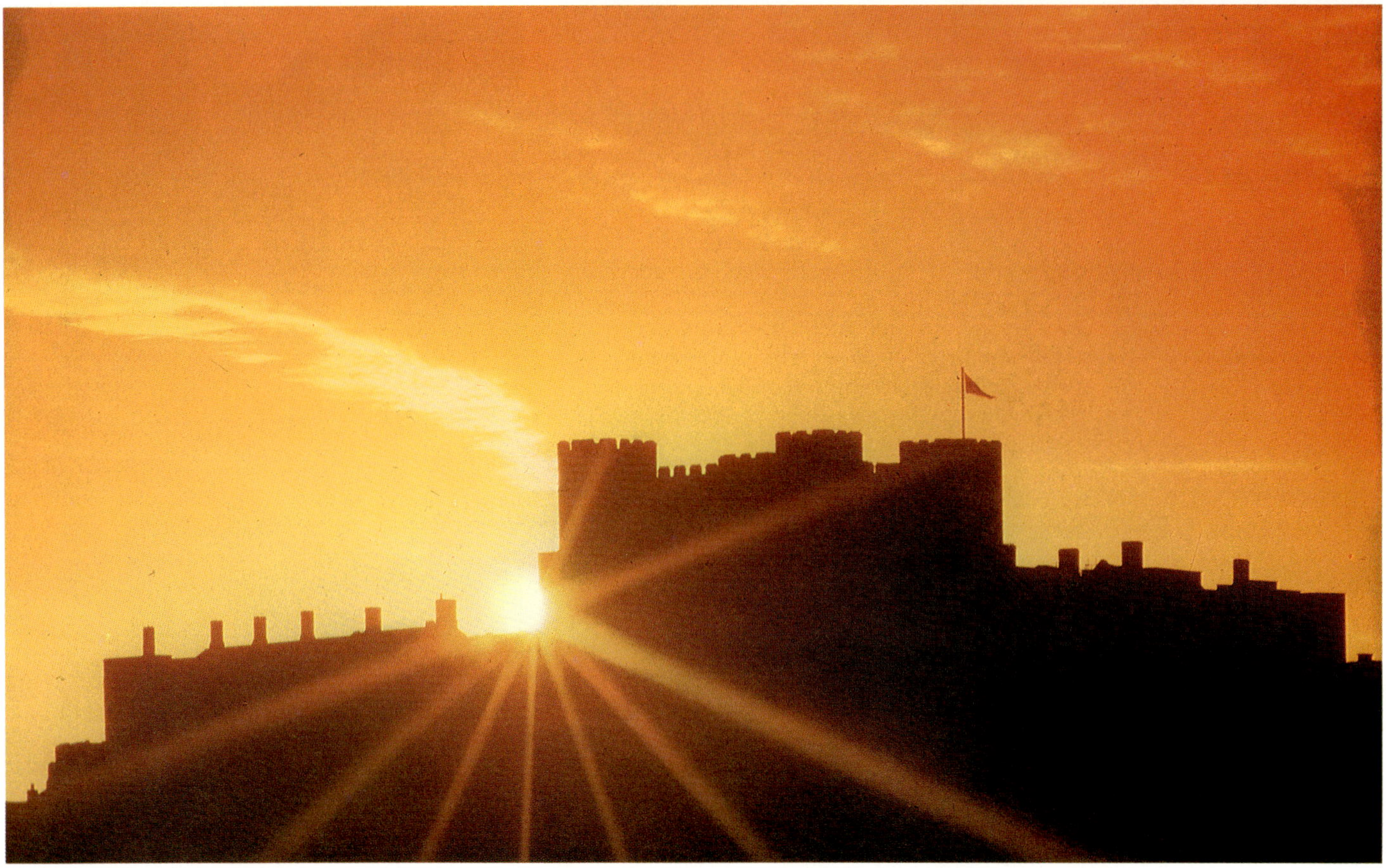

Wide-angle lenses

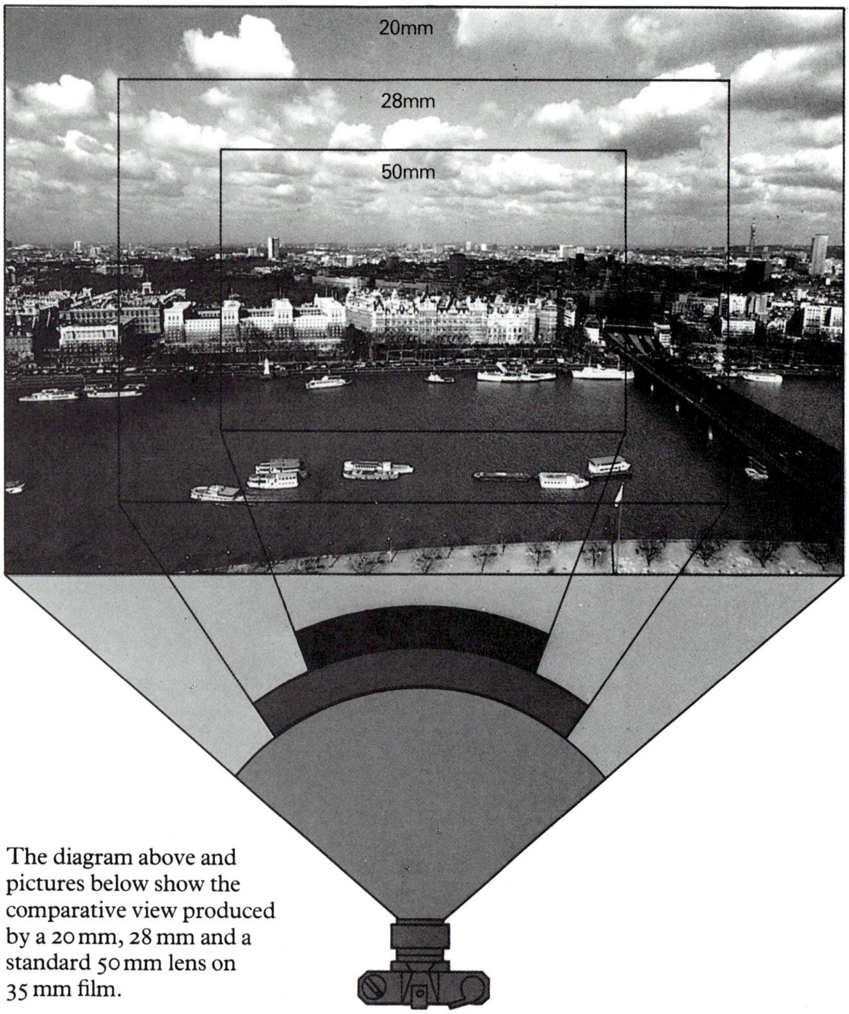

The diagram above and pictures below show the comparative view produced by a 20 mm, 28 mm and a standard 50 mm lens on 35 mm film.

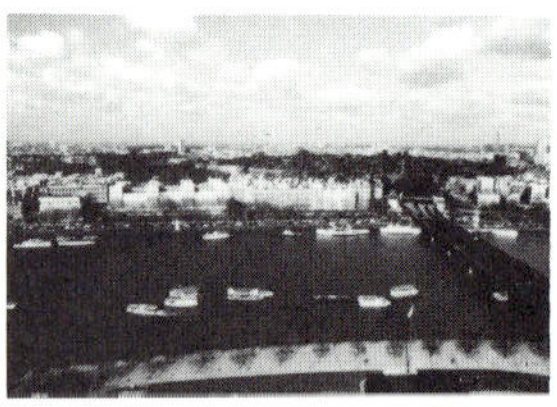

20mm

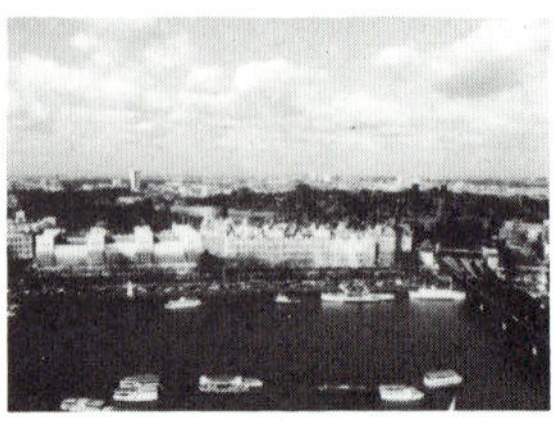

28mm

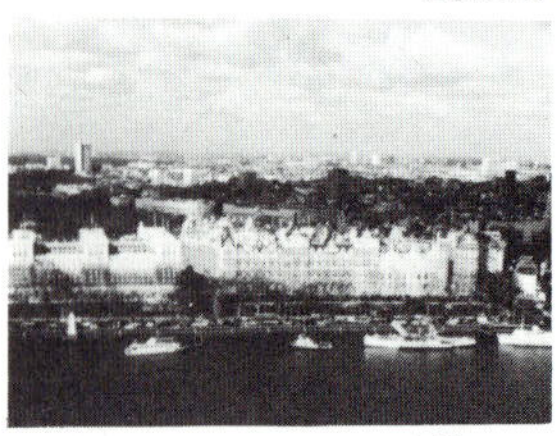

50mm

One of the ways in which a photographer can greatly extend the scope of his camera is by adding a lens of a different focal length to that of the standard lens with which most cameras are supplied. The standard lens is designed to give an angle of view of between forty-five and fifty-five degrees. On a 35 mm camera this requires a focal length of between 4.5 cm and 5.5 cm. A lens with a shorter focal length will give a correspondingly wider angle of view. A 24 mm lens for example will give a field of view of eighty-four degrees. In practical terms this means that the effect seen through the viewfinder of changing from say a 50 mm lens to a 24 mm lens is that the extent of the scene now included in the picture area will have doubled and the size of the objects in it will have halved. The most basic use of a wide-angle lens is therefore simply to enable you to get more of the scene on to the film without having to move the camera further away. Another advantage of the wide-angle lens is its apparently greater depth of field, and even at the wider apertures objects will appear sharper over a greater range of distances. Consequently focusing becomes rather less critical with such a lens and when a very wide-angle lens, such as an 18 or 20 mm, is used at a very small aperture it is possible to obtain a sharp image from only a foot or so in front of the camera out to infinity.

Because a wide-angle lens enables objects which are much closer to the camera to be included in the picture it also has the effect of emphasizing and exaggerating perspective. This is something which can be used to add impact to a picture, but if allowed to occur accidentally will be more likely to give a distorted and unpleasant quality.

As a wide-angle lens is capable of including far more of the subject in the picture and can record almost all the detail equally sharply, it is necessary to give even more consideration to the composition of the image to avoid the main subject being lost and dominated by the surrounding details. The effect of a change of viewpoint will be more dramatic when using a wide-angle lens, and a shift of even a few feet will make a significant difference to the composition of the picture, particularly when there are close foreground details. The effect of both high and low viewpoints will also be emphasized with such a lens.

The choice of a focal length for a wide-angle lens will depend to some extent on the type of subjects you want to photograph. A 35 mm or a

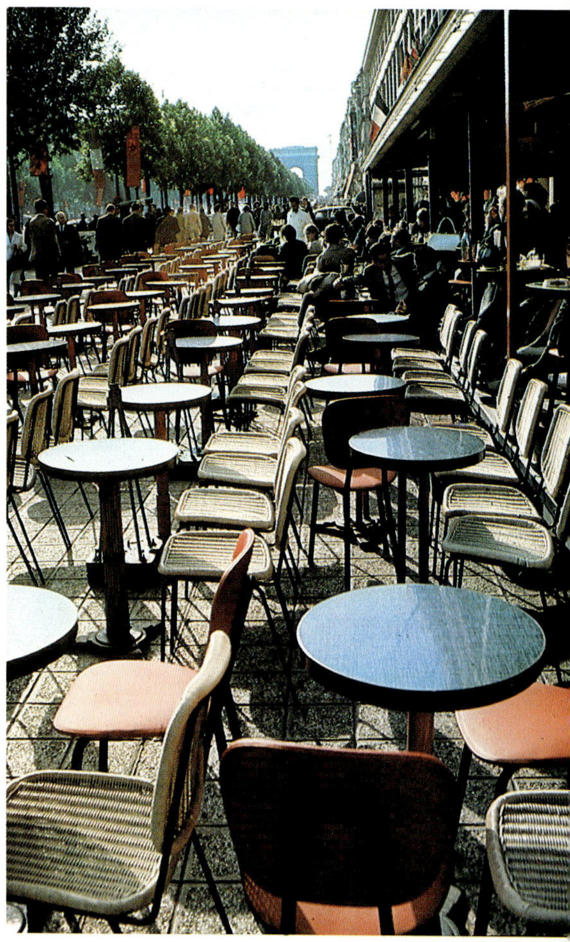

28 mm on a 35 mm camera would be a good length for photographing people, where the perspective exaggerations of a wider angle may be undesirable. For landscape photography a 28 mm or a 24 mm is a good compromise and if you are primarily interested in photographing buildings and interiors it may be worth considering a lens as wide as 20 mm. It should be remembered that with a lens that includes slightly more than is needed it is always possible to crop the picture and obtain the effect of a longer focal length, whereas it is not, of course, possible to produce the effect of a wider angle without another lens.

Once you have acquired a wide-angle lens you will find that you will start to look at your subjects in a slightly different way. You will notice for instance whether or not some interesting foreground details can be included in a landscape to give more depth, or you may find scenes with a strong perspective which can be emphasized. With subjects like architecture a wide-angle lens will make it possible to take pictures in confined spaces, where with a longer focal-length lens you would not be able to consider such pictures. When photographing people you will find that a wide-angle lens will enable you to shoot from a much closer viewpoint and still include all of your subject; or in pictures with people in the foreground you will find that it is possible to include more of the background.

Left: A 24 mm lens was used to take this picture of the Champs Elysées. At an aperture of f 8 the depth is still considerable.

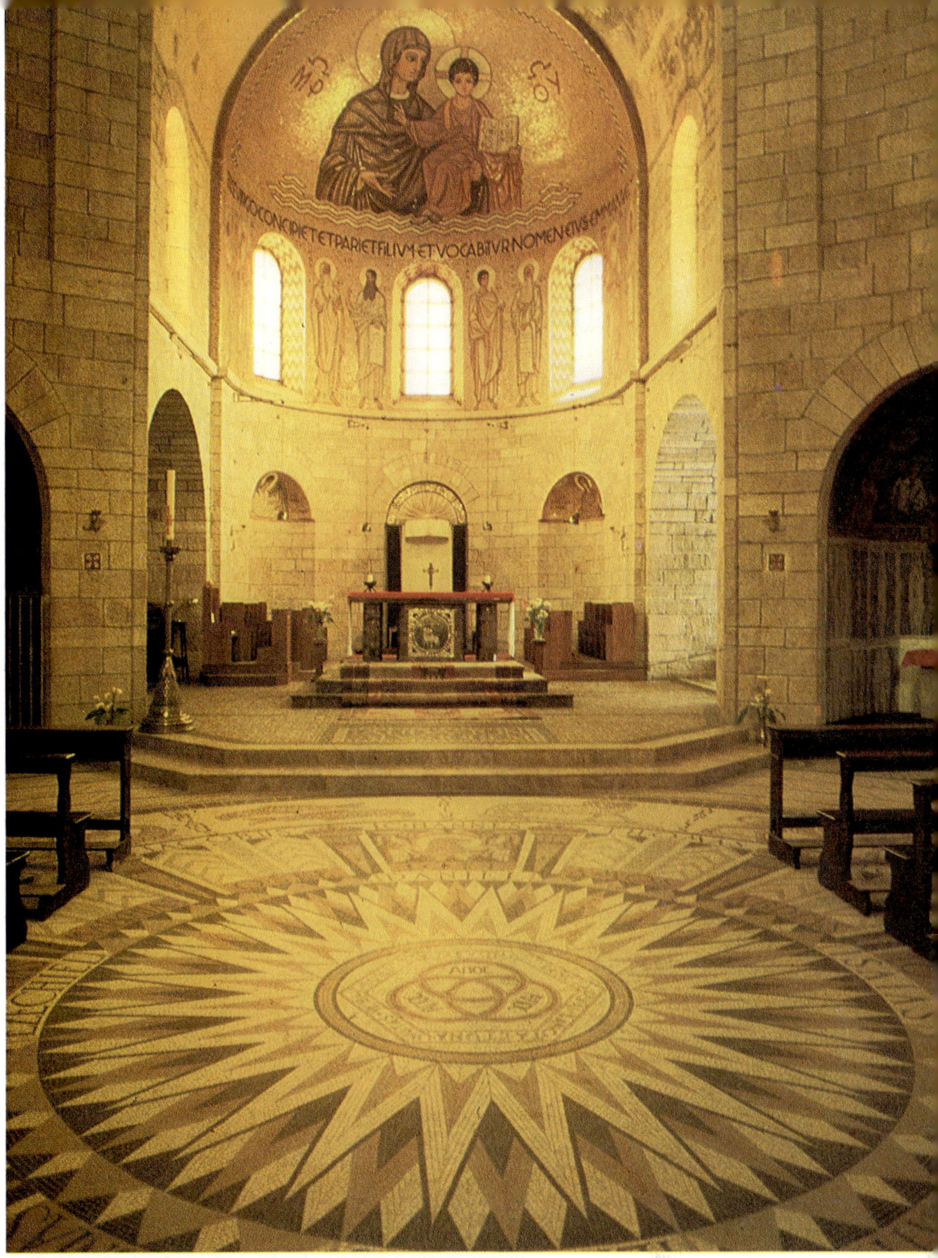

Above: This church interior was taken with a 20 mm lens. The camera was kept vertical to avoid converging uprights.

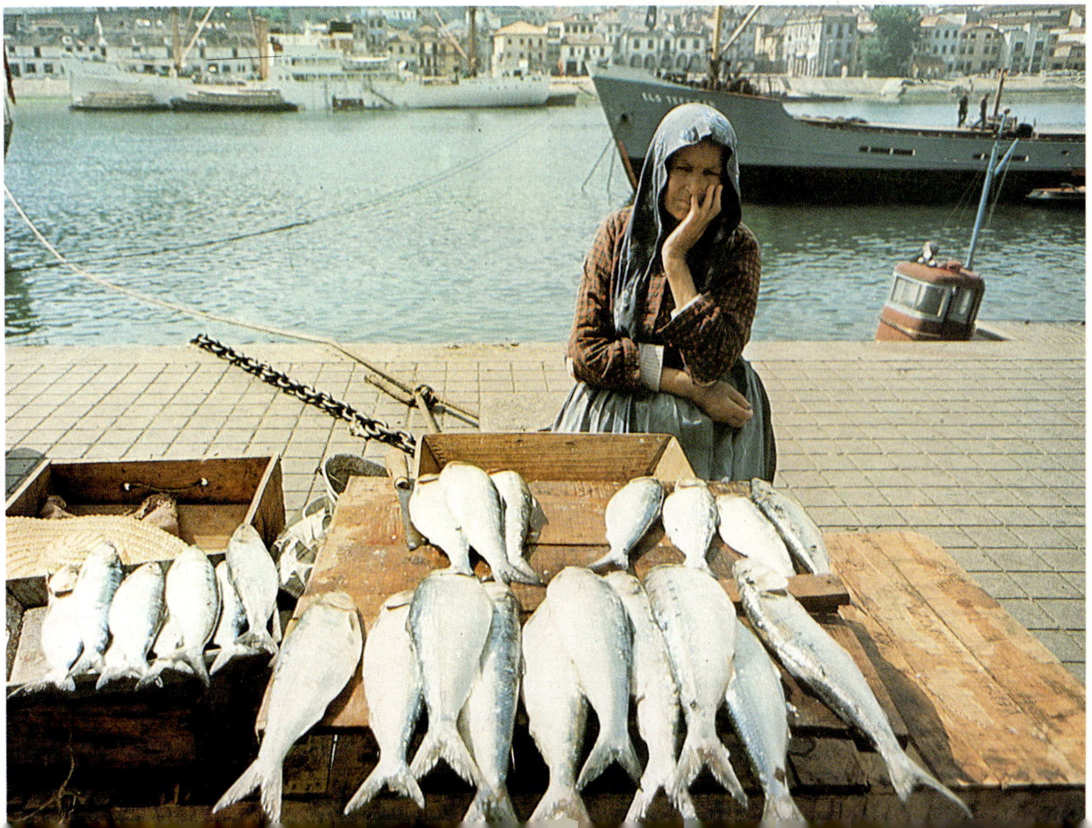

Left: A 28 mm lens enabled the foreground to be included and brought out even though the picture was taken from quite a close viewpoint.

Long-focus lenses

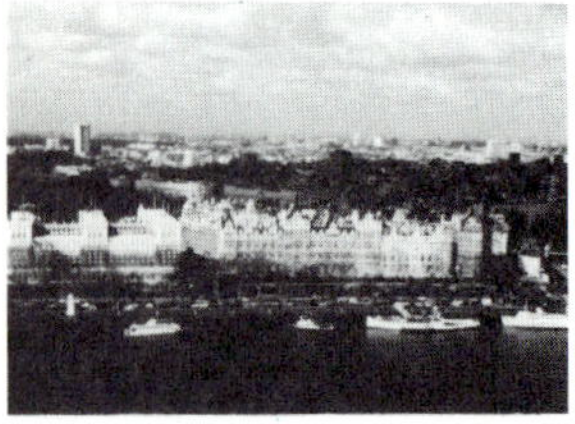

50mm

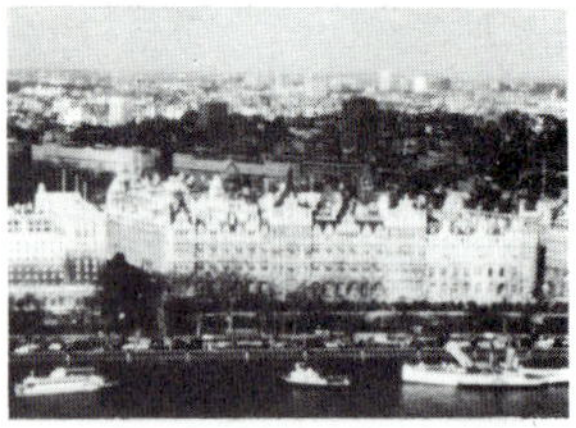

100mm

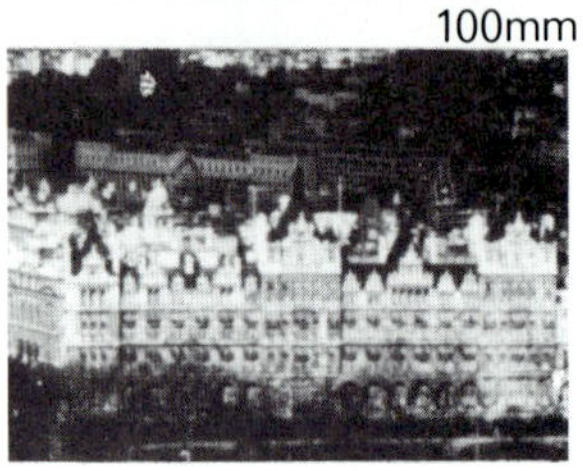

200mm

The diagram (*right*) and pictures (*above*) illustrate the views produced by a 50 mm standard, 100 mm and 200 mm lenses on 35 mm film.

Below: With a 300 mm lens the distant viewpoint and enlarged image accentuates the scale of the sand-dune.

A long-focus or telephoto lens has a narrower angle of view than the standard lens and a correspondingly longer focal length. The most obvious effect of a long-focus lens when looking through the viewfinder is that the picture area is reduced and the subject has been enlarged. For example, a 150 mm lens on a 35 mm camera would increase the size of the subject by three times in comparison to a 50 mm lens. You will also find that the depth of field has been considerably reduced, and that only a limited plane in front and behind the point of focus will be completely sharp. This can be increased by using a small aperture but focusing needs to be quite accurate when using such lenses. In addition it will be found that the problem of camera shake will be exaggerated and that more care will be needed when holding the camera and releasing the shutter. A faster shutter speed is also advisable, and with lenses longer than say 200 mm on 35 mm cameras a tripod is a distinct advantage.

A telephoto lens is simply a long-focus lens which has been designed so that its focusing distance to the film has been optically compressed, making it physically more compact than a straightforward long lens of the same focal length. A mirror lens has a similar effect but an optical mirror is used instead of the compressed lens. Although these lenses are very compact they have an effective focal length of 500 or 1000 mm or more.

The main advantage of a long-focus lens is that it enables a small area of a scene to be isolated and enlarged in the camera without having to move closer to the subject. This has many useful applications: sports photography is an obvious example where a photographer simply cannot get close enough to the action to obtain a large enough image with a standard lens. This ability to reach out optically and isolate small areas of a scene is also very useful in landscape photography and the acquisition of a lens of 135 mm or even 200 mm will literally open up new possibilities with this type of subject. For sports and action photography it may be worth considering an even longer focal-length lens of, say, 300 mm, particularly if your interest lies in arena sports such as football, where the action takes place at a considerable distance from the permitted viewpoints. There are also other occasions where, although it would be possible to approach the subject more closely, it is preferable to keep at a distance and use a longer lens to enlarge the image.

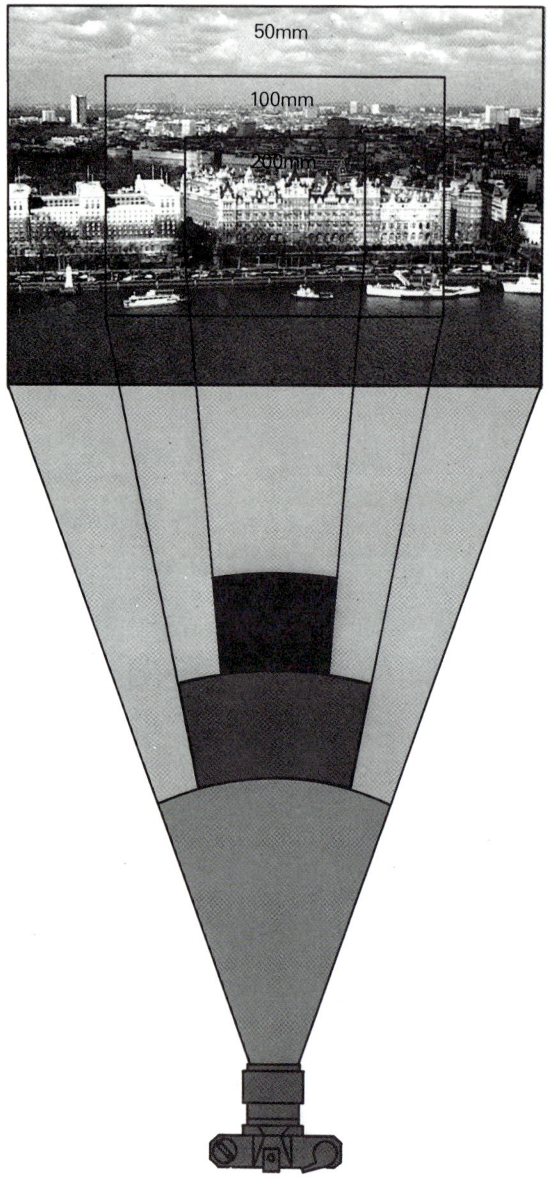

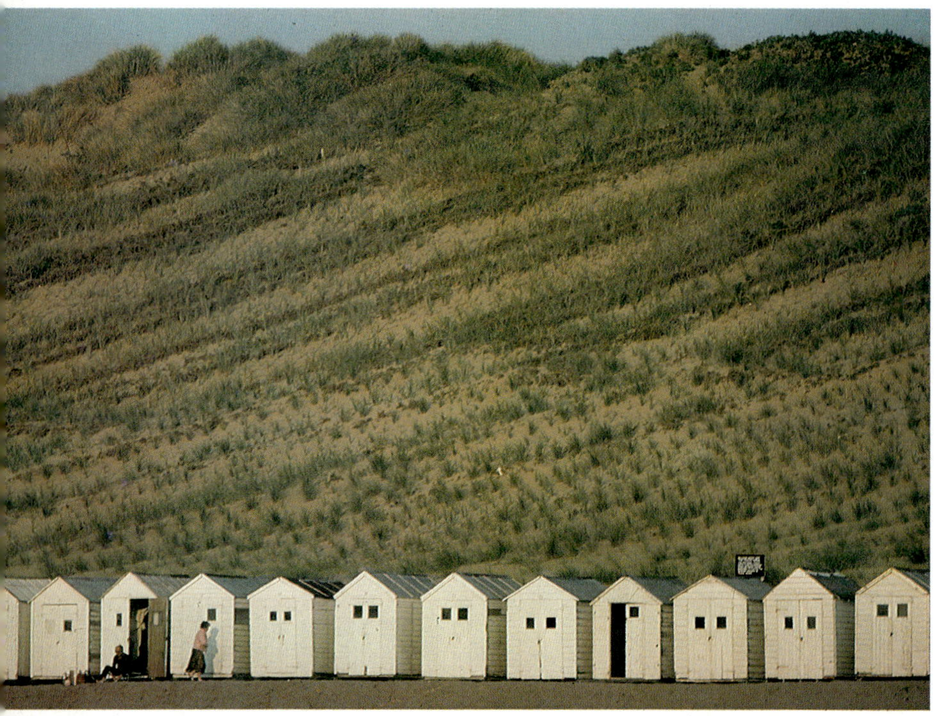

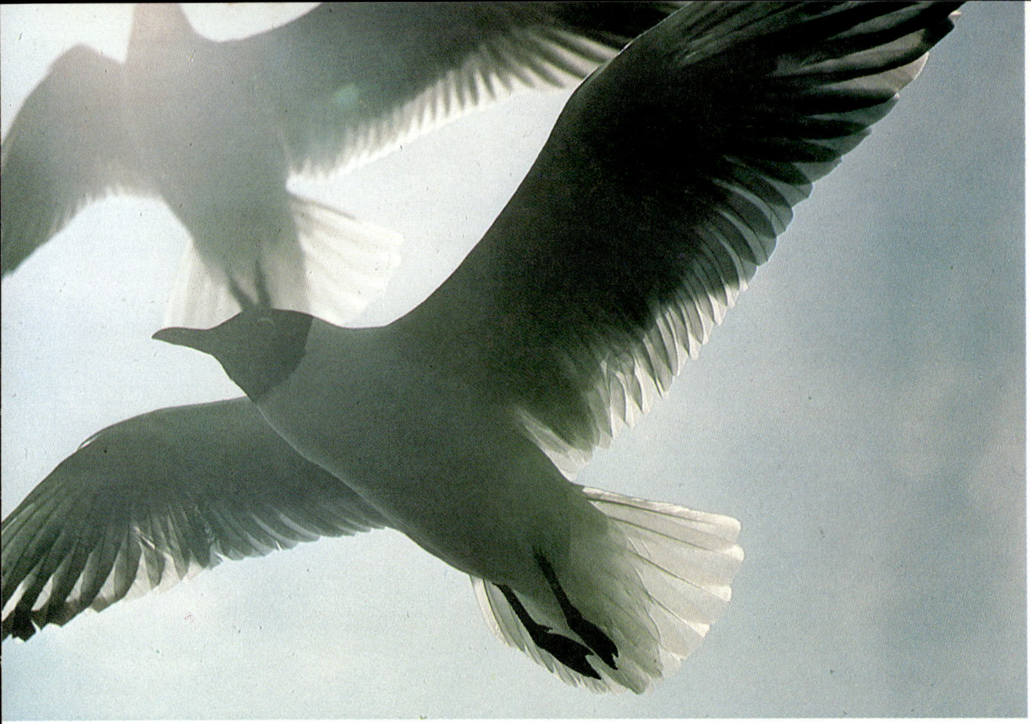

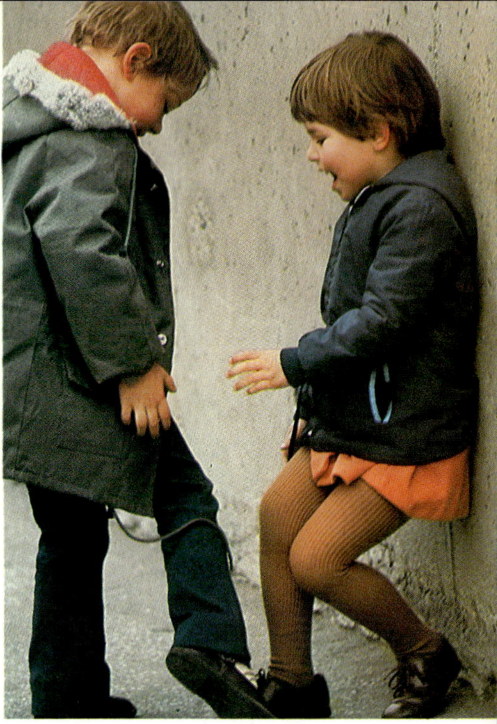

In portraiture, if one approaches the model closely enough to produce a large image of the head with a standard lens there will be a noticeable and often unpleasant exaggeration of perspective, and the model's face will appear somewhat distorted. Shooting from a greater distance with a long lens will also provide a less intimidating atmosphere for the model. When photographing children it is important to avoid disturbing them, and a 105 mm or 135 mm lens is very useful for such photography. With pictures of this type the shallow depth of field which a long lens produces can be a positive advantage since it enables you to focus sharply on the subject while keeping the background well out of focus.

There is now a wide choice available of good quality zoom lenses offering a continuous range of focal lengths within the same lens. For instance a 70–150 mm would provide a very useful choice of settings for someone interested in portraiture, children and reportage photography, while the rather bulkier 70–210 mm lenses could be used for many sport or wildlife subjects as well. Many of these lenses are also provided with a close-focusing or macro facility which makes them ideal for photographing small animals and close-ups of flowers.

The two pictures above were taken using a 70–150 mm zoom lens and the picture below was taken with a 500 mm mirror lens. It can be seen that the depth of field is quite shallow while the sun appears to be enormous.

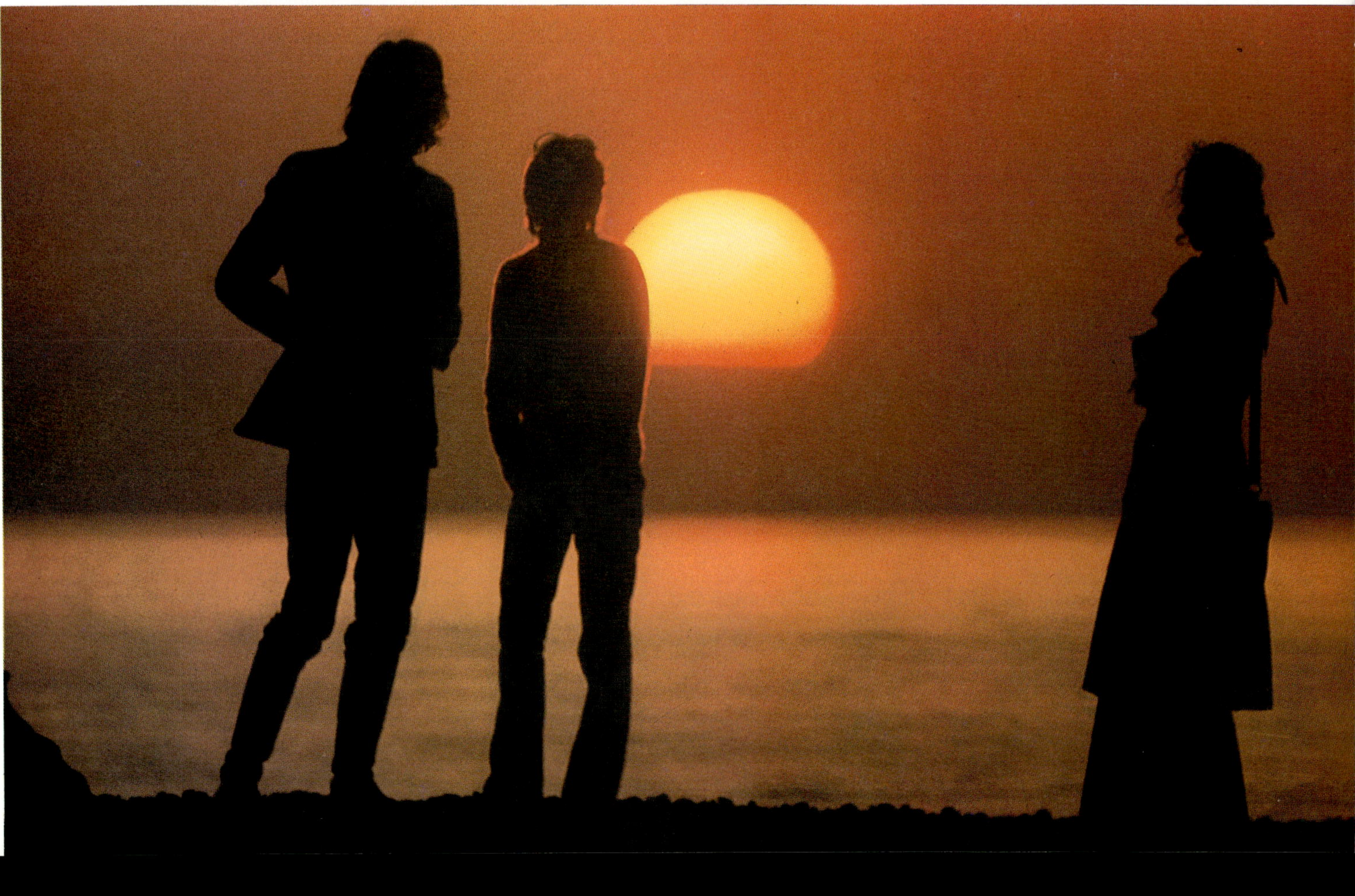

The family album

Below: These two pictures of a children's party were taken using an ultra-fast film and available light, resulting in the minimum of interference of the subject and greater spontaneity.

Many people first take an interest in photography in order to make a record of their family life, taking pictures of children, relations, special occasions and so on. This often leads to a much wider interest in the subject, but unfortunately many enthusiasts who develop photographic skills tend to neglect the family album. A family in which there is a keen photographer tends to have fewer family pictures than the more casual photographer may have. This is, of course, a pity, since a good pictorial record of a family will give a great deal of pleasure to many generations. It is worth taking a little time and trouble as a good photograph of a happy occasion will provide a far more satisfying and pleasurable memory than an indifferent one.

One of the most common faults with pictures of this type is that the taking of the picture becomes an occasion in itself. Everybody stops what they are doing and stand self-consciously staring into the lens. It is far better to take pictures where people are more conscious of the occasion than they are of the camera. At a wedding, for instance, it is customary and indeed desirable to have pictures of the more formal groups of people, but it is invariably the informal pictures, taken when the subjects are unaware of the camera, that provide the real atmosphere of the occasion. Even a formal group can produce a more interesting picture if the photographer tries to get his models to react a little, either making them laugh spontaneously at the moment the exposure is made or taking the picture at a moment when they are talking amongst themselves. Sometimes it is worth taking one shot in a quite composed way and then shooting another immediately after when your subjects are more relaxed.

If you are asked to produce a complete record of an occasion such as a wedding, perhaps in place of a professional photographer, it is vital to plan it carefully beforehand. You should visit the church a day or two earlier, find some suitable backgrounds for the groups and check for permission to shoot inside the church or the vestry. It is also well worthwhile to work out a list of pictures to be taken, including any specially requested, and to decide in what order to take them. It is always a good idea to take the bride and groom away to a quiet pre-selected corner

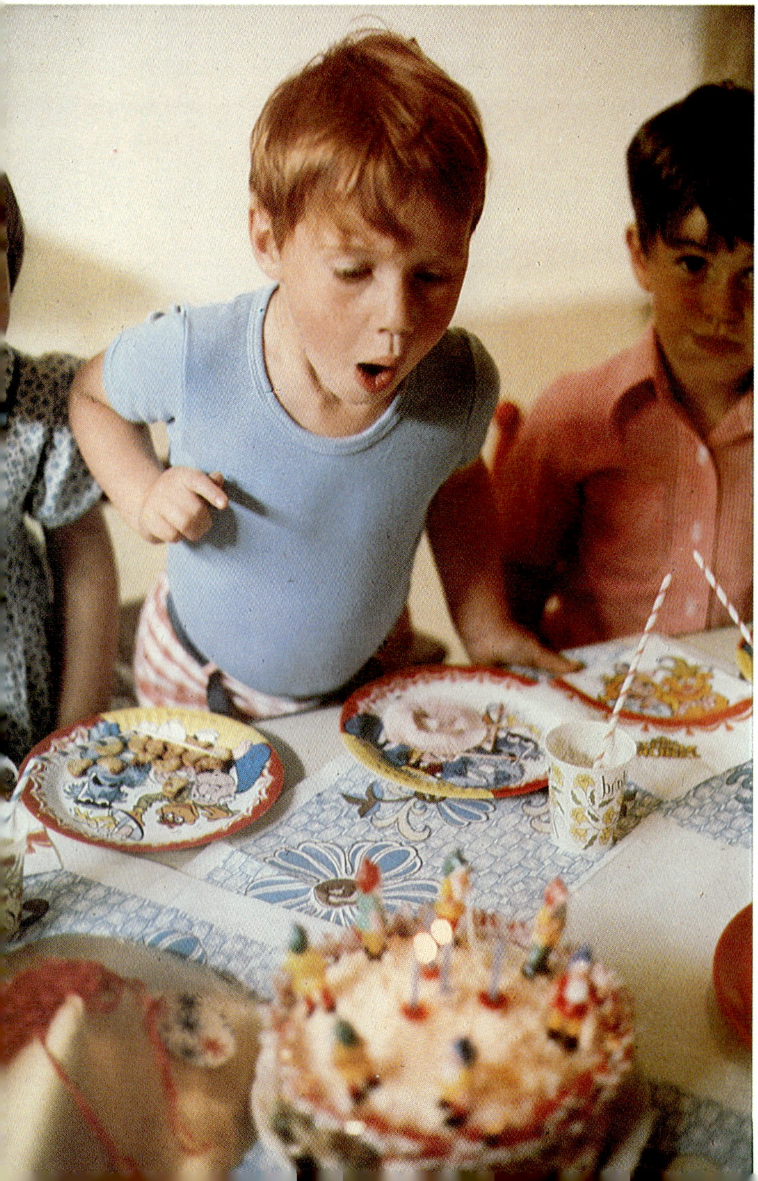

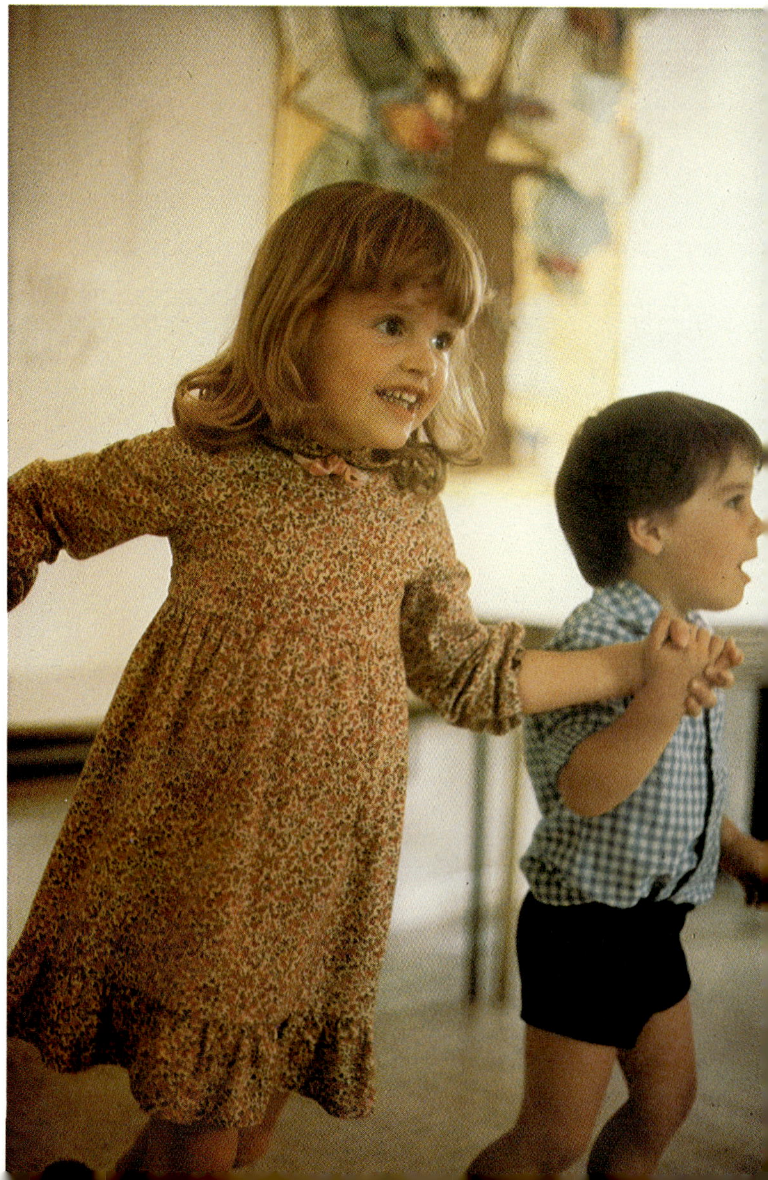

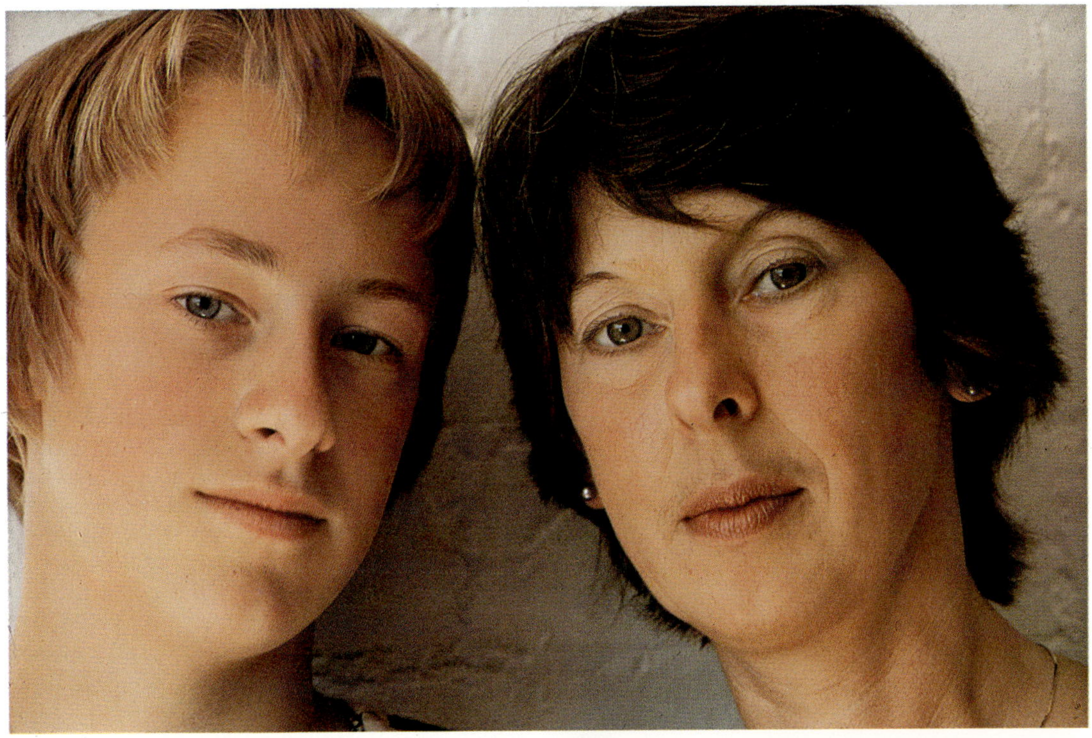

This mother and son portrait was photographed indoors using the light from a window and a white reflector to fill in the shadows.

Below: Framing quite tightly and keeping the background neutral and uncluttered has emphasized the bride's happy and spontaneous expression. Soft lighting has ensured that the inherently high contrast of wedding pictures (white dresses and dark suits) has not become a problem.

aside from the other guests so that you can get them quite relaxed for their own portraits.

With occasions like a children's party or at Christmas a common mistake is to attempt to get too much into the pictures. Although it is nice to have at least one with everyone present included, you are more likely to capture the atmosphere and produce a more interesting photograph by selecting and isolating smaller parts of the scene. At a children's party, for example, a series of close-up pictures of individual faces with lively and spontaneous expressions, blowing out the candles on the cake or putting on a party hat, are more likely to provide a really evocative record of the occasion than a shot of everyone seated round a table.

Another important consideration is the way in which the atmosphere can be successfully captured on film. Often this has a great deal to do with lighting. A subject like a Christmas party, with a tree covered in fairy lights, could be completely spoiled by drowning everything with a powerful flash. It is worthwhile considering using a fast film and making the most of the existing lighting in order to retain the atmosphere of such a scene. While the purpose is to take good pictures of these family occasions no one is going to want to turn them into full-scale photographic sessions and you should aim to shoot as unobtrusively as possible. Often a basic camera and lens with a fast film, coupled with a keen eye, will produce far more satisfying results than trying to shoot with different lenses and flash equipment, which will become an intrusion on the occasion and the mood will be lost.

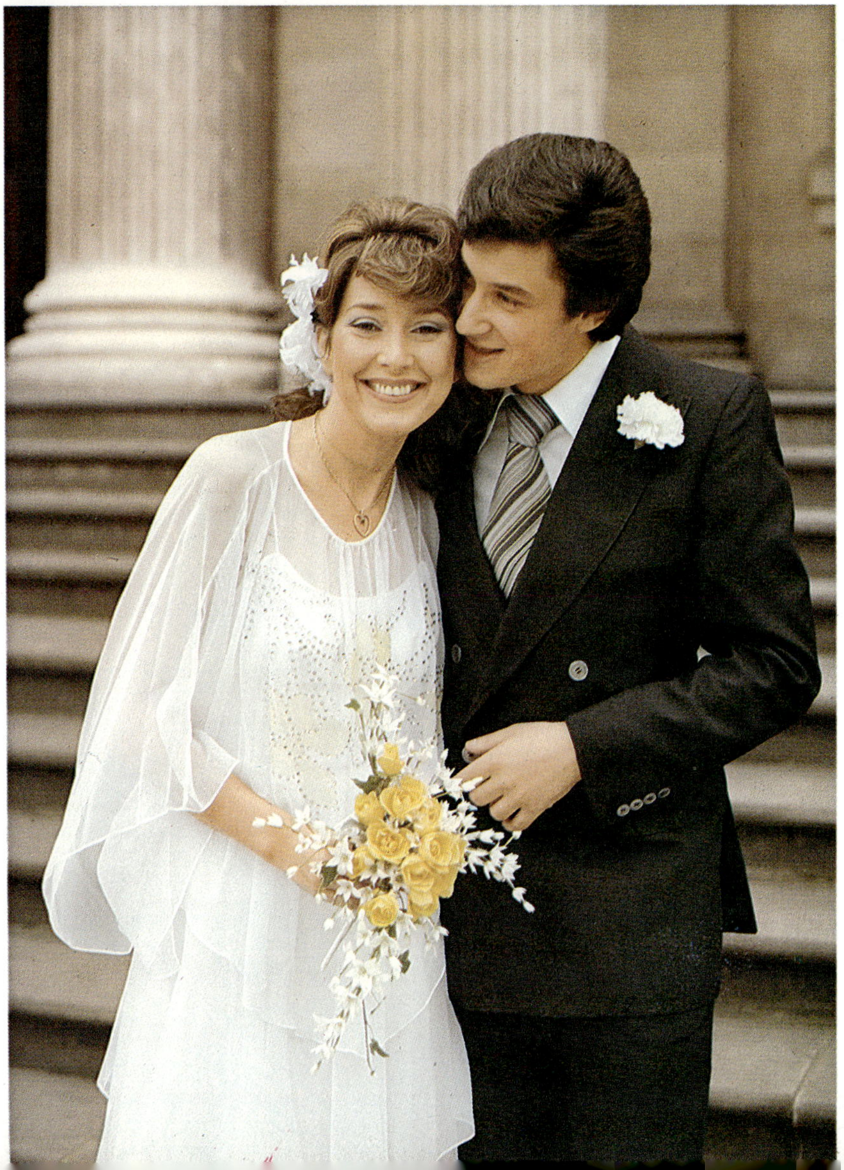

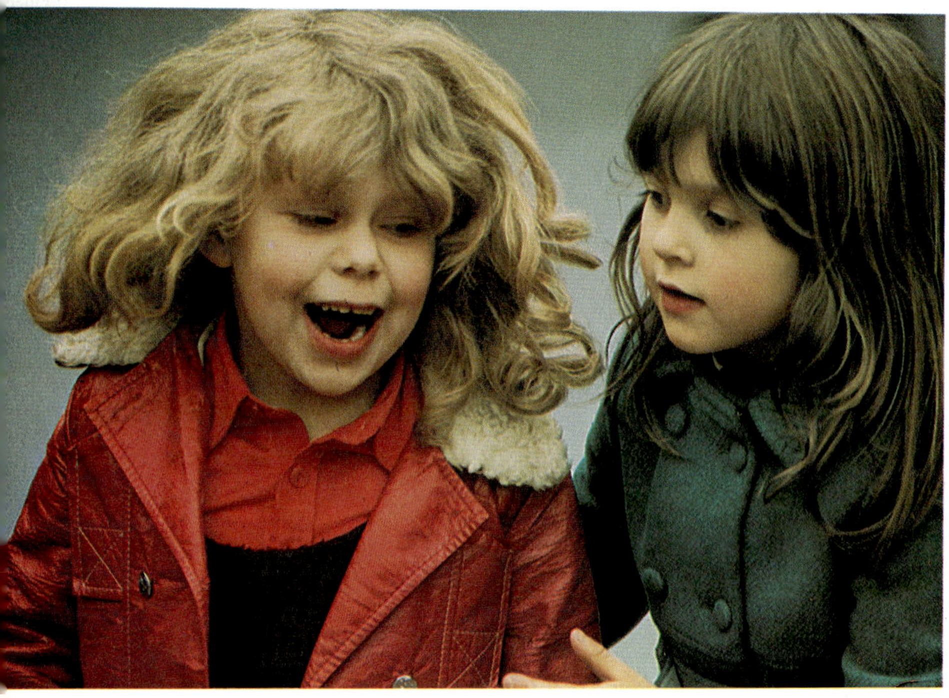

Above: In a school playground the children became less self-conscious as they became less aware of the camera.

Below: A child's preoccupation with play invariably provides a good subject. The bold contrast with the background adds impact to this picture.

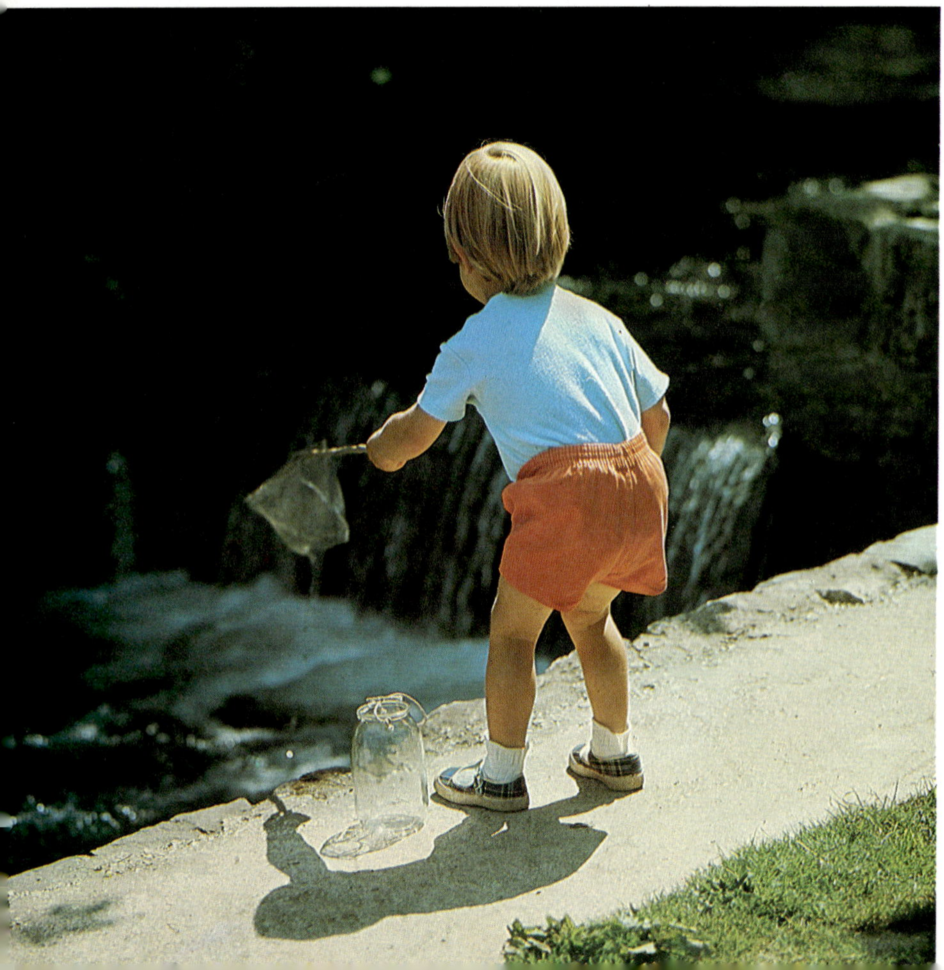

Young children and babies are rewarding subjects for photography as they possess an inherent spontaneity and, if photographed with some consideration, are completely unself-conscious. As they grow older they tend to develop a self-awareness which makes it more difficult to take natural pictures. The formal portrait is the least satisfying way in which to photograph children, although professional photographers produce this type of portrait because, for them, it is convenient and economical. The enthusiastic amateur has a distinct advantage over the professional photographer as he can take the time to become familiar with his subjects.

The essence of a good photograph of a child lies in capturing a lively and spontaneous expression. One of the best ways to achieve this is photographing children at play. Even if they are a little self-conscious and aware of the camera at first, young children will quickly lose their interest in your activities if you allow them to continue with their own amusements and do not attempt to make them pose. A long-focus lens is useful for this type of picture as it will enable you to frame quite tightly without having to approach the children too closely. At the same time the shallow depth of field with such a lens will diffuse distracting backgrounds. It is also often beneficial, with small children, to shoot from a low viewpoint – to come down to their level.

Arrange for them to play in a situation which suits you, where there is a convenient and uncluttered background and the lighting is such that it does not produce heavy shadows which might obscure a small face. A slightly cloudy day when the light is quite soft and the shadows are not too heavy is ideal, as this will enable you to move more freely and follow your subject around without having to worry about unpleasant lighting effects. To ensure that a sharp image is recorded, a fairly fast shutter speed, such as 1/250, is advisable, especially when photographing quite close-up pictures. The best expressions are often quite fleeting and you will need swift responses and the ability to focus quickly and smoothly as your subjects move around.

If you want to take pictures indoors in a more formal setting it is best to find something, like a favourite toy, to amuse your model and occupy his or her interest. If there is a large window and it is a bright day this can be an ideal way of lighting your subject. Position the child near the window and wait until he becomes absorbed in play before you start to take pictures. You should try to position the camera so that strong shadows do not appear on the face and the background is unobtrusive, making sure that the child stands out clearly against it. If you want the child to look into the camera it is far better to wait either until this happens naturally or to attract his or her attention indirectly. If window light is not

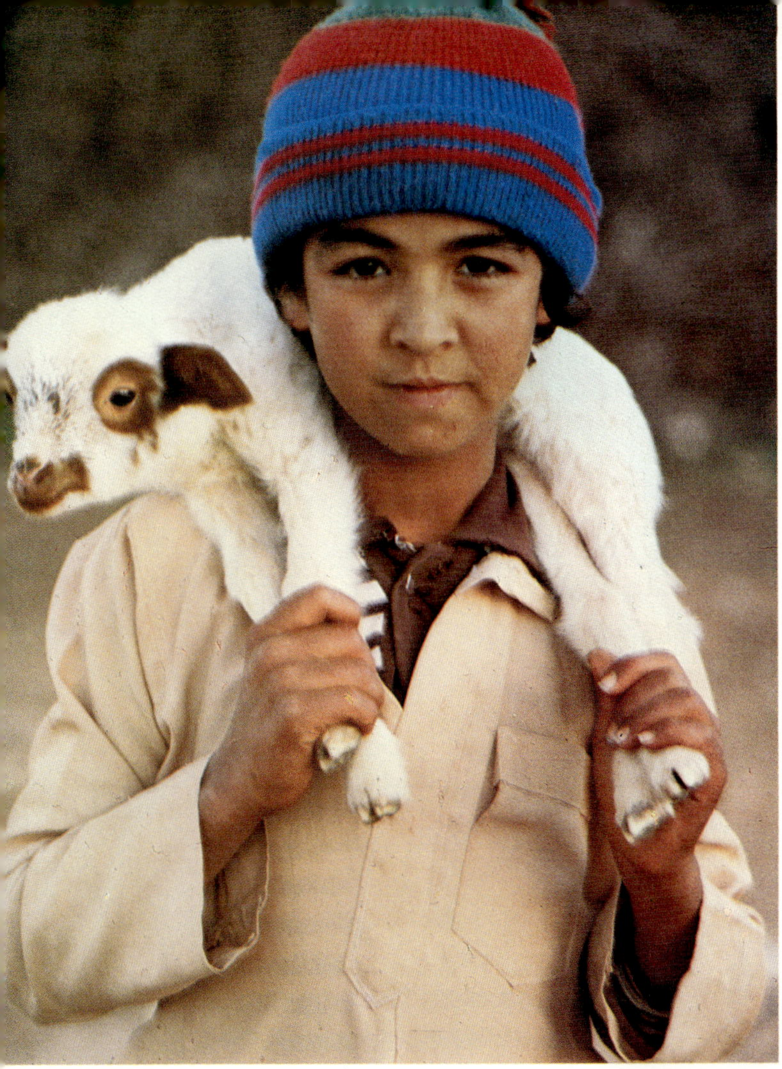

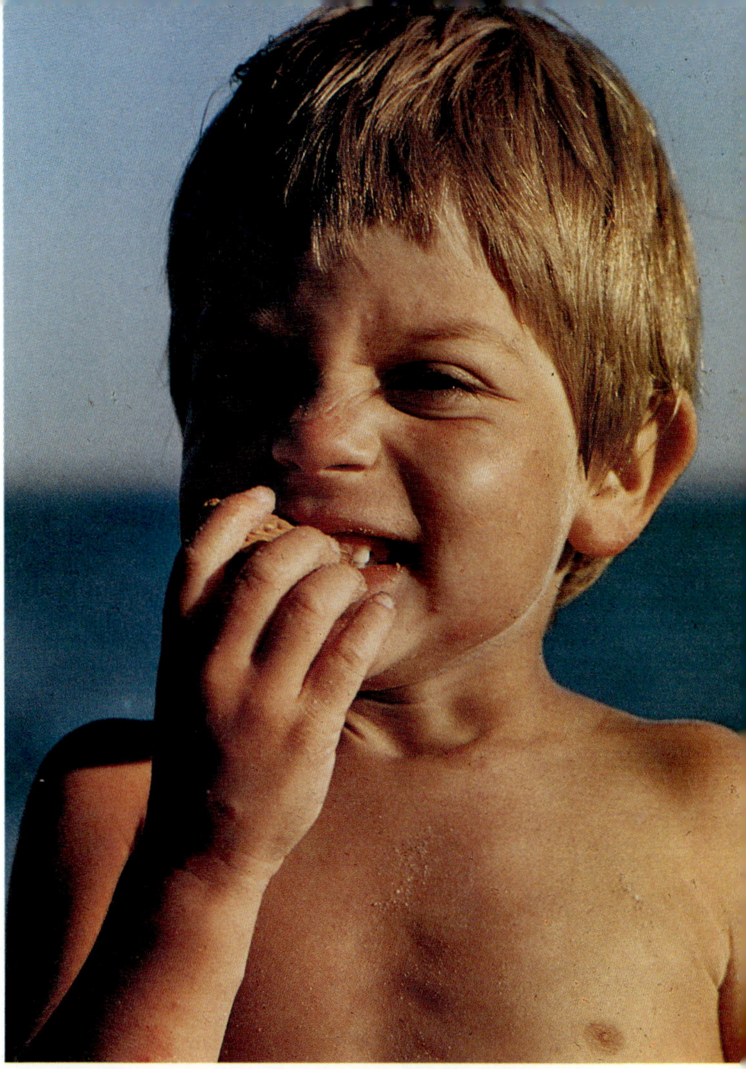

It is often better to frame the picture quite tightly to emphasize the faces and expressions of young subjects.

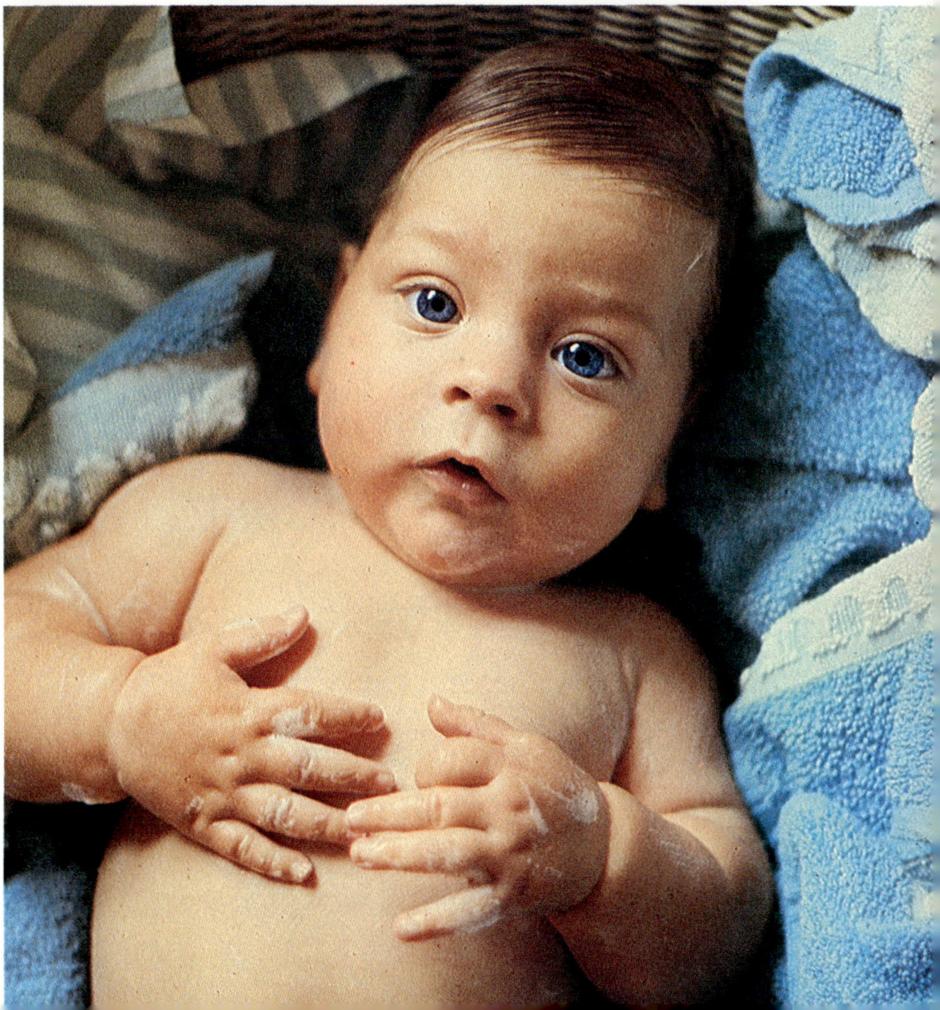

available then a small flash gun bounced from a white ceiling can also be an attractive and convenient way of lighting a child portrait.

Photographing babies presents a slightly different problem as they tend to be less responsive, although of course they are more static and you have far more control over where you take the pictures. It is best to enlist the help of the baby's mother as the baby is more likely to react to her and she will know the sounds and movements that will produce the best expressions. As with children, lively expressions are the essence of such pictures and you should crop quite closely and keep the background plain and unobtrusive. With a very tiny baby it is often an advantage to photograph them being held by a parent. If a portrait of the baby alone is wanted you can simply move in closer using the parent's body as a background, ensuring that they are wearing something quite plain and unobtrusive. This will help to give you a different angle on the baby's face, as the positions of lying on the back or tummy can be restricting both for you and the baby.

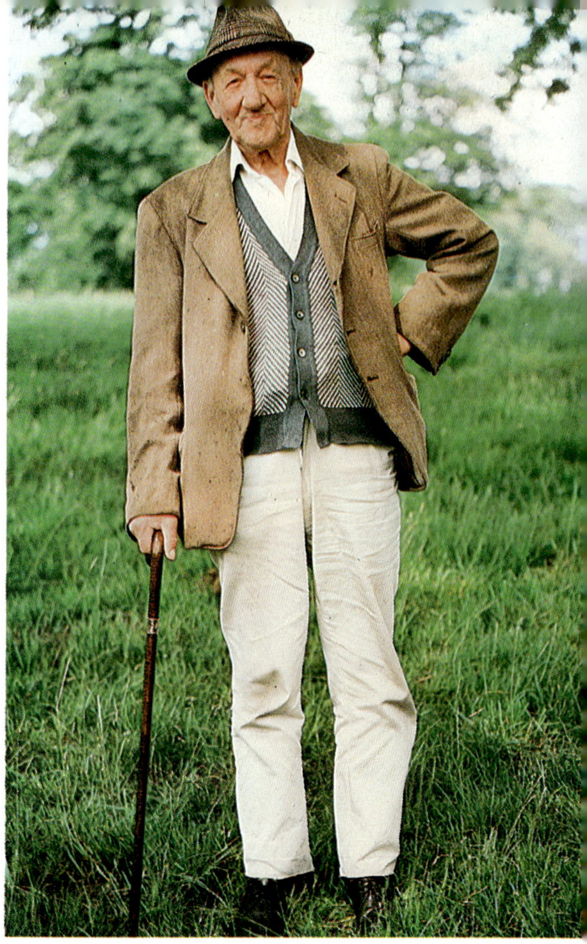

Most photographs of people fall into two categories. One is where the subject of the picture is aware that they are being photographed and will co-operate with the photographer, and the other is where the picture is taken without the subject's knowledge. The term 'portrait' usually implies the former and 'candid' the latter. In a portrait the intention is either to produce a pleasing likeness of the model or to produce a particular effect in which the subject plays a role, as in the case of photographs of models for magazines and advertisements. When you are taking pictures of family or friends the aim is usually to produce a result which *they* will like. This often means you will need to introduce a degree of flattery, photographing them in such a way that their best features are accentuated and the less attractive aspects of their appearance are minimized.

Right: The almost snapshot quality of the portrait of the old man underlines its informal nature and adds charm. This would have been lost by attempting a more controlled picture.

Below: A more formal portrait uses a three-quarter face position with the camera slightly above eye-level, which usually produces a more flattering result.

The majority of people do not, in fact, like having their photograph taken. They tend to feel self-conscious and somewhat vulnerable and an important part of portrait photography is for your model to be relaxed and feel at ease.

If you are going to photograph a friend you will probably already have some idea of the ways in which you can present the best of him or her.

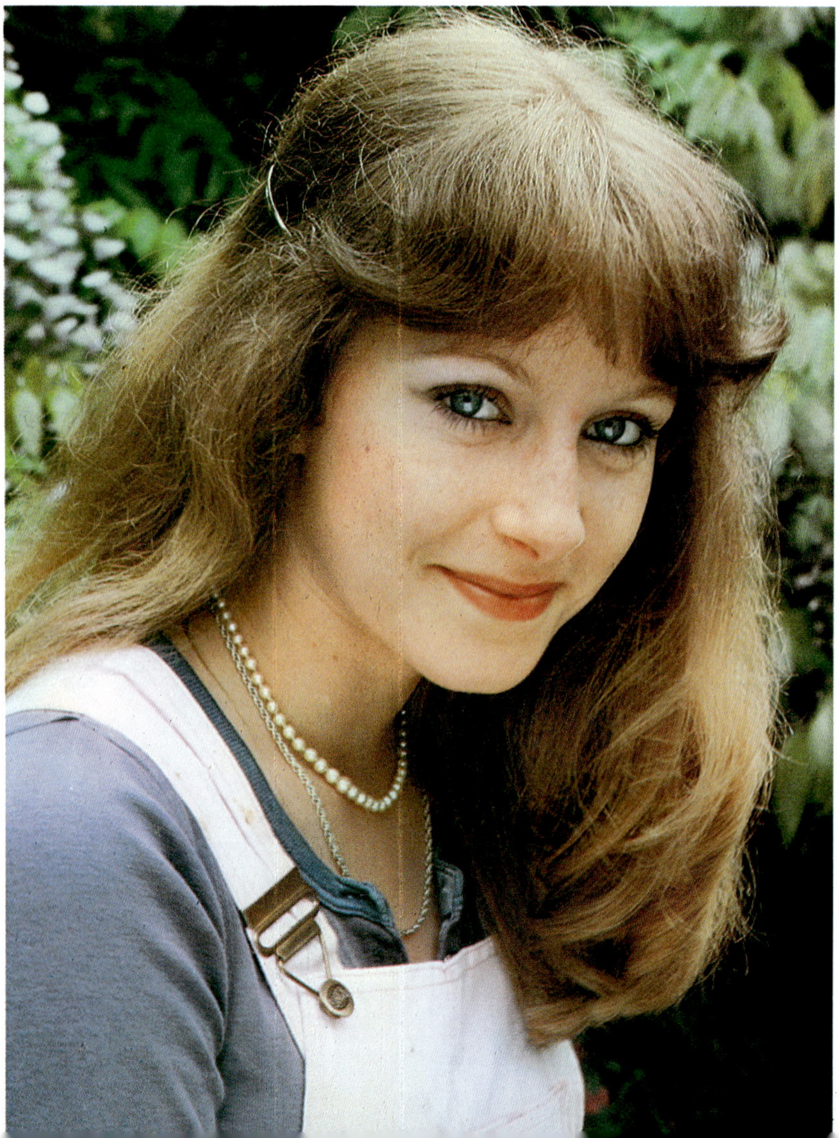

The way you seat your model, the position of the camera and the angle of the model's head should all be designed to show the model in the most complimentary way. For example, a model with a chubby round face would be better photographed in three-quarter profile rather than with the face square on to the camera. In general it is preferable to seat your model in a relaxed way so that their body does not appear tense. It often helps if they can lean forward on to the arm or back of a chair rather than sitting bolt upright. In most cases it is best to avoid the model's shoulders being square on to the camera, as most people look better when their head is turned slightly towards the camera and their body slightly away. This gives a little life and movement instead of the static symmetrical quality so typical of the average passport picture. Once you have your model comfortably settled you can begin to start manoeuvring him or her into the best position. It is better to do this indirectly and to avoid issuing positive directions such as 'move that arm' or 'turn your head' which tend to be rather inhibiting and produce a self-conscious response. It is also important to carry on a conversation and to offer some encouragement when you are beginning to shoot.

A tripod is a definite advantage for this type of picture as it enables you to position and focus the camera while leaving you free to communicate more directly with your subject rather than remaining glued to the viewfinder. A long-focus lens is best for portraits where anything closer

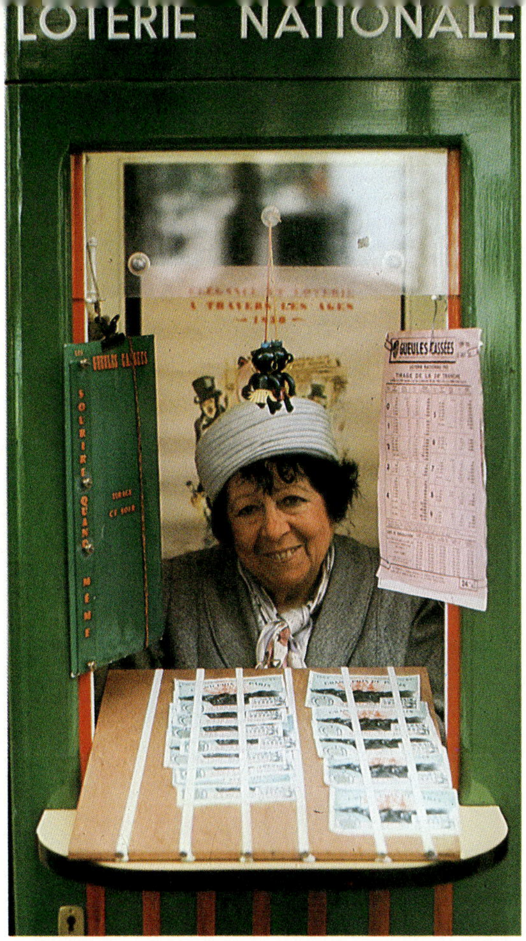

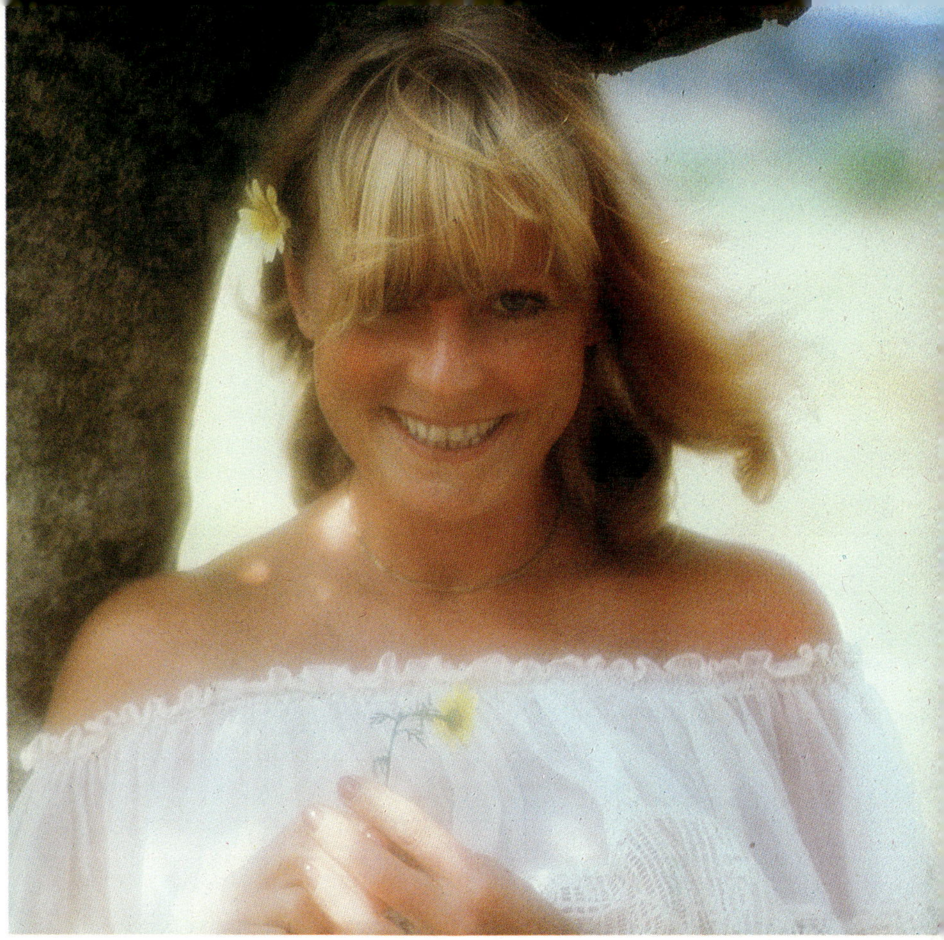

than waist up is required. This will help avoid exaggerated perspectives and enables you to shoot from a more comfortable distance. The model's eyes are the best point at which to focus, and when photographing faces quite close-up use a small enough aperture to ensure adequate depth of field.

The most flattering lighting for portrait photography is a soft light directed from quite close to the camera position. This will avoid the formation of heavy shadows and will minimize skin texture and facial lines. If you are using artificial lighting it is important to avoid using more lights than are necessary. A single, soft light which gives just a little modelling in the face, with a reflector to brighten up the shadows and possibly a further light from behind the model to create highlights on the hair, is all that is necessary for most pictures. Using more than one light source on either side of the camera will, unless you are careful, result in multiple shadows on the model's face.

If the purpose of the picture is to create a mood or to emphasize the character of the model then it is possible to be rather more adventurous. Lighting which is directed from much further to the side of the camera will give an image with a greater impression of depth and form and the features and skin texture will be accentuated. In this type of portrait you should aim to emphasize both the individual features of the subject and characteristic expressions: choose camera angles, head positions and lighting quality with this in mind.

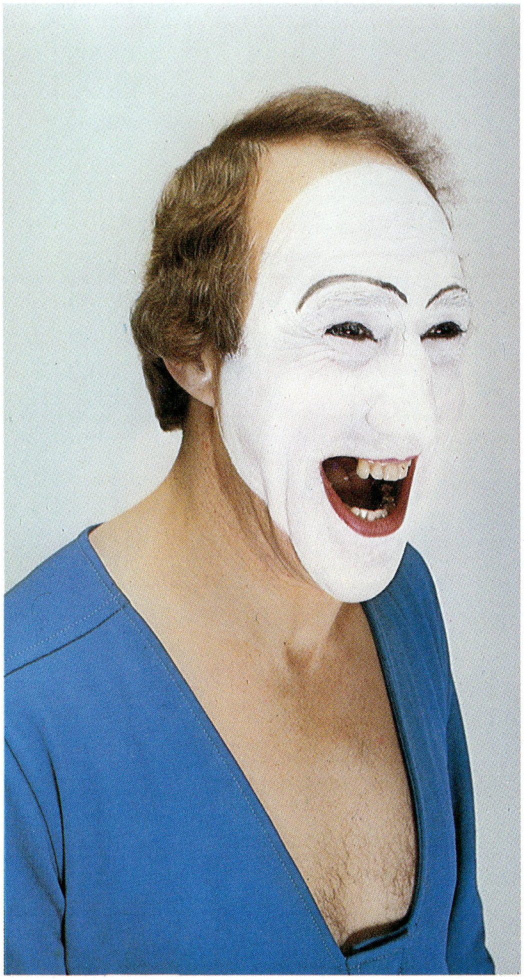

Above left: An impromptu portrait of a lottery-ticket lady has been given more impact by using her kiosk as a frame.

Above: A soft-focus attachment has been used to produce this romantic portrait of a girl. Soft lighting was achieved by shooting in the shade of a tree.

Revealing character is usually achieved by exaggerating features and expressions.

Using daylight

Portrait photography is usually thought of in terms of a studio with artificial lighting, but daylight, if used with a little care, can provide a far more convenient, inexpensive and equally effective light source for many types of portrait pictures. In fact, some of the world's leading portrait photographers prefer to use daylight whenever possible. A few simple accessories which can easily be made from ordinary materials can be used in conjunction with both outdoor and indoor daylight to produce a wide range of lighting effects. Even a careful choice of camera position and placing of the model can greatly improve the results that are obtained by haphazard photography outdoors. Although one cannot alter the direction of the light itself it is a simple matter to vary and control the quality of daylight when shooting pictures of people.

Bright, unobscured sunlight is rarely satisfactory for this type of picture because it creates strong shadows with hard edges, accentuates skin texture – often unpleasantly – and above all is uncomfortable for the model, causing him or her to squint or frown. On a sunny day it is preferable to find an area of open shade cast by a tree or a building in which to position the model. Alternatively you can shoot against the light so that the model's face is in its own shade: this has the additional advantage of creating an attractive halo of light around the hair or the profile. The problem with this approach is that it tends to produce a very high brightness range, or contrast, and the difference between the highlights and the shadows is too great for the film to accommodate. One solution is simply to calculate the exposure from the shadow areas – the face itself – and to allow the highlights to overexpose. In many cases this will not matter and can, in fact, look very attractive. Another method is to use a white reflector – a piece of card or painted hardboard would be fine – ideally about 3 × 4 feet, placed close to the model just in front of the camera. With a very close-up shot even the pages of a magazine or a large white handkerchief placed very near the face will help considerably. This has the effect of bouncing the light back into the shadows and reducing the contrast. Even on a cloudy day this technique can be worth adopting, as the light on such days, coming from almost directly above, tends to give heavy shadows under the eyes which a reflector will minimize. Another solution would be to position your model just under a tree or in an open doorway to shield the face.

Daylight can provide an equally effective light source for indoor photography providing you are working in a room with a large window. The window provides a smaller and more concentrated light source – even on a cloudy day it will tend to give more contrast – and, therefore, the use of a reflector is even more important. By

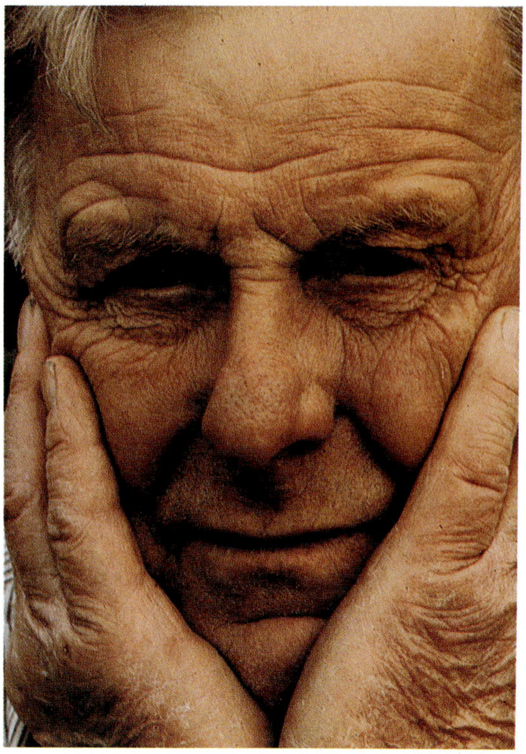

Right: This close-up portrait was taken in the soft light of an overcast day. Strong sunlight would have created harsh shadows on the face.

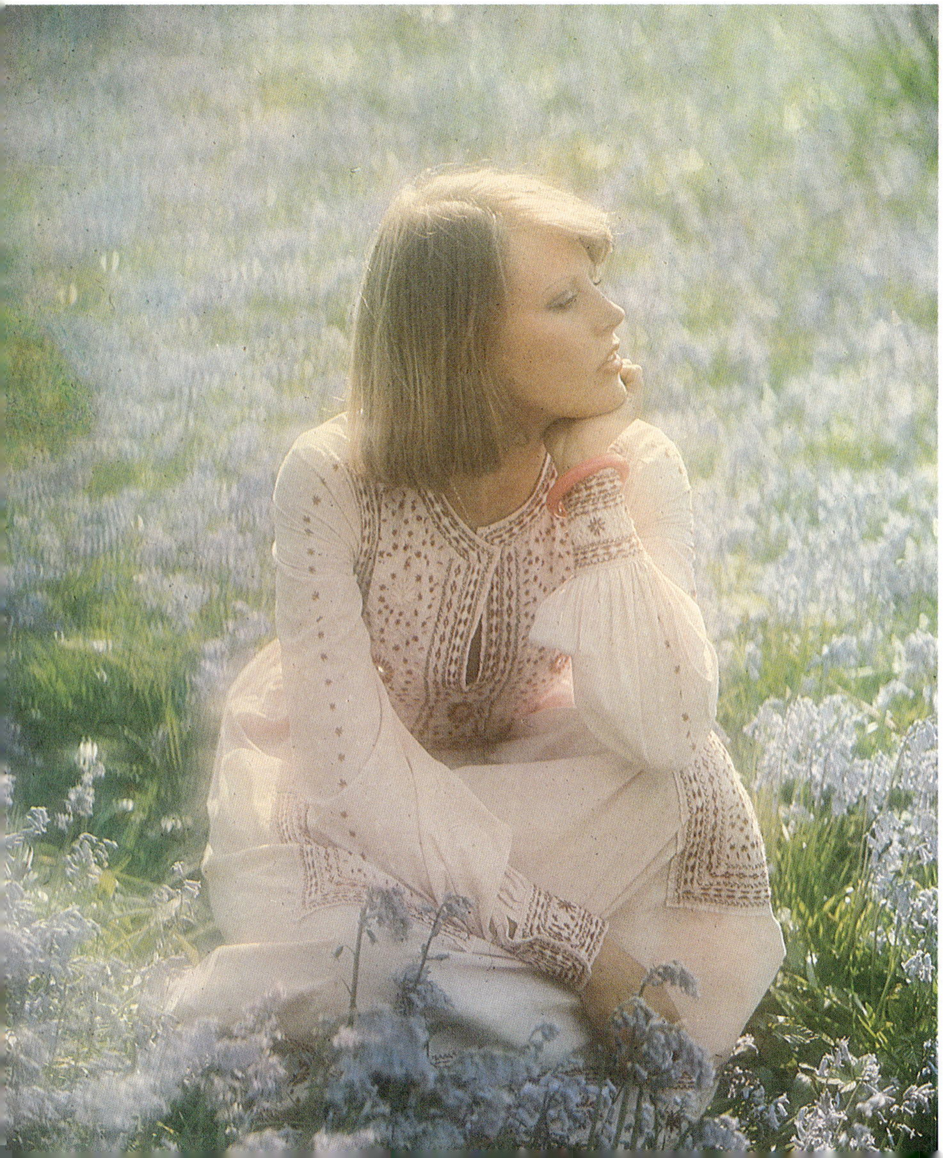

Below: Shooting into the light, slight overexposure and a soft-focus attachment have helped to produce the pastel effect.

varying the position of the model and the camera in relation to the window it is possible to utilize quite a wide variety of lighting effects. With the window running alongside a line between the camera and the model a strong side lighting can be produced, and with the window behind the camera and the model facing towards it a flat, frontal lighting will result. By moving the reflector closer to and further away from the model the depth of the shadows which the window light casts can be controlled. A useful way of judging the contrast of the lighting, whether outdoors or indoors, is to view your subject through half-closed eyes: often the contrast is much higher than you think, because normal eyesight tends to compensate for the extremes.

Below: Although lit by sunlight, the young girl's face has been angled away from its direct light, and a reflector placed just in front of her to lighten the shadows.

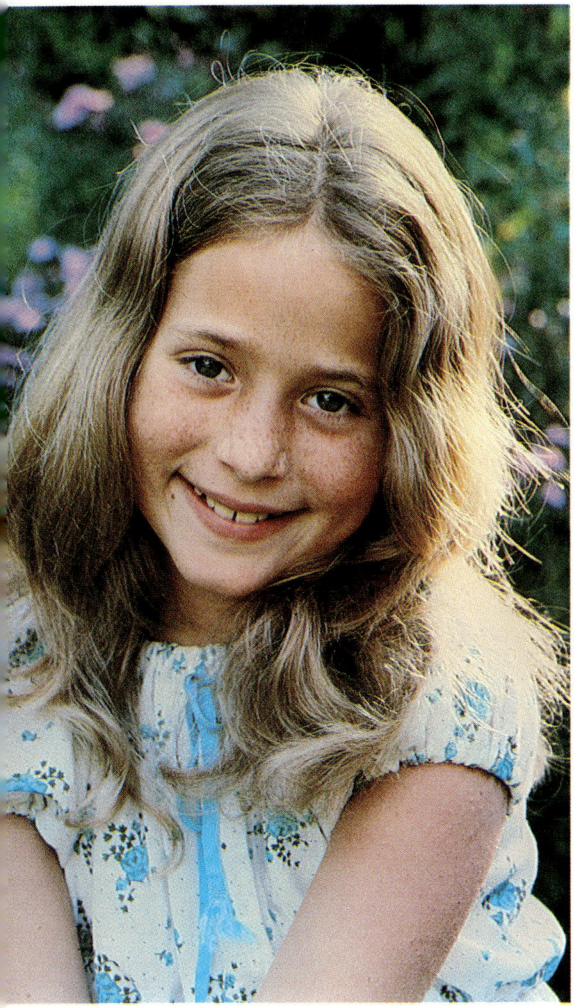

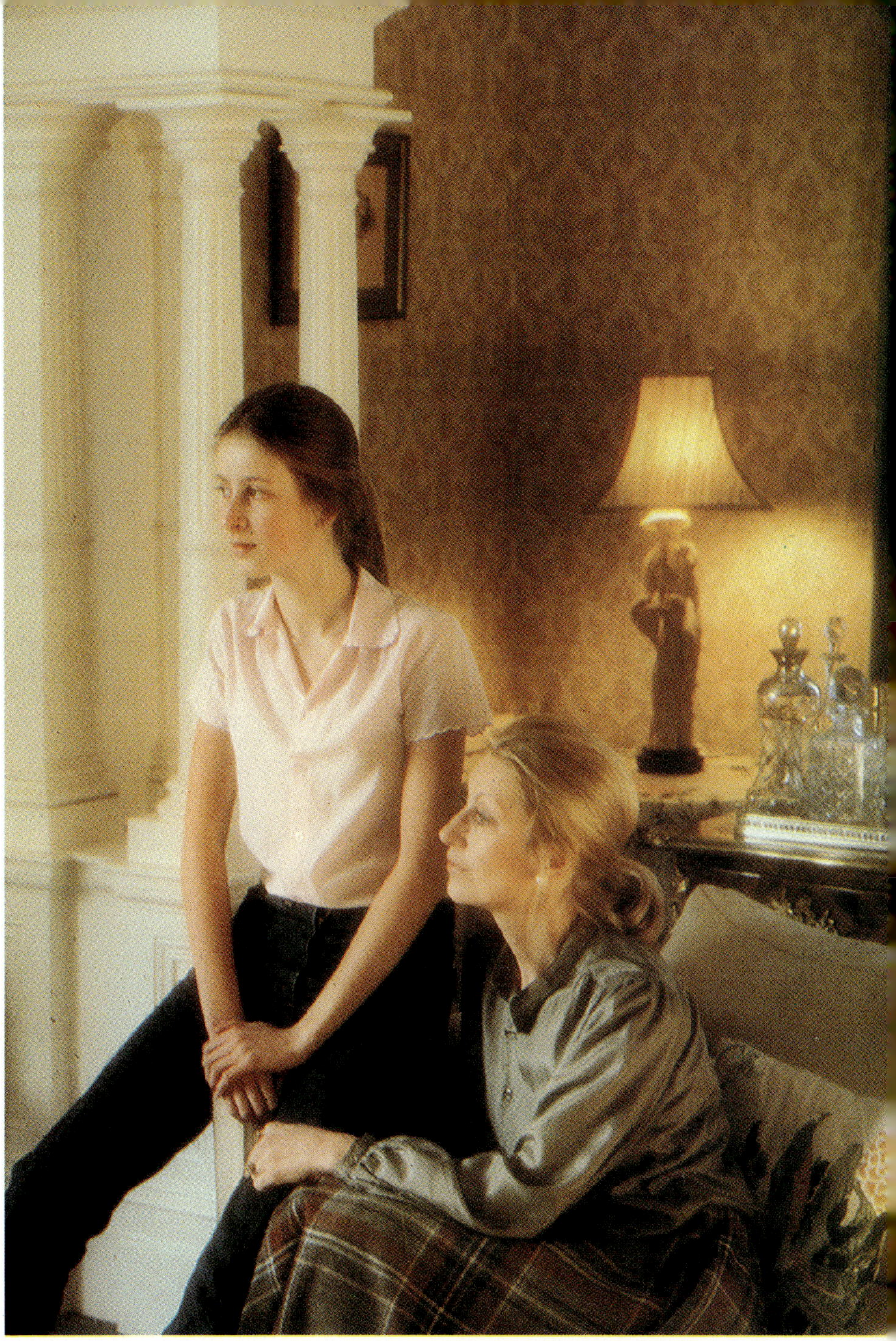

Light from a window has been used for this indoor portrait of a mother and daughter. The table lamp adds a warm touch in the background on the daylight film. For this type of formal portrait it is preferable to have the camera mounted on a tripod, enabling it to be positioned quite accurately and the picture to be composed more carefully.

The background

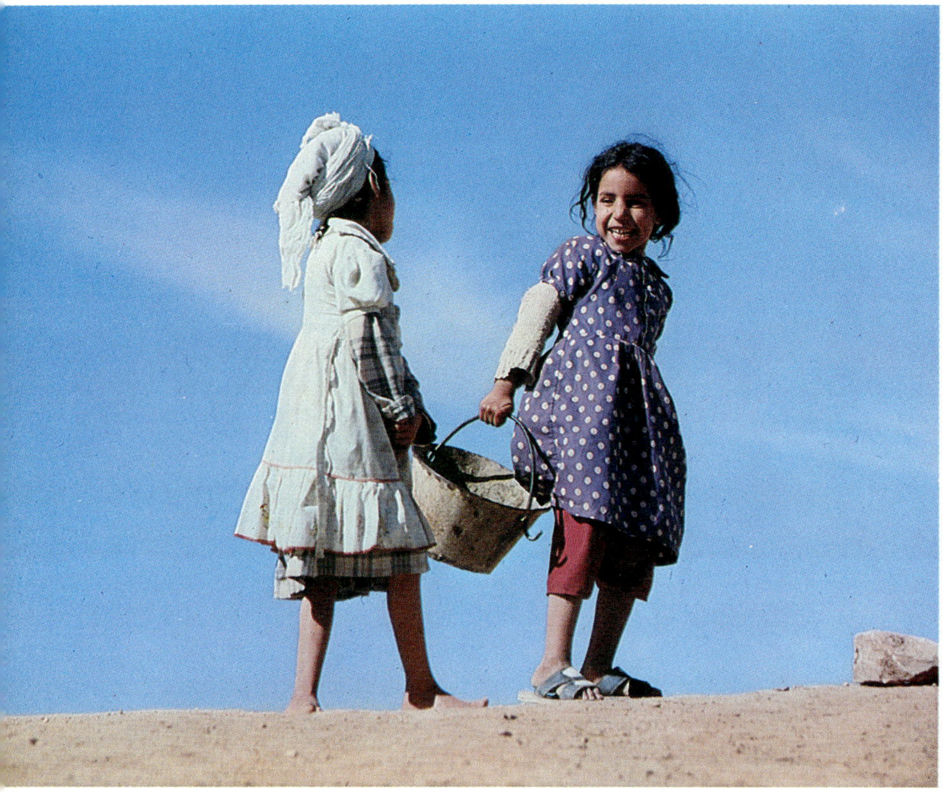

Above: This picture of two Moroccan children, taken from a low viewpoint, uses a blue sky as a plain background, emphasizing the shape of the children.

Below: A plain white wall is the background for this studio shot of two youths. Soft light and distance between the subject and the background has kept it shadow-free.

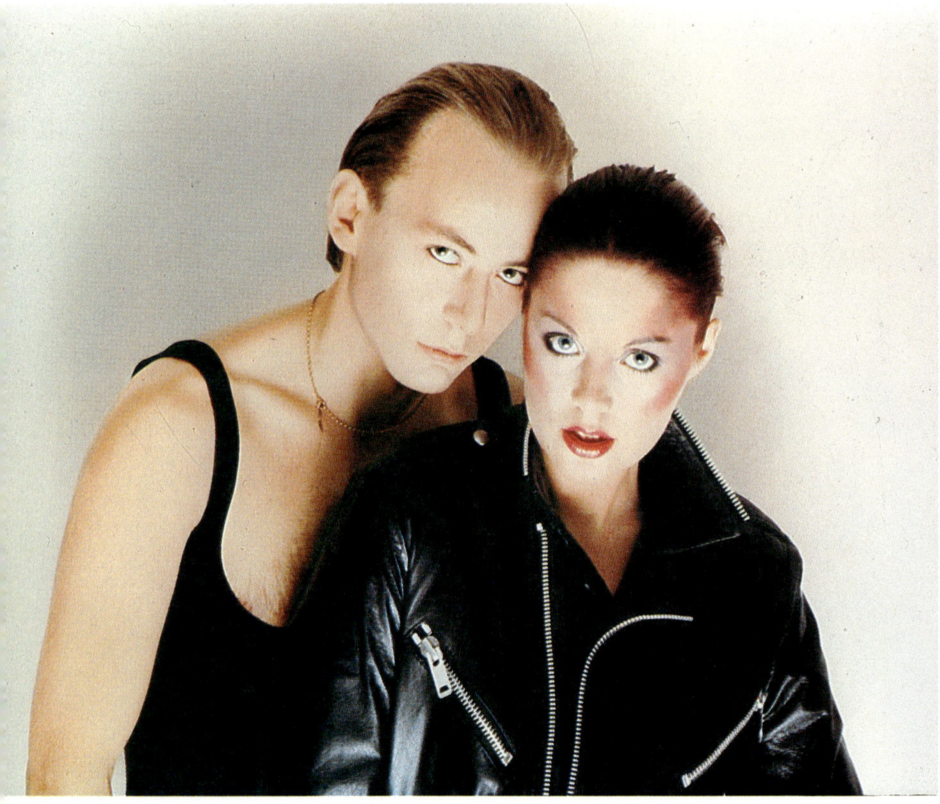

Inexperienced photographers rarely give thought to what goes on behind the subject in a photograph, and yet an ill-chosen or fussy background is responsible for spoiling a great many pictures which might otherwise have been excellent. The background of a picture needs to be considered as carefully as any of the other elements of an image. The background can contribute to a picture in two basic ways. One is as an unobtrusive neutral area against which the subject itself is clearly shown, and the other is as an area of additional interest which increases the impact and meaning of the photograph. With either way the background must be thought of as part of the overall picture and not be allowed simply to appear haphazardly.

If the background is intended to provide an unobtrusive tone against which the subject can contrast, as in a formal portrait taken indoors, this can be achieved most easily by using plain paper or fabric behind the model – even a plain wall in the room you are using will often be satisfactory. You should ensure that enough space is allowed between the model and the background so that shadows are not thrown on to it by the main light source, and if fabric is used it should be tightly stretched so that no wrinkles are visible. If you are shooting in black-and-white you should ensure that there is enough tonal difference between the model and the background to provide a degree of contrast; with colour pictures the background should be of a colour which either complements the colour of the model's clothes or provides a pleasant contrast. Bright, saturated colours such as red or green should be avoided in portrait photographs as the skin tones in a face are quite subtle and could easily be overwhelmed by bold background colours. It may be desirable to have a background with a little tonal variation, in which case you could use a fabric which has a texture or spray a piece of hardboard with an aerosol paint to give a soft cloud-like effect. In either case it is best to keep the background well out of focus.

When shooting outdoors rather different methods need to be employed to find unobtrusive backgrounds. A plain wall of a suitable colour would be an obvious choice but in many situations it is necessary to be a little more creative to achieve good results. The simplest technique for obtaining an unobtrusive tone as a background is to ensure that there is as much distance as possible between the model and the nearest details and to use a long lens with a fairly wide aperture. This will ensure that the background area falls well outside the depth of field and all but the obvious details will be reduced to a vague blur. Another technique is to choose a camera position that enables you to use a difference in light levels. If, for example, your subject is in quite bright light it is usually

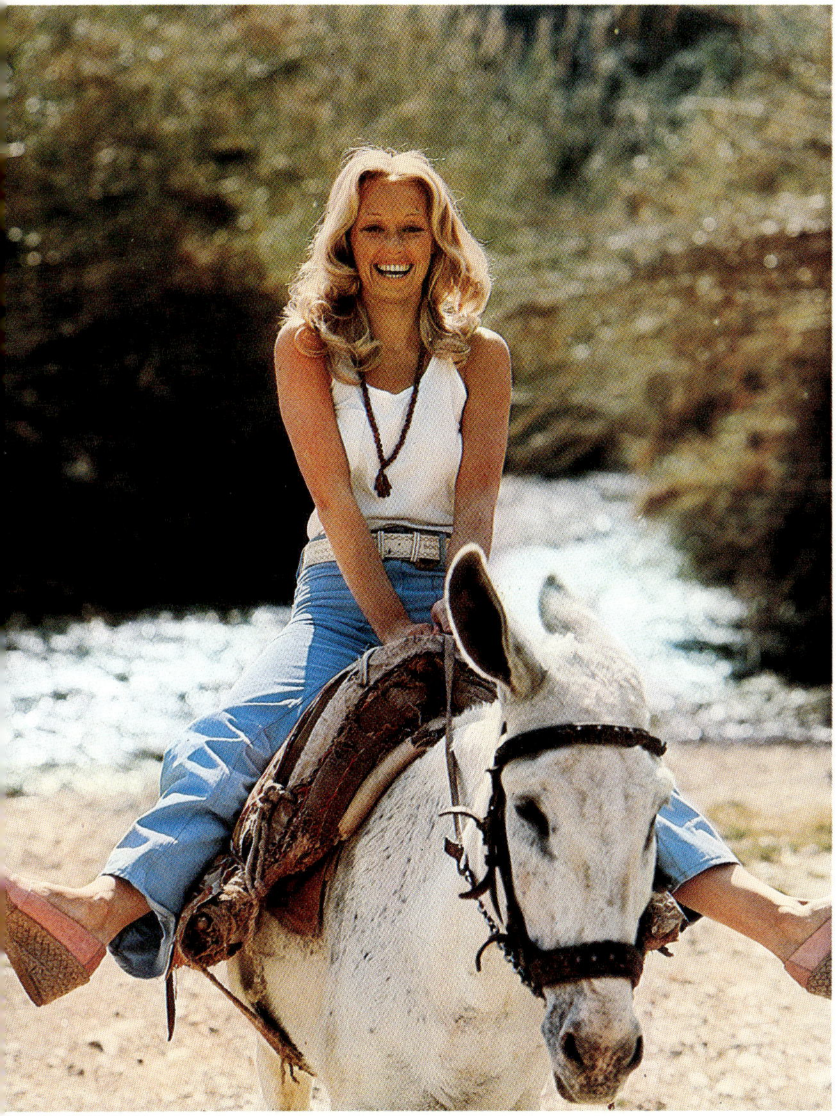

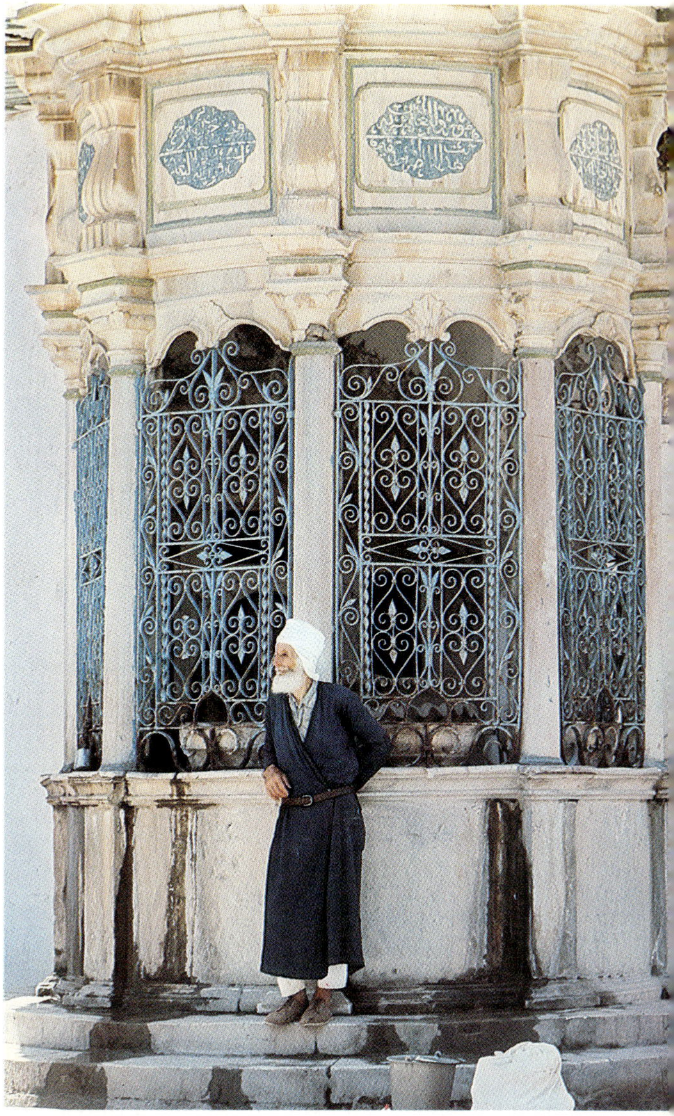

possible to find a camera angle which will position a shadow area behind the subject so that any details will be lost in the shadows. Conversely, with a model positioned in open shade it is usually possible to shoot so that a more brightly lit area forms the background tone, and the unwanted details will be lost in overexposure. Where the subject's immediate background is too fussy and it is not possible to move further back it can sometimes help to shoot from a high or low viewpoint, allowing the ground or the sky to become the background.

The background can play a much more active role in many pictures and add to both the interest and the impact. A suitably furnished and decorated room can contribute to the mood of a picture taken indoors. It is important, however, to ensure that such backgrounds do not dominate and complicate the picture. The subject should be carefully positioned so that the eye is led automatically to that part of the picture. Depth of field can again be a useful way of slightly subduing such backgrounds; by making sure that they are sufficiently out of focus the sharply focused model remains the most dominant feature of the photograph. It is also very important to watch out for unwanted highlights or splashes of bright colour occurring where they might distract from the subject. With indoor photographs this is often caused by reflections in pictures on the wall or ornaments and they are quite easy to overlook, although glaringly obvious when your film is processed.

An effective way of using a background in a setting either indoors or outdoors is to compose the picture in the viewfinder without the model, so that a balanced and pleasing composition is achieved on its own, but mentally to leave a 'hole' for the model in a predominant position. This is the way fashion photographers often work; they see a setting which can be composed into a balanced image and imagine the presence of the model, who then can simply be put in position when the photographer is ready to shoot.

Above left: Although the background adds to the mood of this picture, a shallow depth of field, produced with a long-focus lens and a wide aperture, has prevented it from becoming obtrusive.

Above: In this picture the background is of almost equal importance as the subject and it has been composed so that the figure is part of the overall composition.

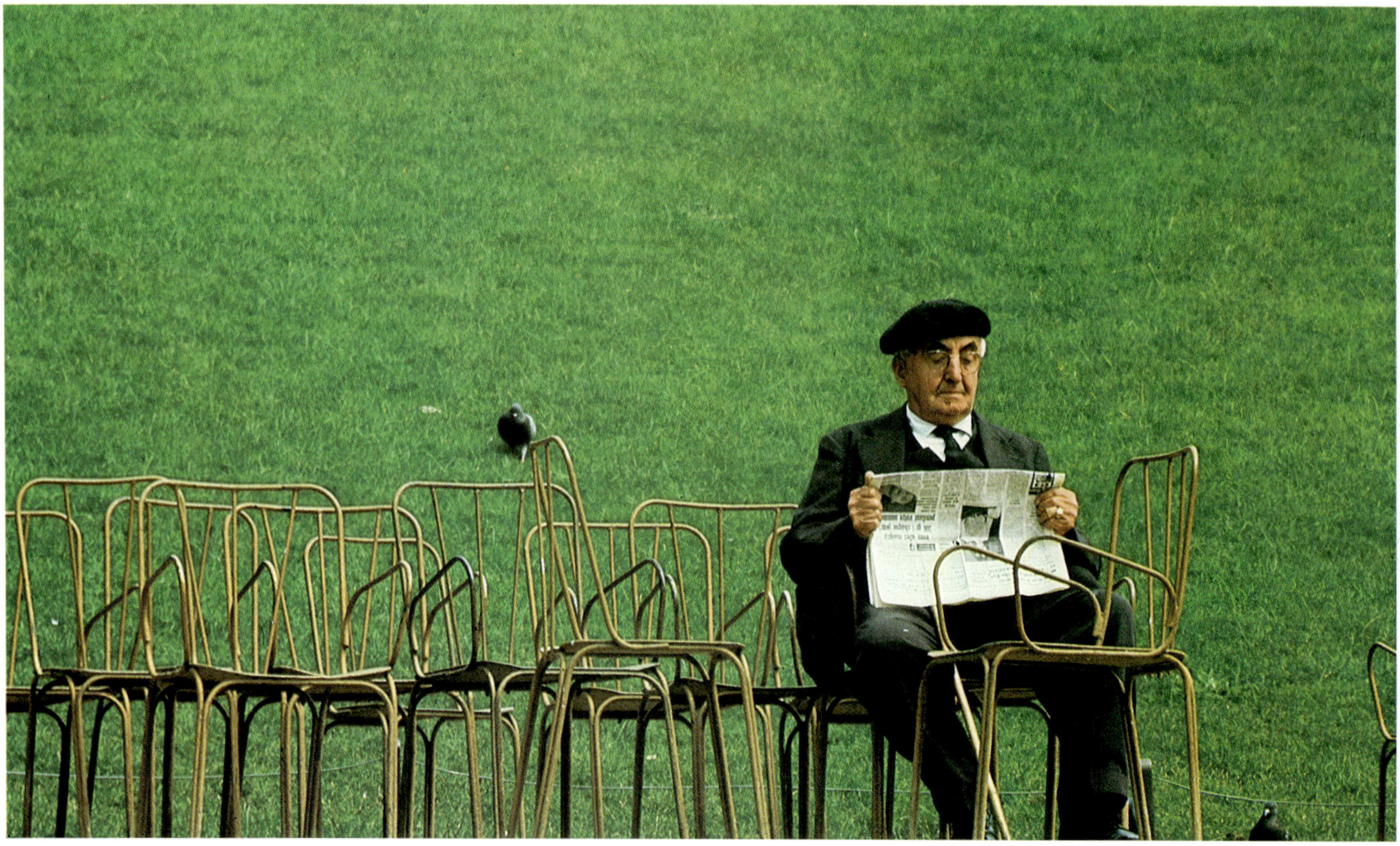

A long-focus lens enabled the photograph to be taken at a distance which did not attract the subject's attention. His pre-occupation with his newspaper made this relatively simple.

As with children and their toys, it is possible to photograph more natural and relaxed responses when your adult subjects are preoccupied with their work or hobbies, or merely engrossed in conversation. This 'candid' approach can add much interest to the picture in purely visual terms, and will express much more about the subject.

It is vital for this type of picture that you are completely familiar with your camera and equipment. The purpose is, of course, to take the pictures as quickly and unobtrusively as possible; any fumbling or hesitancy is likely to attract the attention of your subject. A little experience will soon teach you how close you need to be to frame the picture correctly without having to use the viewfinder, and having found the right viewpoint you should pre-set the focusing and the exposure setting still without aiming the camera at your subject. Again with a little practice it is quite easy to take an exposure reading from an area of similar tones before you even approach your subject – an automatic camera is, of course, ideal for this type of shot. All you need to do now is raise the camera quickly to the shooting position and fire the shutter. Cameras with a waist-level viewfinder, such as a twin lens reflex, are often easier to use unobtrusively, as they do not have to be raised to the eye. A long lens can be an advantage when shooting candid pictures as it is possible to remain some distance away from your subject but still produce a large image: a 105 or 135 mm lens on 35 mm cameras is a useful focal length but you will need to be considerably more careful with the focusing. It is still an advantage to pre-set the distance as accurately as possible, but with a rangefinder or SLR camera you can usually make a quick last-second adjustment before shooting. Since you will need to use a fairly fast shutter speed and often a small aperture to offset focusing errors and increase depth of field, it is an advantage to use a fast film in all but the best lighting condititions. With some situations it can be helpful to use a wide-angle lens, although this usually means having a much closer viewpoint and your subject is more likely to be aware of your presence. However, it is possible to use a wide-angle lens in such a way that they will not realize that they are the object of your interest, as in many cases the camera will not be aimed directly at them, and focusing and the depth of field are also less of a problem.

When you are taking pictures of strangers, on holiday perhaps, or abroad, it is even more important to avoid attracting too much attention to yourself. You should avoid using an ostentatious camera bag and simply carry your camera in your hand, not slung round your neck, with maybe an extra lens and some film in a pocket. The best way to take candid pictures of people in places where the presence of a stranger or a

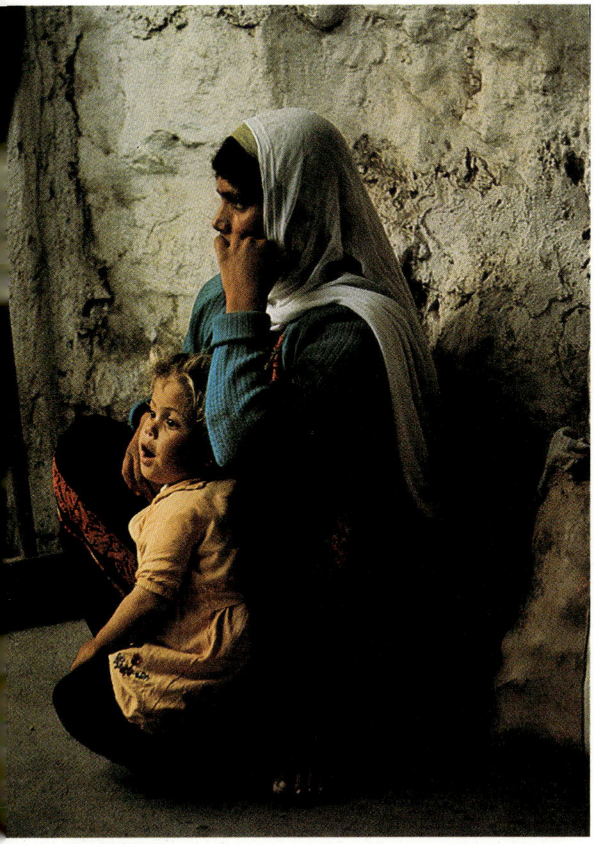

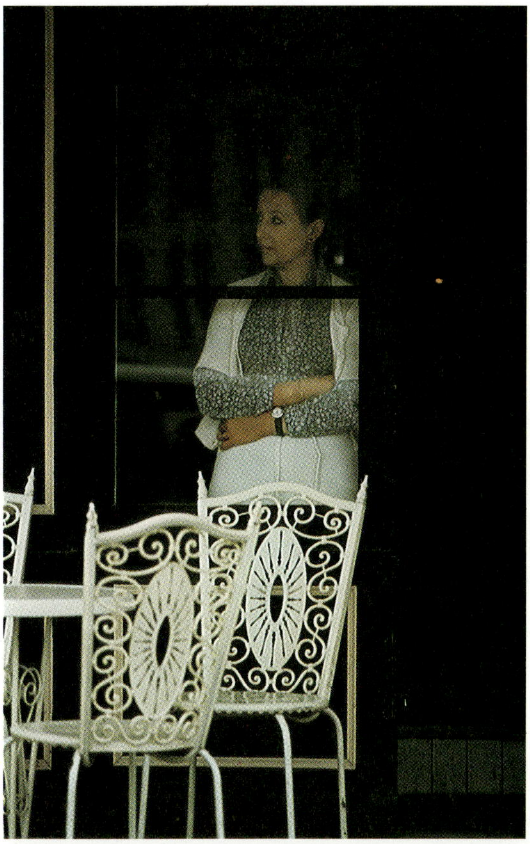

Far left: This picture, taken from quite close quarters, was possible because the subjects had become accustomed to the presence of a camera and were no longer self-conscious.

Left: The picture of the waitress was taken by presetting the camera and shooting quickly before her attention was attracted.

foreigner is very obvious is to lounge around for a while until your presence is accepted and ceases to be of interest. It does not usually take long for people to become accustomed to, and quickly forget, what might initially be an object of curiosity. In this type of situation, it is even more important to be discreet as far as equipment is concerned and it is best to do such things as loading film and changing lenses well out of sight of the people you intend to photograph.

Indoor daylight through a window can be ideal for taking interior candid photographs. In the interests of spontaneity, it is usually best not to use reflectors to aid the lighting in this type of picture and when you are shooting in black-and-white you can make use of room lighting to help fill in shadows. With daylight film in colour you must be careful, as interior tungsten light will produce an orange cast and fluorescent tubes tend to create a rather unpleasant green cast. Providing the main subject is lighted predominantly with daylight and any other lighting is only secondary this need not present a problem, but you should remember that the effect of such colour casts tends to be rather more pronounced on film than it appears to the eye. You can also add light to the darker shadows by using a small amount of electronic flash as this is indistinguishable from daylight in colour quality.

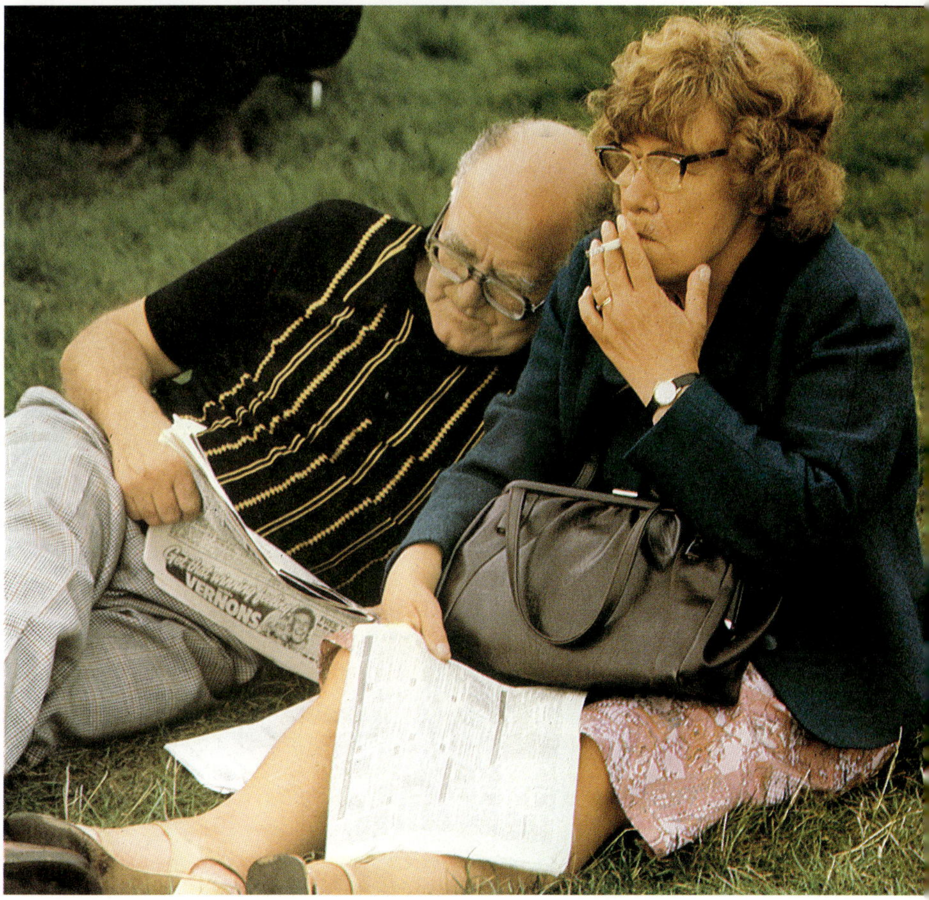

This couple picnicking at a race course were photographed from a considerable distance with a 300 mm lens, making several exposures possible.

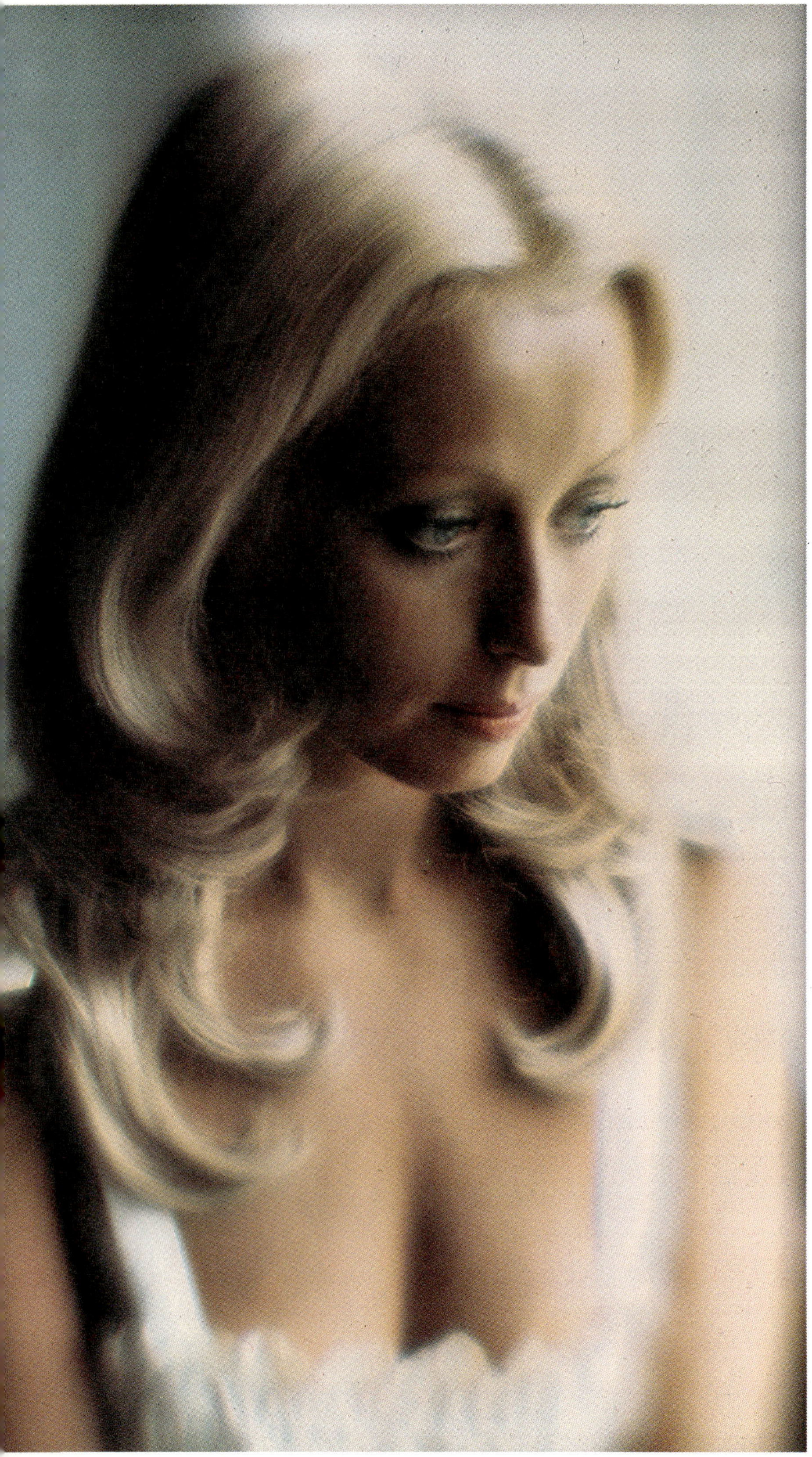

Above: This picture was taken using soft, hazy sunlight with a reflector. The soft-focus effect was achieved by stretching sellotape across the lens hood, leaving a small clear area in the centre. A long-focus lens helped to separate the face from the background.

Cameras and pretty girls seem to have a natural affinity and there are many ways in which they can provide both the inspiration and the means for producing great pictures. The most important aspect of this type of photography is, like portraiture, the ability of the photographer both to relax and to inspire confidence in his model. Whether your subject is your wife, a girlfriend or a professional model it is ultimately this factor which will be responsible for the success of the pictures. Familiarity with your equipment is vital as nothing is more likely to ruin the atmosphere than if you appear uncertain or hesitant in the way you use your camera.

There is a considerable difference between taking a conventional portrait and one in which you will want the subject to project both her personality and sexuality. Finding a suitable model is the first problem for most people and unless you intend to employ a professional model this will probably mean approaching someone who has not been photographed in this way before. Whether your model is someone you know well or a stranger, the first step is to convince them that you are a competent photographer and that you will take good pictures of them. Unless your first model is a good friend it is probably better to make use of the first session to establish a rapport between you and convince her of the abilities you both have. It may even be best merely to shoot some good portraits and attempt nothing more adventurous on the first occasion.

Having found a model the next major concern is where to shoot the pictures – indoors or outdoors, countryside or beach? The novice would do best to avoid a studio session, particularly with an inexperienced model, since it is far more difficult to create a relaxed atmosphere in the rather stark surroundings of a studio and to contend with lighting equipment and backgrounds. Using daylight in an indoor setting is a good way of starting. If you want to take nude or semi-nude pictures an indoor setting is usually more comfortable, convenient and, of course, private, than an outdoor location, particularly. Also you have the use of furniture and decor both as props for the picture and to help the model feel more relaxed. Often something quite simple such as a chair or the corner of a sofa can help the model to provide more varied and graceful body angles and shapes. If you want to take pictures which have a strong sexual appeal you will find that this is more easily achieved when your model is not completely nude. Sensuality is often created as much by what is only implied in a picture as by what is revealed, and nude pictures where the model is openly provocative can easily look somewhat tasteless.

Texture plays an important role in building an

erotic image. The textures of skin and hair can be enhanced by introducing other elements into the photograph, such as silk or fur; even oil or water on the skin can help to give a stronger tactile quality in the photograph. Clothing is an important element in evoking a glamorous atmosphere and often the idea for a particular picture can be based on an attractive piece of clothing, such as a see-through top or a pretty bikini.

The nude body can provide a limitless source of images for a photographer. The variety of effects that can be produced by subtle changes in lighting and body angles enables you to create images ranging from the sensual to completely abstract. Daylight is an ideal source of light for nude photography, both indoors and out, and with the aid of a reflector or two it can be controlled effectively. Skin quality is if anything even more important than the shape of the model's body. Blemishes tend to be exaggerated when recorded on film, and in particular you should make sure that there are no marks on the skin caused by tight clothing, such as the waist band of a skirt or underclothes. Time should be allowed for these to disappear before starting to shoot as they look unattractive if visible in the photograph. Do not hesitate to ask the model to use a little make-up on her body to cover any blemishes.

A very effective way of shooting nude pictures is to isolate quite small areas of the body and make use of the infinite variety of shapes and contours which can be produced by the movement and angle of the limbs. A long-focus lens is useful for this type of picture and a tripod will be of great help, particularly as small apertures and correspondingly longer exposures will be needed to ensure adequate depth of field when shooting close-ups.

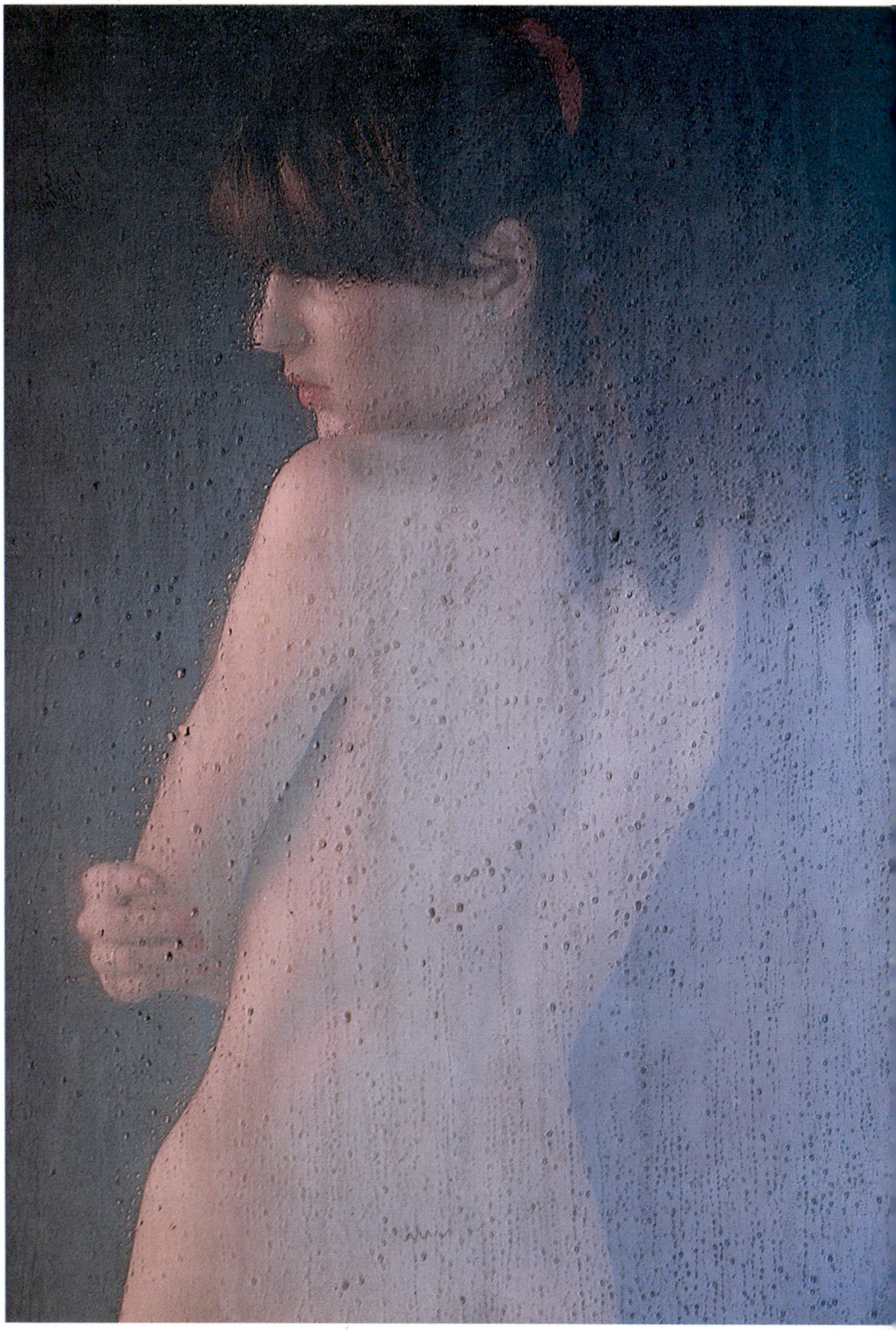

Above: The sheet of glass was sprayed with water and picked up the light of a white reflector. The figure was illuminated separately by a soft light from behind the glass, over which a reddish filter was used to add an interesting colour element.

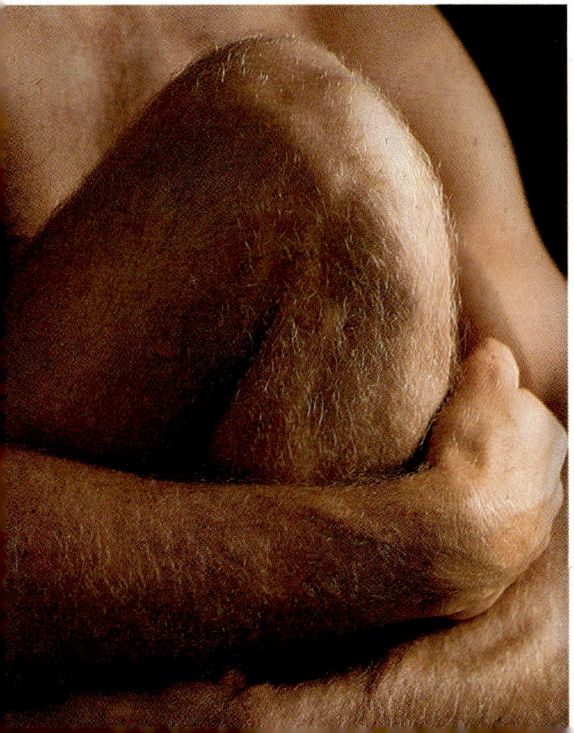

Left: Soft but direct studio lighting has accentuated the form and texture of the model's limbs.

One particularly pleasurable aspect of photography is that it can be combined with other hobbies and interests. This is certainly true of sport and the ability to take good photographs of sporting events will greatly extend the knowledge of photography and often of the sport as well. Even if you are not a sports enthusiast shooting this type of event can still provide a stimulating and exciting subject for photography. The equipment and techniques you need will to a large extent depend on the particular sport and type of event which interests you. At large spectator sports, such as football matches, the use of a long-focus lens is essential since the main action takes place at some distance from the spectator areas. Even more confined sports such as tennis need a fairly long-focus lens to enable you to move in on the action and isolate your subject.

A low viewpoint, a very fast shutter speed, a pre-focused camera and precise timing all combined to freeze the action of this long-jumper.

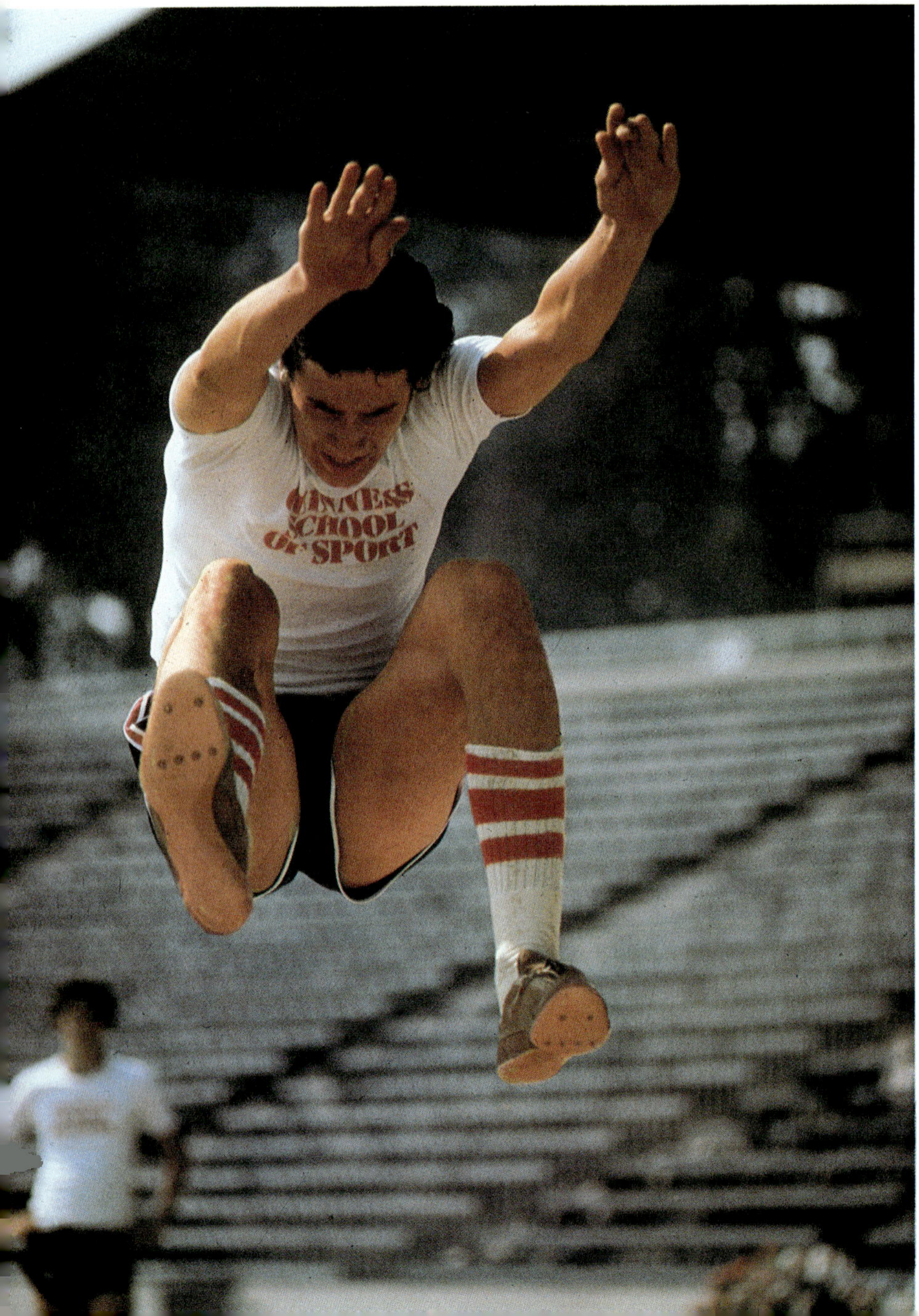

Choosing a viewpoint is one of the most important considerations and obviously a knowledge of the sport in question will help to establish the best position. At large public events this choice is usually restricted unless you are able to obtain special facilities. If your interest is primarily photographic it can be far better to select events and sports which allow you more freedom to choose a camera position and to approach your subject quite closely. In terms of its purely pictorial possibilities a school sports day, for instance, provides just as much action and excitement as a major athletic event, albeit less polished. In many ways you are far more likely to produce good photographs at the smaller, less formal occasions even if the subjects of your pictures are not household names.

While the first consideration in choosing a viewpoint will be to ensure that you are well placed to capture the liveliest and most dramatic action, it is also vital to remember both the background and the lighting. Once again the effect of even the most dramatic moment will be greatly diminished if the subject is lost against a confusing and cluttered background or if it is badly lit with heavy shadows. When you are working at quite close quarters to your subject it is often possible to avoid a cluttered background by shooting from a very low viewpoint and using the sky behind the action; and with some subjects, such as steeplechasing, it will also add a more dramatic quality to the photograph. A long-focus lens is a positive advantage since it enables the subject to be in sharp focus while the shallow depth of field subdues even the most obtrusive background. This type of image is usually more effective when it is tightly framed and isolated from its surroundings.

Accurate focusing can be a real problem when dealing with a moving subject. With long lenses in particular it is almost impossible to change the focus accurately as the subject moves, especially when this movement is directed towards the camera. The best method in most situations is to anticipate the point at which you wish to shoot the picture, pre-focus and then wait until your subject moves into position before firing the shutter. An electric winder or a motor drive is an advantage in this type of photography as the film is advanced automatically after the shutter has fired, giving you a chance at another shot. The motor drive can be set to fire at a continuous rate of up to six frames a second, or even more with specialist cameras.

Whether it is an expression on a competitor's face or the body shape created at a moment of stress, the point at which the most powerful picture can be taken is usually there for only a fraction of a second – it is the ability to anticipate this moment and react swiftly that produces the best pictures.

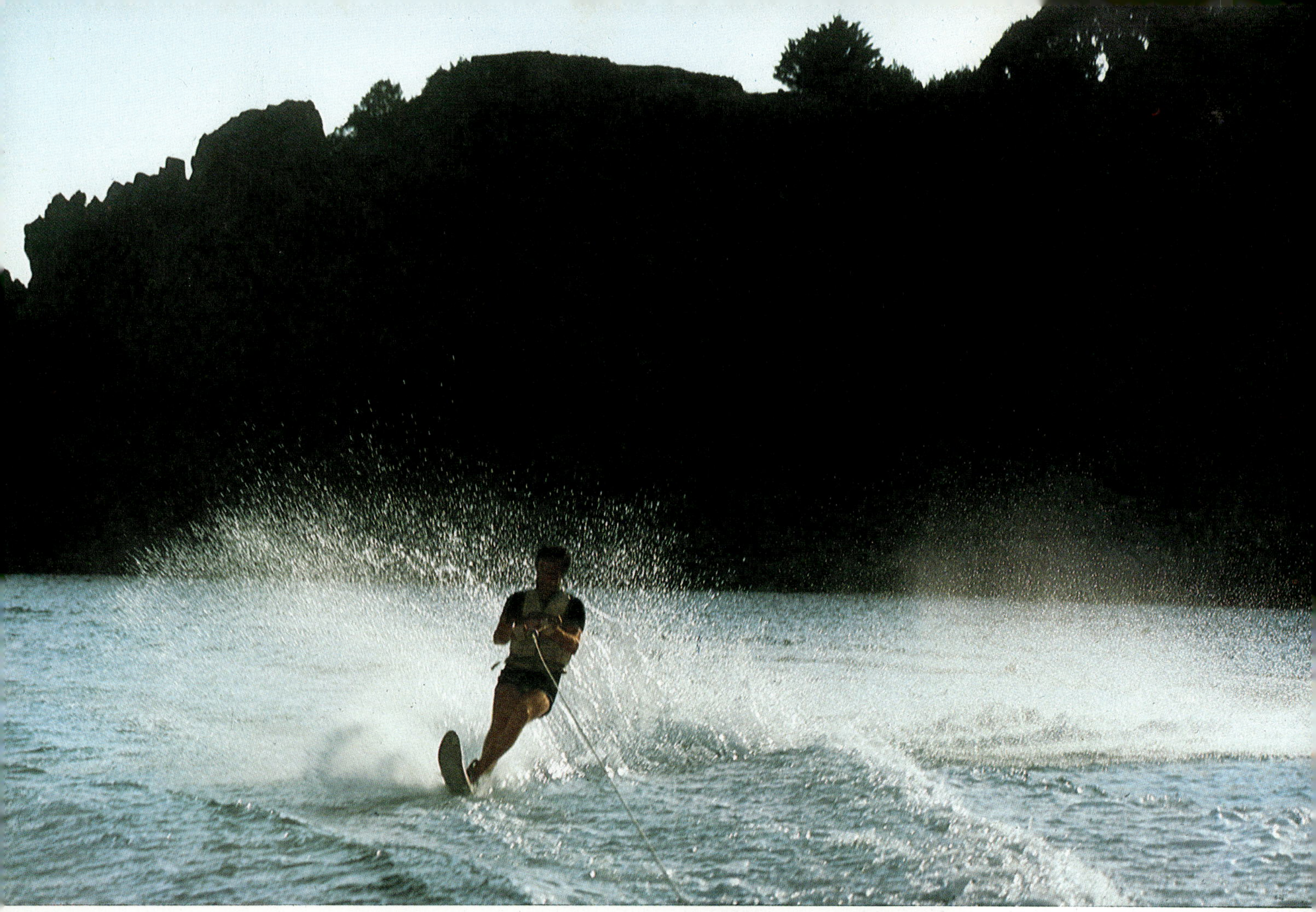

A fairly fast shutter speed has frozen the movement of the water as the skier makes a turn. The spray is drawn out by the back-lighting and the dark background.

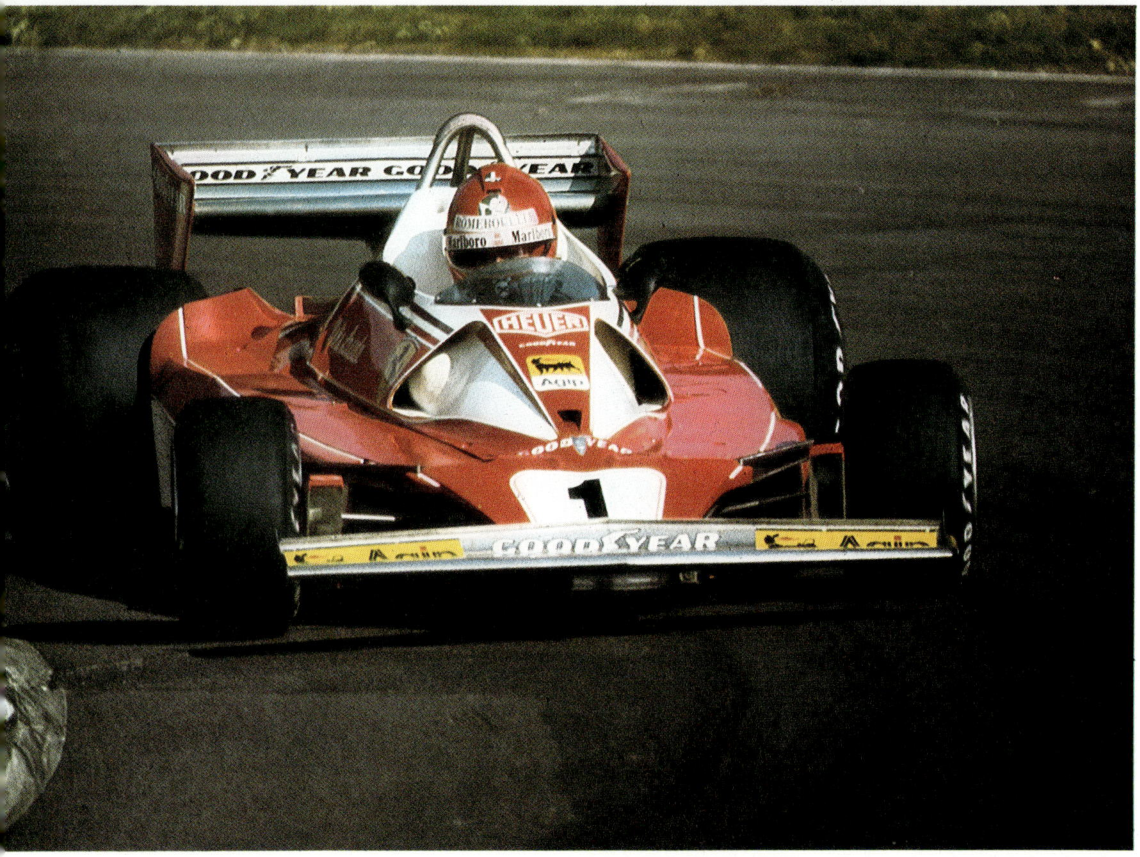

A sharp image has been recorded of this racing car by photographing at the apex of a tight corner with a fairly slow shutter speed.

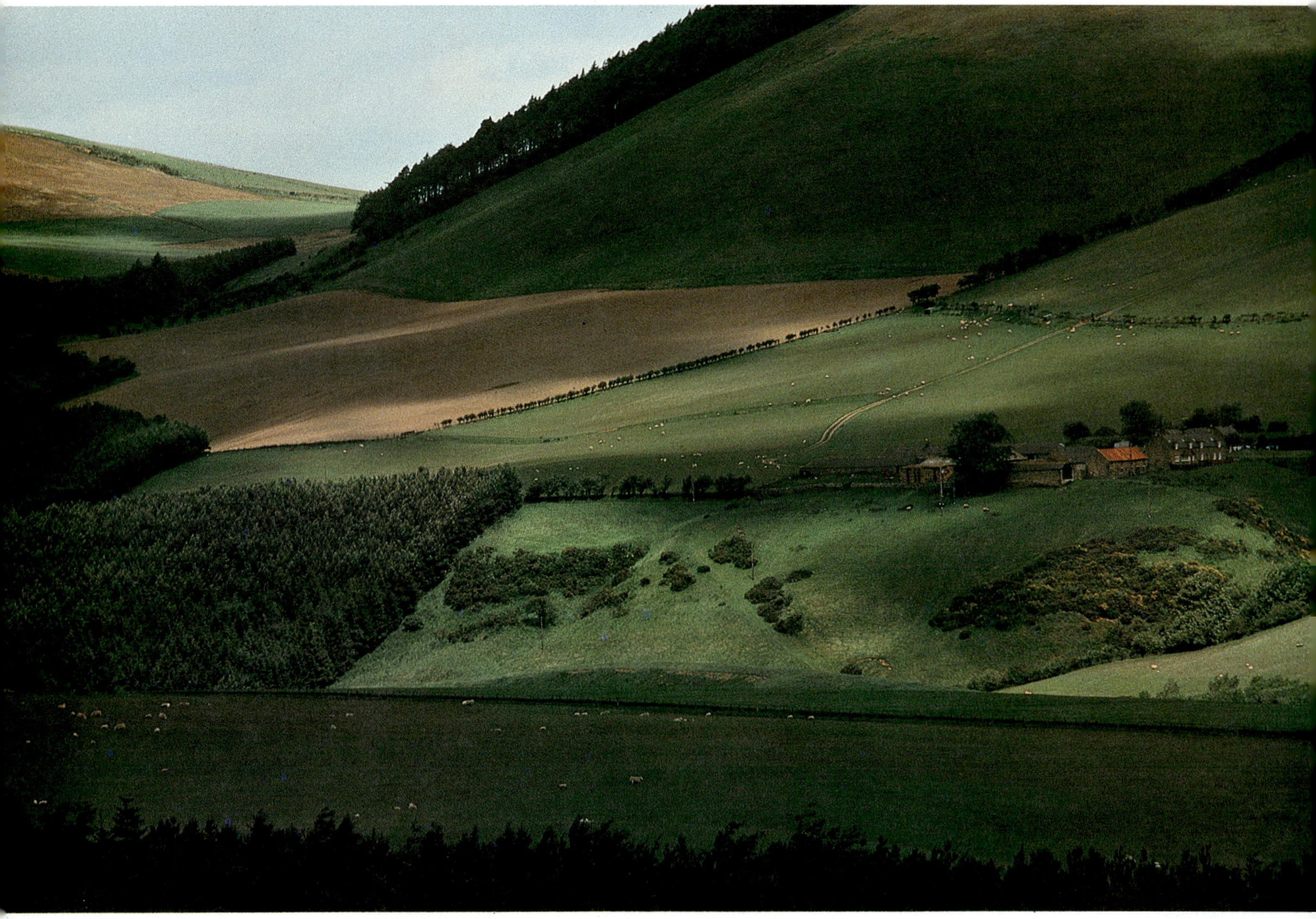

A long-focus lens and a distant viewpoint have helped to emphasize the scale of this landscape; the buildings appear to be dwarfed by the surrounding hills.

Opposite below: The presence of a human figure in this picture has given a sense of space as well as adding interest.

A lovely view of open countryside is inspiring to most photographers, but very often the photographic results of such a scene are disappointing. In many ways landscape photography needs even more care and thought in terms of selection, framing and composition than other subjects. A good landscape photograph is rarely one that simply shows a straightforward open view, no matter how beautiful the countryside. Always establish a centre of interest in a landscape picture. This may be something quite subtle, a tree or a rock, for instance, or there may be a much more obvious focal point such as a church or a bridge; but there should *always* be a place in the image to which the eye is more strongly attracted and around which the rest of the picture is balanced and composed. In a colour photograph this can be achieved by contrasting a single colour against a background of harmonizing colours, such as a single field of buttercups in a landscape of green fields and a blue sky. Even where there is no obvious focal point it is usually possible to find one that gives prominence to some feature of the scene. A human figure will always provide a very effective focal point to a landscape picture. Even when very small within the frame a figure will always draw the viewer's eye, and this also helps to establish a sense of scale.

Perspective plays an important role in landscape photography and to a large extent the choice of lens will decide the effect of your pictures. A long-focus lens can be invaluable for isolating small areas of a scene and creating tightly framed images. It will produce images which emphasize the scale of the scene: a distant view of a group of trees with mountains in the background would be shown very much more in their true perspective when photographed with a long-focus lens. A wide-angle lens, on the other hand, would drastically alter the scale of the picture and the distant mountains, instead of appearing imposing, would be reduced to a small detail in the background. While a long-focus lens helps you to emphasize scale, a wide-angle lens will exploit the impression of depth more fully.

The ability to include close foreground details in the picture area, together with the exaggeration of perspective which this tends to give, is an important factor in this type of photograph. When using perspective in this way you should ensure that the resulting lines of demarcation – from a receding wall or the furrows in a field, for example – lead the eye towards your main centre of interest rather than away from it. Open views of countryside often benefit from the inclusion of foreground interest, such as an overhanging branch of a tree or a farm gate. This not only enhances the feeling of depth but also aids composition by creating a frame for the picture which helps to contain and concentrate the viewer's attention.

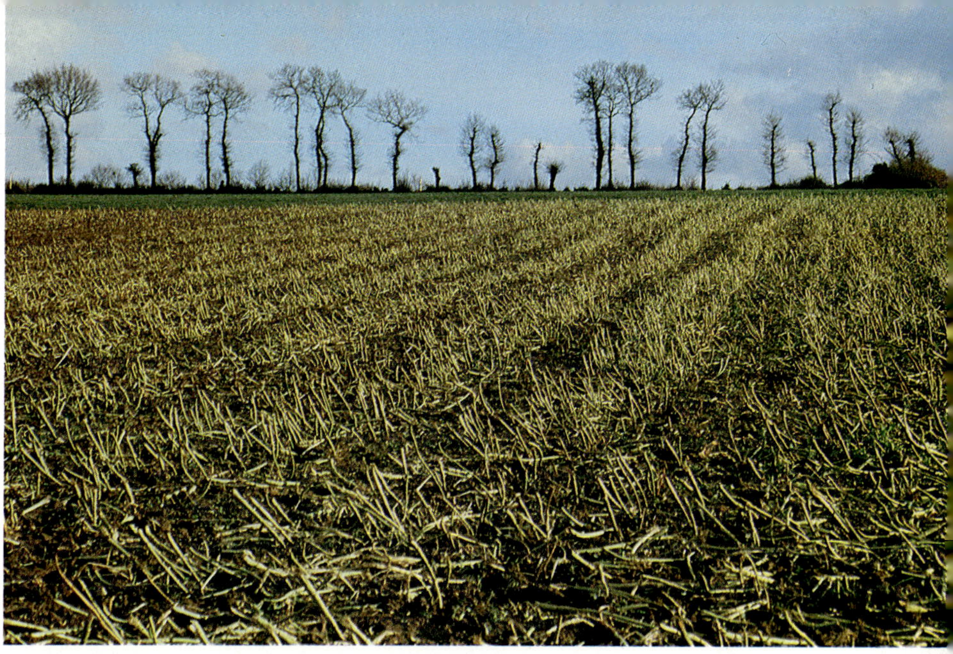

Above: A wide-angle lens has been used in this picture to accentuate the lines of perspective and feeling of depth.

Invariably, the position of the horizon strongly divides the image and the way it is placed in the frame will have a considerable effect on both the composition and mood of the photograph. For example, when it is near the base of the picture, it throws much more emphasis on the sky and tends to give a stronger feeling of space. The horizon which is near the top of the frame produces a more contained image with greater emphasis on the land mass. In general, it is best to avoid having the horizon too near the centre of the frame, since this will just divide the interest between the top and bottom halves of the picture. An exception to this is where the picture is dependent on a symmetrical quality or where there are strong shapes which break into the horizon line and provide an additional element in the composition. Wherever the horizon line is placed you should aim to produce a picture where the main weight or emphasis is based firmly in one half of the image or the other.

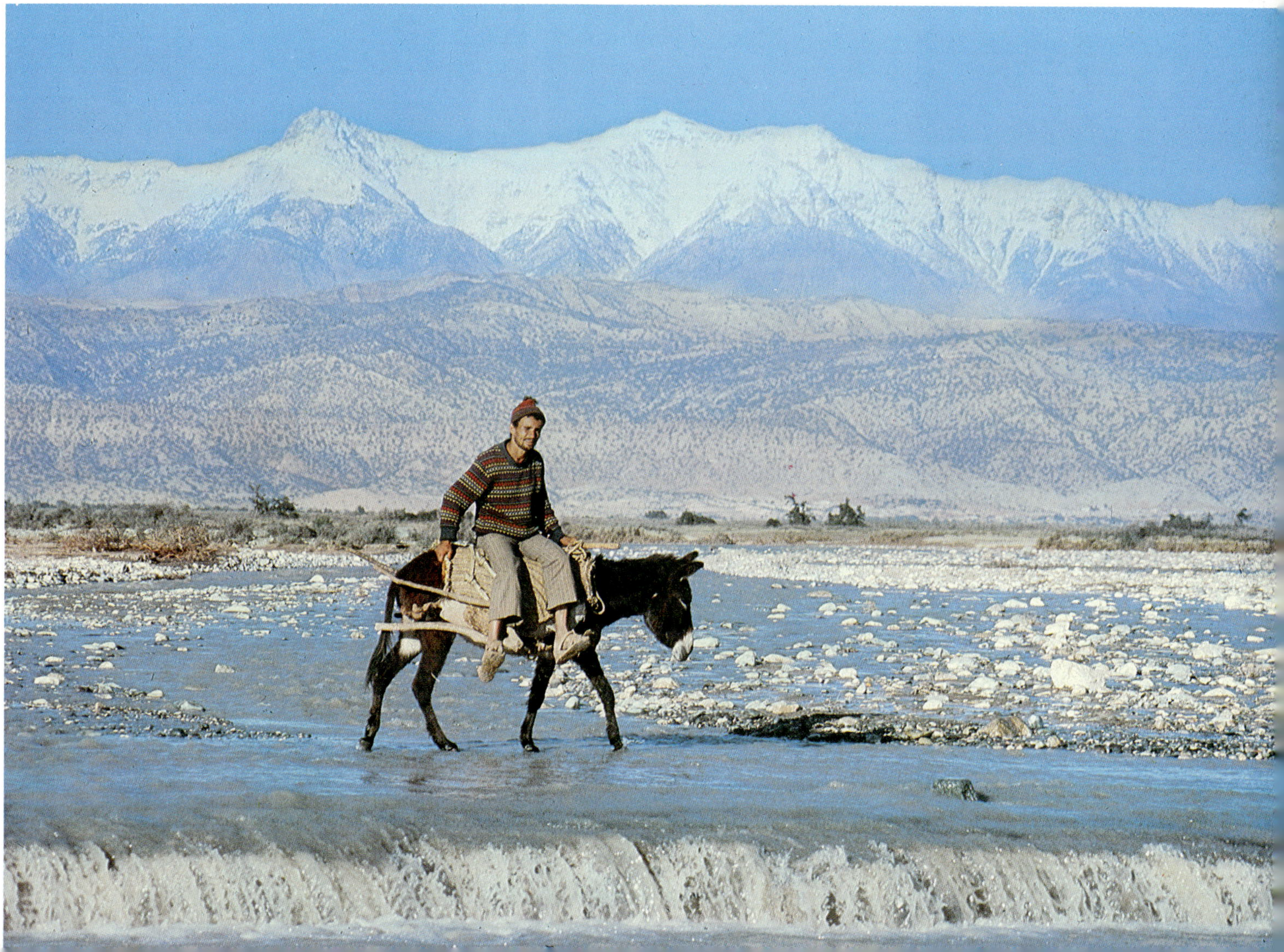

The quality of the light is largely responsible for the mood of a landscape photograph and it is important to be aware of the way that changes in both the lighting and the weather can be used to provide different effects. Many landscape photographers like to shoot early or late in the day when the sun is lower in the sky and the shadows are longer, creating images where both the form and the texture of the landscape are emphasized, and in which details are more clearly defined. This is particularly effective when shooting pictures of open countryside or more distant views where the overhead sunlight in the middle of the day can give a rather flat image with less clarity. It is, however, not only the quality of the lighting that you should consider but also the mood you wish to create – it could well be, for example, that a photograph of a desert landscape may more effectively convey an atmosphere of starkness and heat when lit by midday sunlight.

Another consideration is the nature of the landscape itself. While the long shadows created by evening sunlight would add to the quality of an open landscape, in a mountain area the same light might well result in large areas of dense shadow with no detail. The relationship between light and landscape is one that is constantly changing and rarely repeats itself; a scene which looks visually exciting one moment may lose that quality within minutes when the light has changed. A scene which had escaped your notice could well be inspiring on another occasion.

A day when there is a lot of cloud with small patches of blue sky is ideal for landscape photography as small pools of sunlight are projected on to the countryside, highlighting some areas and leaving others in shadow. The sky itself is more interesting than on a cloudless day, and just before or just after a storm are ideal conditions in which to shoot dramatic landscape pictures. A very good way of increasing your awareness of these effects is to revisit a particular scene over a period of time, and see how much it changes under various conditions – you will find that you are able to take a number of quite different pictures. The same landscape will also, of course, undergo dramatic changes throughout the seasons. Countryside that was soft and green in spring may be transformed into a harsh and rugged view in winter when the trees are bare and the fields ploughed. One of the great pleasures of landscape photography is that there is always something new, even in a familiar environment.

Although the majority of landscape pictures are taken when the sun is shining and there is a blue sky, many of the best results are obtained by quite deliberately seeking the effects of what is

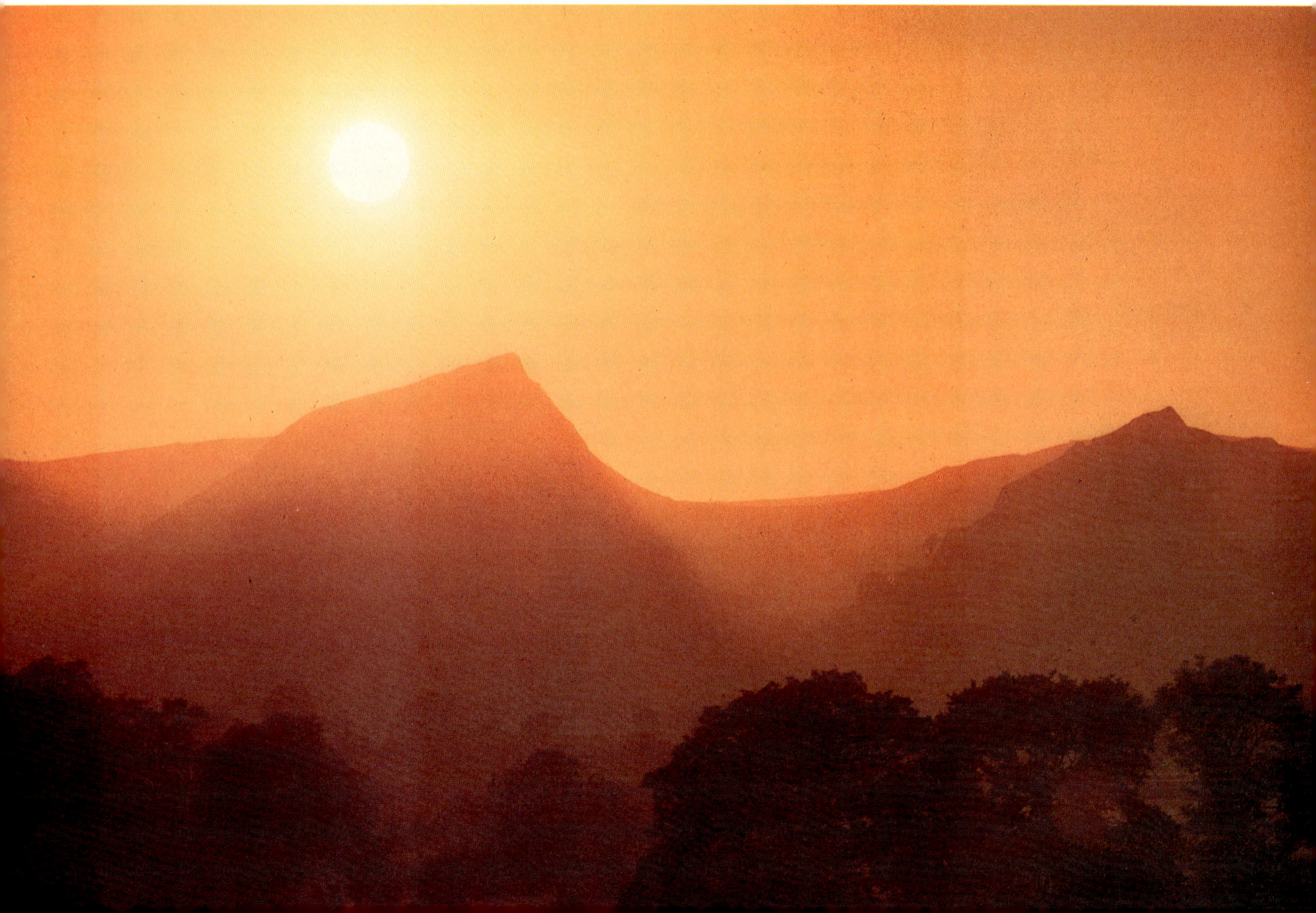

It was possible to include the sun in the frame by photographing in late evening when it had begun to sink into a slight mist. A tobacco-coloured graduated filter was used to add tone and colour to the sky.

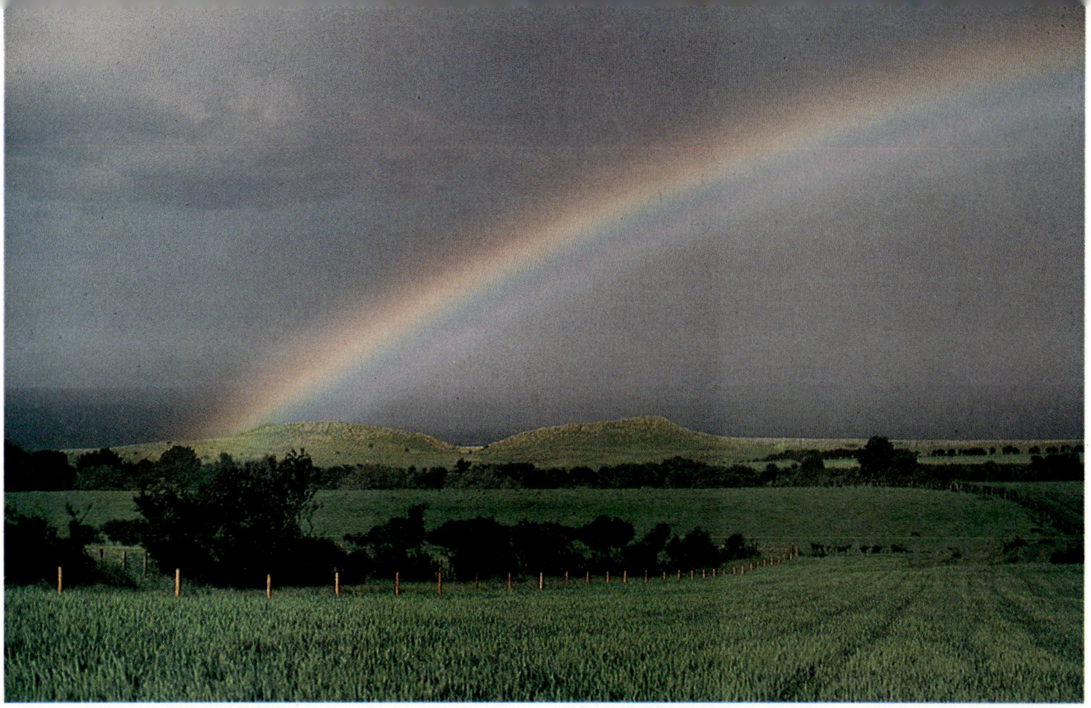

Immediately after a storm is often a good time for landscape photography. In this case a rainbow has added interest and mood to the picture. A long-focus lens was used to isolate a small area of the scene.

considered poor light and bad weather. There is a certain predictability about sunny pictures and unless there is particularly strong interest in the subject matter or the composition they can easily possess the rather boring and repetitive qualities of picture postcards. It is far more rewarding to explore the possibilities of the changes in light and weather than to wait for a bright, sunny day before you take your camera out. Mist, rain and snow or even just a dull day will often impart an interesting mood to a picture. With colour photographs the pictures produced on a dull day, or at dusk when the sun has gone down, have a much softer quality and the colours are more subtle and subdued. This type of light is best when the picture contains quite bold shapes and contours, as fine details and textures may be lost.

Exposure needs to be judged accurately because the brightness range of the subject is usually much lower than with a sunlit scene. Overexposure will result in pictures which are pale and colourless and underexposure will result in images with grey and muddy tones. A good method is to take an average reading from both the lightest and darkest areas of the scene, and it is also advisable to bracket your exposures either side of the calculated setting. Mist and fog give a similar effect, subduing colour and detail and emphasizing the shape rather than the form of the subject. Rain, on the other hand, can enhance the quality of texture by creating highlights on wet surfaces, such as foliage or a country lane, and adding sparkle to the image. Many people hesitate to use their cameras in such conditions in case they are damaged by moisture. However, it is a simple matter to protect the camera from rain by encasing it in a loose-fitting plastic bag with holes cut into it for the lens and viewfinder window. A little damp won't harm the camera providing it is dried carefully with a soft cloth as soon as possible after use. Salt water, such as sea spray, is very harmful and should be avoided as it has a corrosive action.

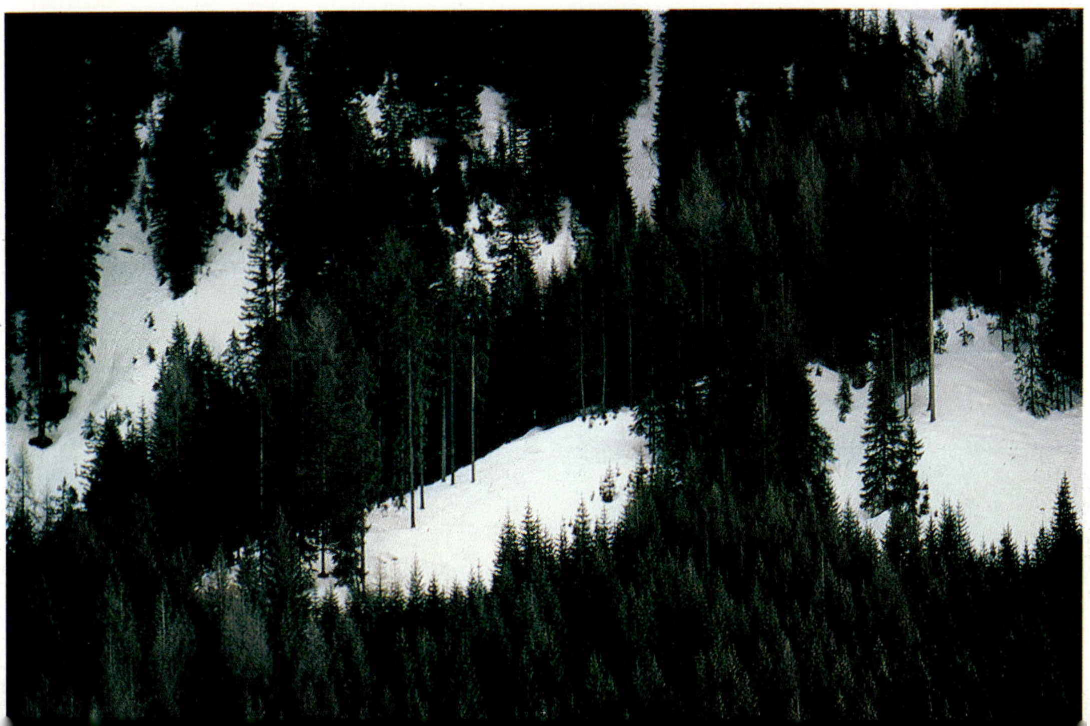

A dull day producing a soft light was used to photograph this snow-covered mountainside. The absence of a sky-line and a limited colour range have resulted in a somewhat sombre picture.

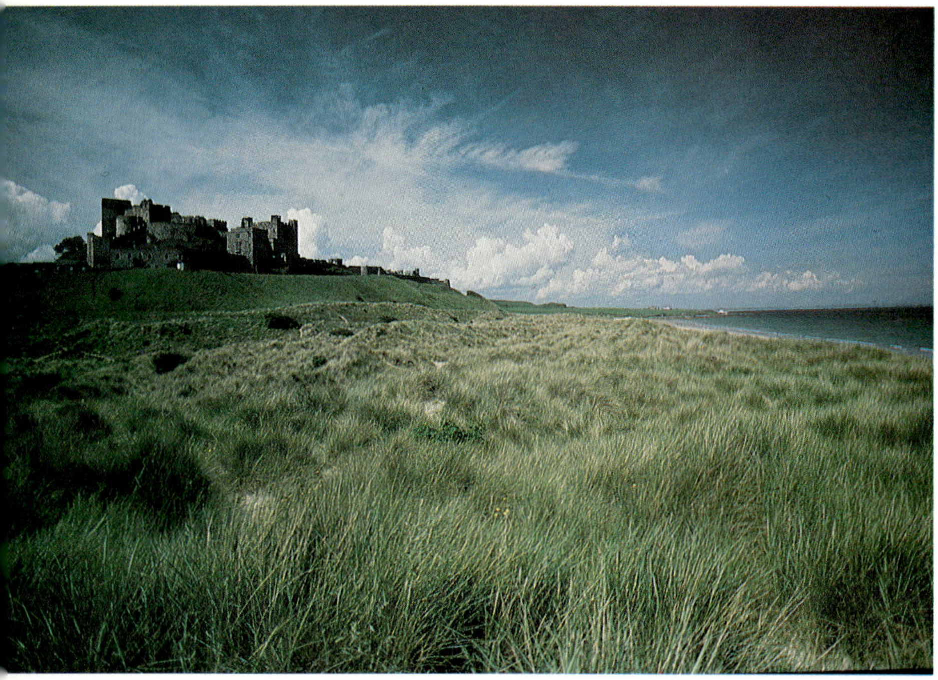

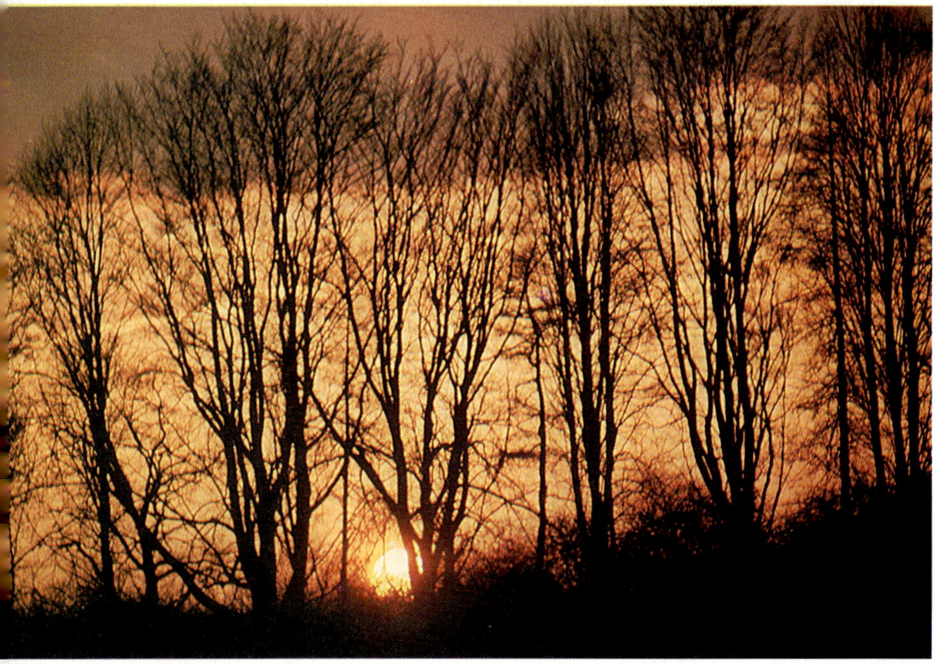

Top: A blue sky and dramatic clouds have been emphasized by using a polarizing filter.

Above: Slight underexposure has produced the rich colours and silhouetted trees in this sunset picture.

The sky plays an important role in landscape photography and needs to be given special consideration in order to produce the best results. The sky is part of the light source in most pictures, acting rather like a reflector in a studio lamp, and an exposure which is calculated to record detail on the land will result in the sky itself being somewhat overexposed.

In black-and-white photography this can be compensated for during the printing process by printing the sky darker or shading it in. A blue sky can also be made to record as a darker tone in black-and-white photographs by using a yellow, orange or, for the strongest effect, a red filter; this will also make white clouds stand out in much stronger relief and create a more dramatic effect.

With colour pictures it is not possible to use such filters, and other methods must be used to help produce adequate tones in the sky. It is vital to avoid overexposure when the sky is important to the picture, and in such cases it is often effective to underexpose deliberately and allow the foreground to be partially silhouetted. A polarizing filter is very useful as it will record a blue sky as a darker and richer blue without altering the other colours in the scene. The effect will vary accordingly to the position of the sun in relation to the area of sky you are photographing, and the filter must be rotated to give the optimum result. As with a red filter in black-and-white pictures, white clouds will be made to stand out in quite dramatic relief.

Graduated filters are also very effective in adding depth and quality to sky tones and, unlike the polarizing filter, can be used when no blue sky is present. As their name implies they affect only part of the image: half the filter is quite clear, and there is a gradual transition to a tone or a colour, so that the foreground or landscape part of the image remains unaffected and the sky can be made darker or a colour introduced quite independently. They are available in two strengths and in a range of colours which includes a neutral grey. The circular variety is fixed in position to affect approximately half of the picture but the square variety can be positioned in the filter mount to offer a finer adjustment. When using between-the-lens metering systems it is important to measure the exposure before fitting the filter to obtain its full effect. A wide-angle lens will invariably enable a more dramatic quality to be obtained when photographing skies, and the effect of all of these filters tends to be much stronger with one.

Photographing a sunset presents a similar problem of overexposure, and as the sun itself is usually within or very near the picture area this tendency is even greater. The colours will appear much weaker and there is less detail than appears to the naked eye. It is usually quite impossible to give an exposure which will both record adequate detail in the foreground and produce a rich and colourful sunset. Graduated filters can be of help in some situations and the coloured versions such as tobacco or mauve can add dramatic colour in addition to making the sky darker. The best solution is to use an interesting shape in the foreground which can be exposed to create a silhouette: a tree or a city sky-line. Another method is to use a lake or sea in the foreground as this will reflect the colours of the sunset and add foreground interest. One mistake is to photograph the sunset too early when the sky is still very bright, and even with underexposure this will cause a considerable loss of detail and tone. Very often the best time to shoot a sunset is just before or even just after the sun has disappeared below the horizon. Sometimes it can be very effective to include the sun in the picture, although this is best left until it is very low in the sky or is weakened by mist. In some situations it is possible partially to obscure the sun behind some foreground details, such as the branches of a tree, in order to reduce its power.

Calculating exposure can be quite difficult with a sunset. One method which gives a reliable result in most situations is to take a reading from the area of the sky directly overhead rather than attempting to read from the area of sky included in the picture. It is advisable to bracket exposures as it is quite difficult to predict results accurately even with some experience.

When the sun is still fairly strong a wide-angle lens will often produce a starburst effect without the aid of any lens attachments – quite a dramatic effect when combined with underexposure and the inclusion of some interesting foreground details. A long-focus lens can also produce pictures of considerable impact if you juxtapose the sun against some distant object, a building for instance – the lack of perspective will create the impression that the sun is much larger than it would otherwise appear.

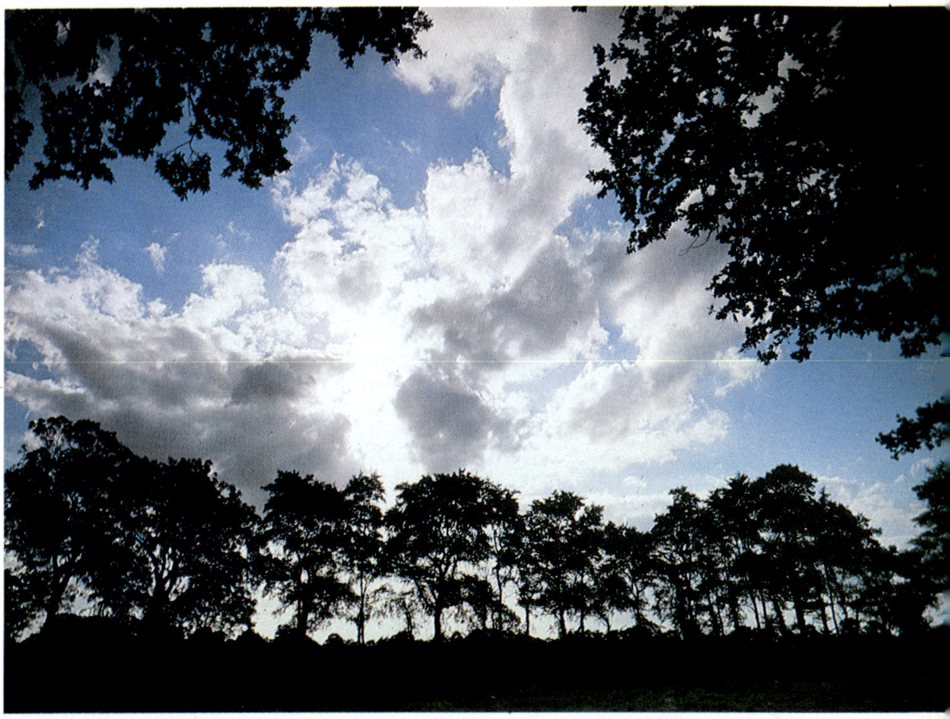

Above: Considerable underexposure has transformed an ordinary summer sky into a powerful image.

Below: A tobacco-coloured graduated filter has added both depth and colour to the sky in this late evening scene.

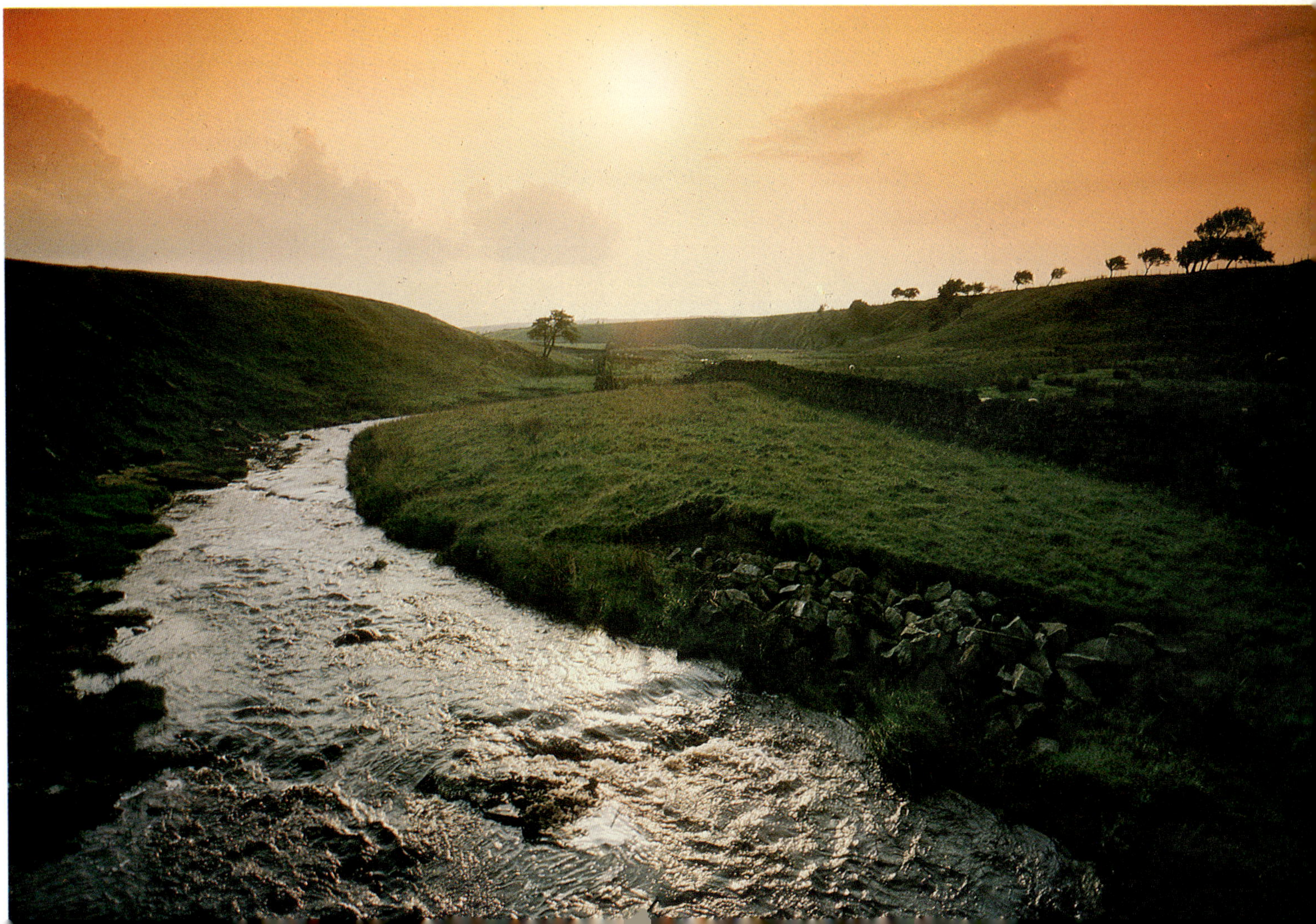

Lakes & seascapes

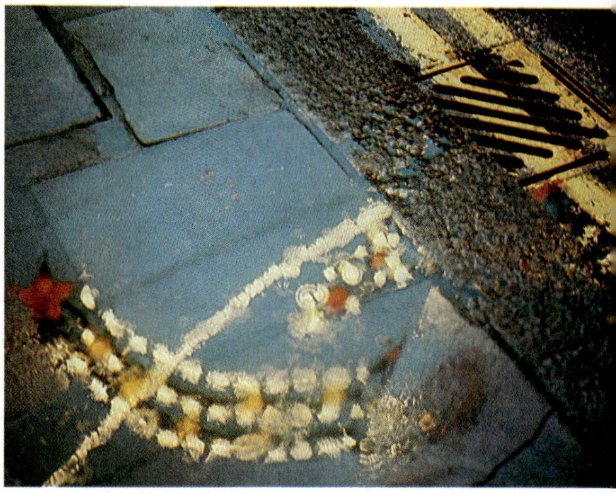

Right: Christmas street lights reflected in a puddle have given semi-abstract effect.

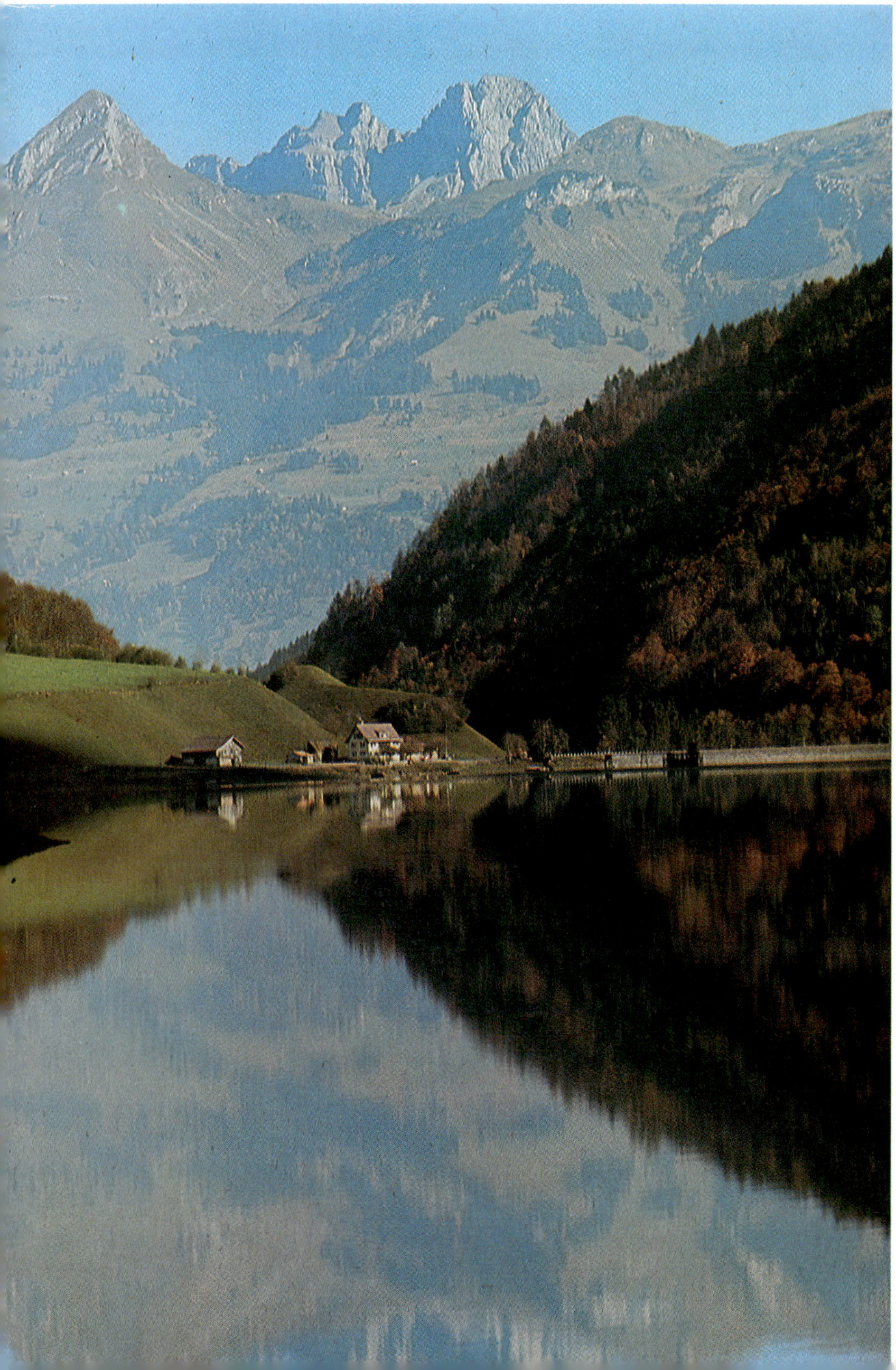

Below: Very still water and evening light falling on the distant mountains have produced an almost mirror image in this lake scene. A long-focus lens was used to isolate a small area.

Water in a natural setting has a powerful visual appeal, from the passive tranquillity of a mountain lake to the fierce, sometimes frightening, thunder of surf on an exposed coastline. It is this wide variety of moods that provides such a challenging and rewarding subject for photography, and the presence of water is invariably a powerful element in a picture.

Still water, such as a lake, can create beautiful reflections forming a mirror image of the landscape around it. This effect is most powerful when the lake is very calm and when the light is strongest on the land beyond it, as in the early morning or late evening. You should explore all possibilities before deciding on your picture – a wide-angle shot may be the most effective, showing a vast expanse of water with the reflections clearly seen and maybe a boat or an overhanging tree in the foreground to give the picture some depth; or a long-focus lens may isolate some small aspect of the distant landscape mirrored in the lake with a small fringe of land to establish the setting.

In addition to the surrounding landscape, still water also reflects the sky – it is the nature of the sky that is responsible for the appearance of the water. Blue sky will produce a smooth, even quality, whereas dramatic cloud formations will give a rich variety of tones and textures on the surface of the water.

Water rarely makes an effective picture on its own and it should be seen as one element of the complete picture, as part of the overall composition. Often in lake scenes there is a little mist present, particularly early or late in the day, and this can result in very soft images with muted colours, reducing the landscape and its reflections to simple shapes and contours. Do not overlook the possibilities offered by isolating very small details such as a group of reeds or an overhanging tree. When there is a slight breeze causing ripples on the surface of the water, the reflections will appear distorted to the point where almost abstract pictures can be taken.

It is interesting to experiment by varying the shutter speeds. Slow speeds will produce soft flowing swirls of tone and colour, whereas quite fast shutter speeds will record the surface as a hard-edged texture. This effect can be found just as easily in a small pond or even in a puddle. Running water, such as a river or a waterfall, also provides a variety of images and, again, explore the effects which the choice of shutter speeds can provide. With the camera mounted on a tripod and an exposure of a second or even longer, moving water can provide the most beautiful images – but be sure to include some static objects in the picture, such as rocks or trees, to obtain the best effect.

The sea is also subject to an infinite variety of

moods conditioned by the weather and the light, ranging from the limpid turquoise translucence of a Mediterranean cove to the threatening grey waves breaking over rocks on the Atlantic coast. Capturing the quality of clear blue sea to its best advantage requires a day when the sky is deep blue and the sea is quite calm or is sheltered. It will also appear a deeper, richer colour when you shoot down on to it from a high viewpoint. In these conditions a polarizing filter can have a quite dramatic effect; by removing some of the surface reflections it will make the water appear more translucent, revealing a wider range of colours and tones. Do not forget to include both foreground and distant details as this will give a greater feeling of depth and provide a balanced composition.

It is, of course, vital, as with all photographs, to establish a centre of interest – a fishing boat, for example, or it may be simply a rock or a swirl of colour in the sea. When the sea is slightly disturbed by small waves it can be very effective to shoot towards the sun, resulting in a myriad of tiny highlights on the surface. Exposure can be misleading in these circumstances as these bright highlights indicate far less exposure than is really needed, which will result in underexposure unless an allowance is made. This is particularly important when you have included foreground details in your pictures. It is best to take your reading well to one side of the area you are photographing, including only a fringe of the highlighted water; or, alternatively, you can take your reading from the foreground details. If you can find an interesting shape which can be silhouetted in the foreground, a tree perhaps, it can be effective to underexpose, as this will make the sparkle on the water far more dramatic, and if you shoot with a long-focus lens with a fairly wide aperture the highlights will appear as large, luminous, overlapping circles.

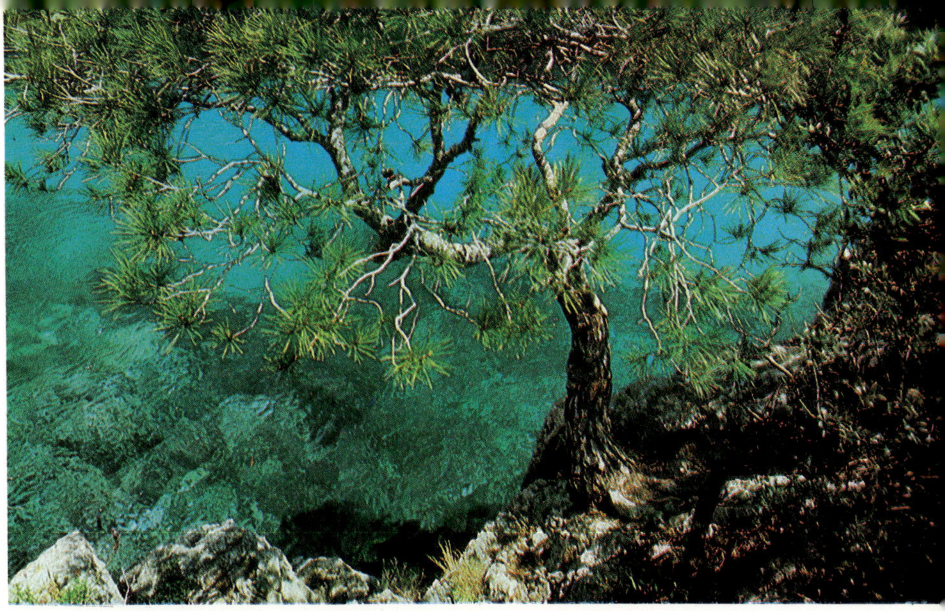

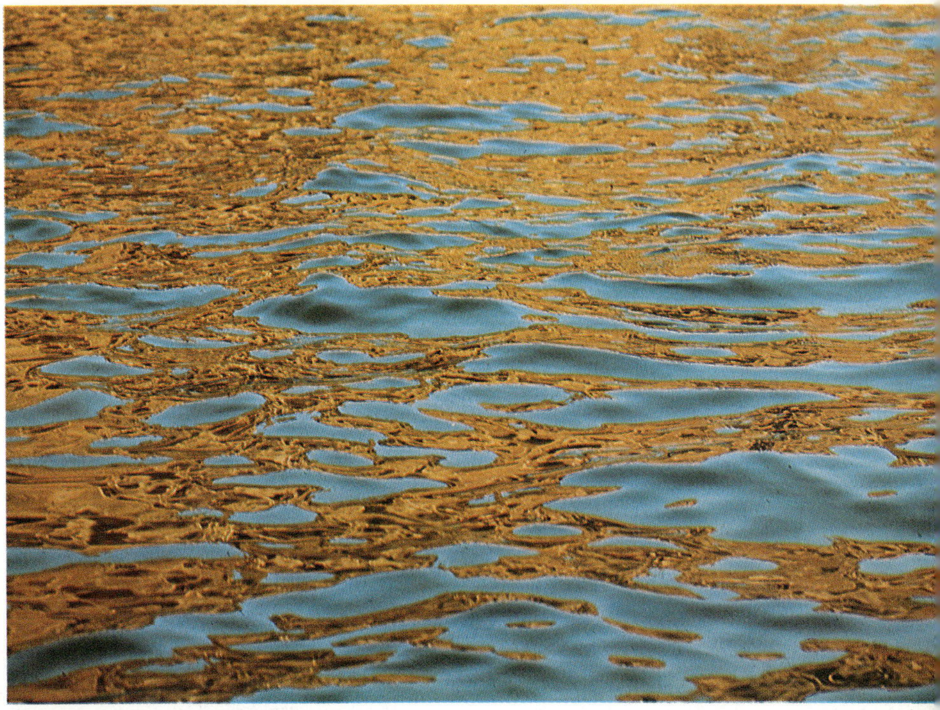

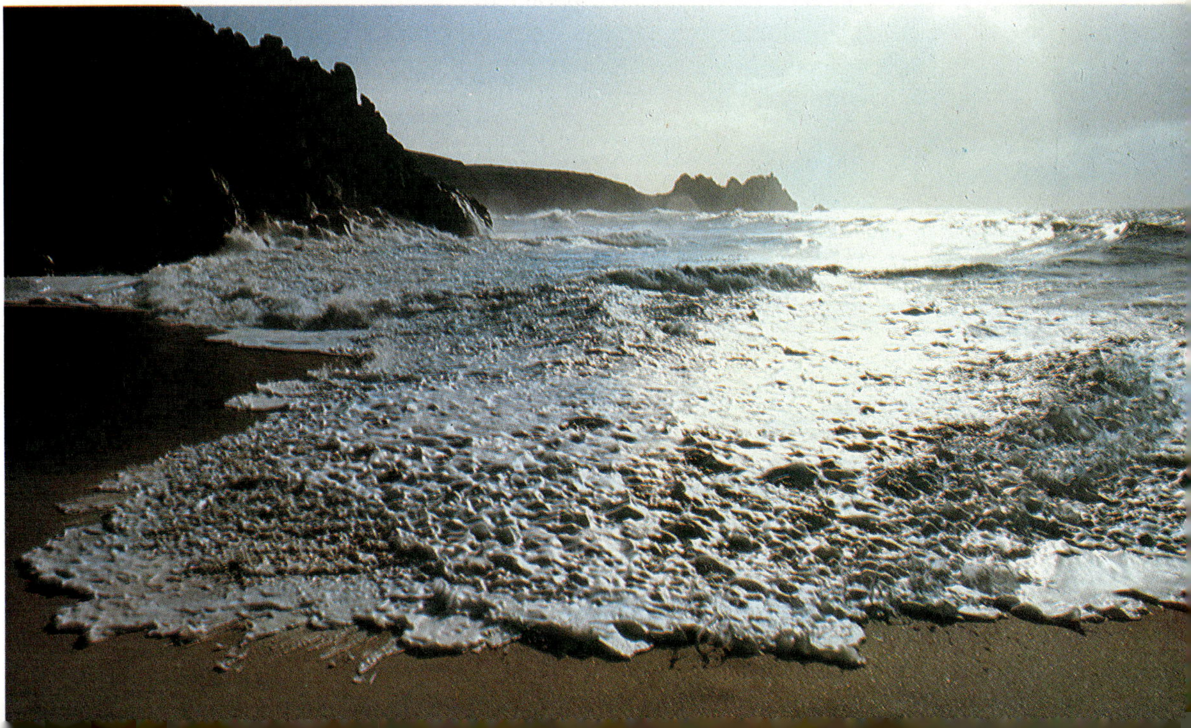

Top right: A polarizing filter was used to emphasize the translucent quality of this Mediterranean cove.

Above right: Brightly-lit buildings reflected in the rippled surface of a Venetian canal have produced an impressionistic pattern.

Below right: Shooting into the light with a fast shutter speed and a wide-angle lens was used to capture this solitary moment of surf breaking on to a beach.

Below: A macro lens was used to isolate this single bloom.

Bottom: A wide-angle lens has emphasized the shape of this sprawling beech tree.

Nature provides us with such an abundance and variety of subjects to photograph that we usually take them for granted, and it is only the more dramatic and unusual things that attract our attention. It is often, however, the more colourful and obvious subjects, such as a cascade of brightly coloured flowers in a park or a riot of colour in an autumn woodland scene, that can lead to disappointing pictures unless care is taken. These subjects need to be approached with a perceptive and selective eye to produce good photographs.

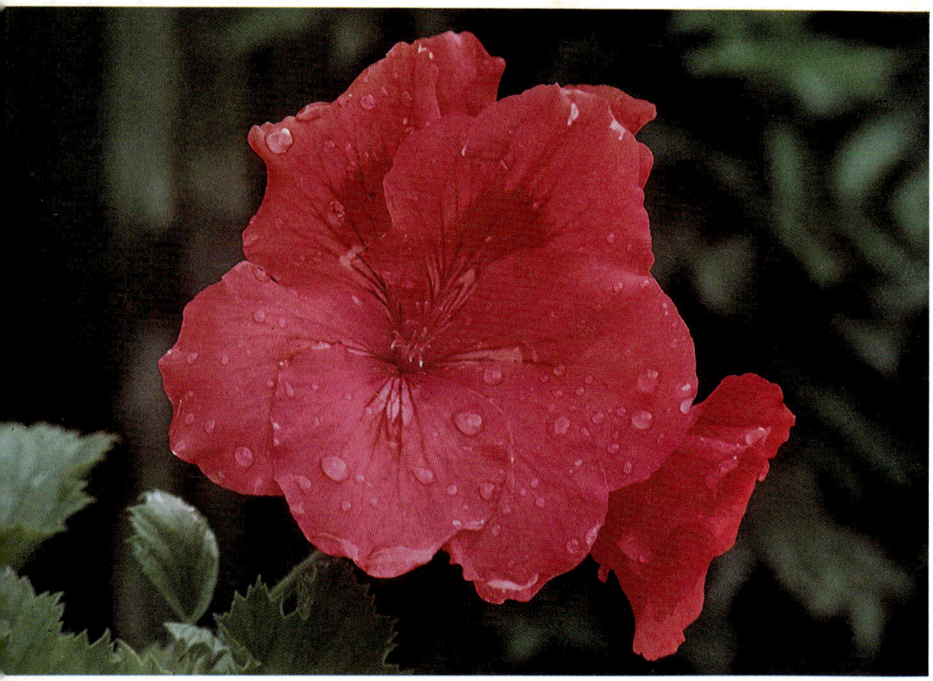

A single bloom glistening with raindrops is more likely to provide a dramatic picture than a view of a flower bed, and a single, well-shaped tree is more pleasing than the wide expanse of a wood. Most photographers experience days when they are simply unable to find a suitable scene, and yet one never really has very far to look – just maybe a little closer and harder. The problem is not a lack of subject matter but the inability to see and isolate individual elements from what can easily appear as an overwhelming mass of detail.

One of the easier aspects of photographing natural subjects is that at least Mother Nature does have a remarkably good colour sense. There is almost always a balanced harmony or a pleasing contrast in the flowers of the field or with leaves and trees, and once you begin to appreciate the rather less obvious nuances of a natural setting you will find it difficult to take a *bad* picture.

Inexperienced photographers often believe that flowers and trees will only look their best on bright sunny days. The opposite is usually true, however, as strong sunlight gives hard, dense shadows and brilliant highlights and many of the subtleties of colour and texture will be lost. Soft, hazy sunlight is far preferable and even a dull day can provide good lighting conditions for photographing rich colours, when flowers in particular will look fresher and more appealing.

When you are taking quite close-up pictures of

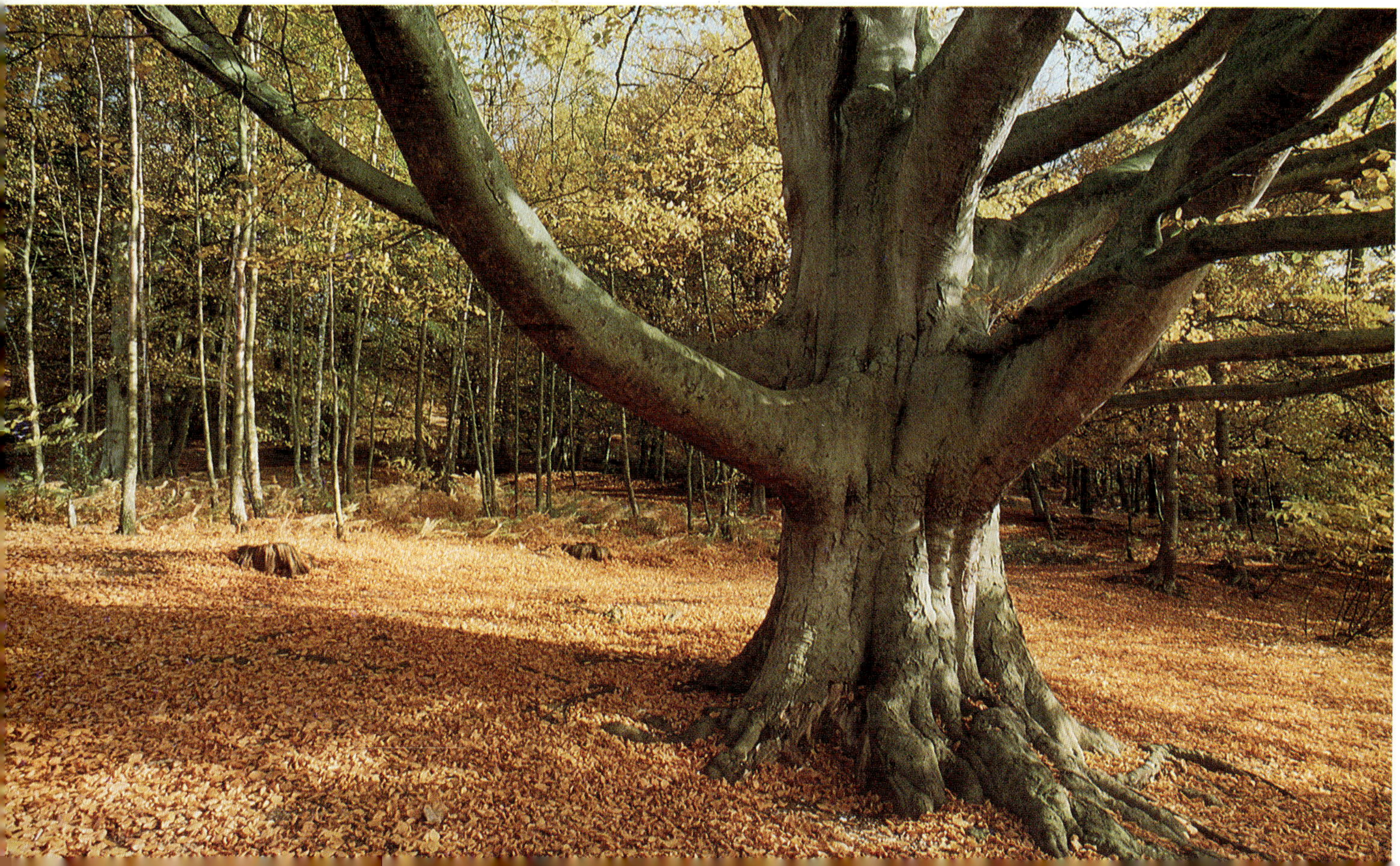

individual blooms a tripod is a great help since it will enable you to position the camera more carefully and ensure that there is no camera shake. Slow shutter speeds are often needed to allow a small enough aperture to be used to give adequate depth of field, but don't stop down too much, otherwise background details will be brought into focus and detract from your main subject. A long-focus lens is often an advantage with this type of picture as it will help to keep the background out of focus and will also allow you to shoot from a more comfortable distance. Subject movement can also be a problem with close-up pictures, particularly if there is a breeze, and it can be very helpful to erect a small windshield – a piece of card will do – close to the subject and just outside the camera's view.

You should choose a camera viewpoint which enables an area of contrasting tone or colour to be brought into view behind your subject to help it stand out more clearly. When you are taking pictures of a broad expanse of flowers, in a field for instance, it is very effective to focus on quite close foreground details and use a wide aperture: this will cause the more distant details to form a backdrop of soft mottled colours while your subject remains in sharp relief.

Trees have a natural elegance and if you choose a viewpoint that isolates them from their surroundings, they can provide a strong element of design in a photograph. In winter and in the spring, when the foliage is not so dense, the patterns created by the tracery of the branches of a tree can make very attractive pictures, for example, when partially silhouetted against the sky. The elements of pattern and texture are found in abundance in a woodland setting. A perceptive photographer can find many ways of exploiting these qualities to produce effective pictures but, again, remember that they are part of a considered composition and not the only reason for the photograph. A misty day is often ideal for this type of subject as it reduces the effect of smaller details and simplifies the image, allowing the trees and branches to form bolder shapes against the partially obscured background.

Autumn is a time when few photographers can resist the temptations offered by the rich orange and brown colours of a woodland setting, but great care is needed to avoid a confused image with no obvious centre of interest. Viewpoints must be carefully chosen to isolate the most effective elements of the scene and, as with the photography of flowers, the best pictures are likely to be those which feature relatively small areas of the scene rather than the broader view. The discreet use of a warm filter, such as a Wratten 81B or 81C, can often add a degree of richness to autumn hues, and a slight amount of underexposure will provide additional help.

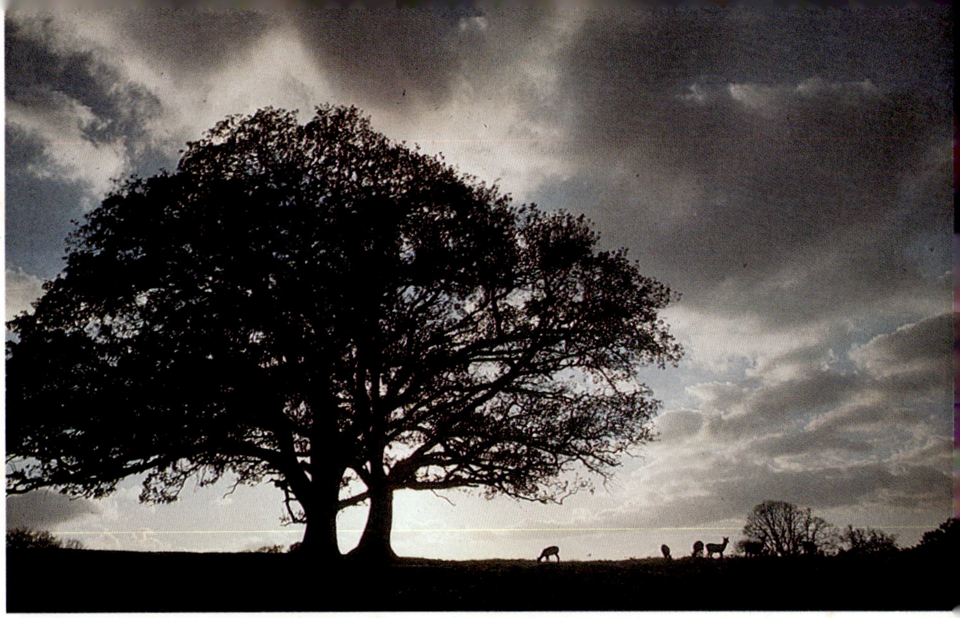

Above: A low viewpoint and slight underexposure have produced this silhouette of a tree.

Below: A long-focus lens and a wide aperture have isolated this small section of a flower-filled field from its surroundings.

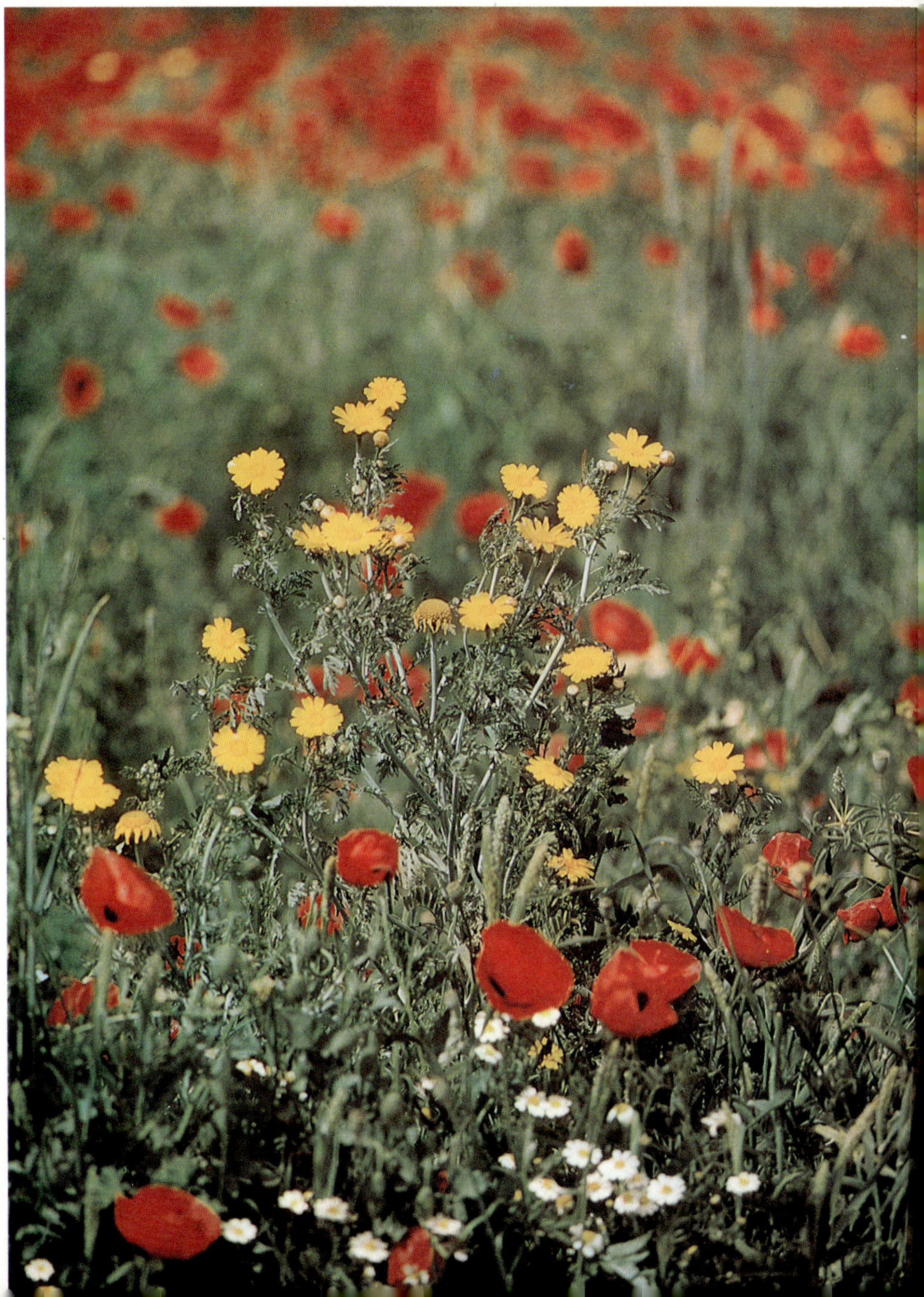

Like children, animals make ideal subjects for photography because they have instant viewer appeal. You don't require any particular skills or equipment to photograph animals, at least for the domestic variety, and all you need is a little patience. The easiest subjects to start with are household pets. They are more familiar with you and are more likely to respond to a little control and direction. Cats and dogs are probably the most photographed of all animals and are a permanently popular subject for calendars, books and greeting cards. The least satisfying way of photographing animals, from a photographer's point of view, is the rather artificially posed picture in a studio setting. Pictures which show animals behaving and responding naturally in an appropriate setting are more likely to produce a pleasing result.

Right: A 300 mm long-focus lens was used to photograph this bird from a distant viewpoint.

Below: A shallow depth of field, using a wide aperture and back-lighting, have helped to isolate these animals from their background.

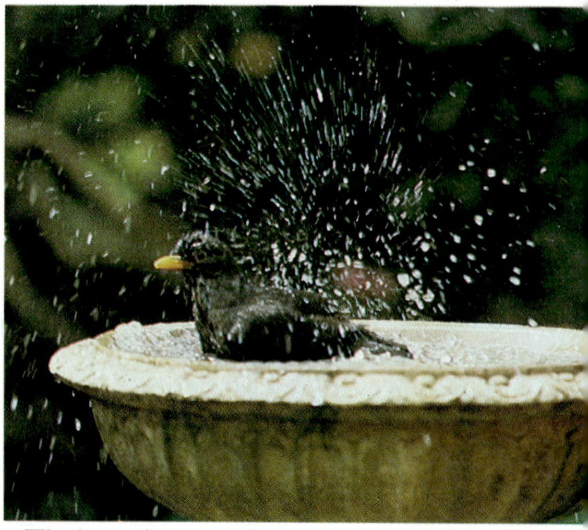

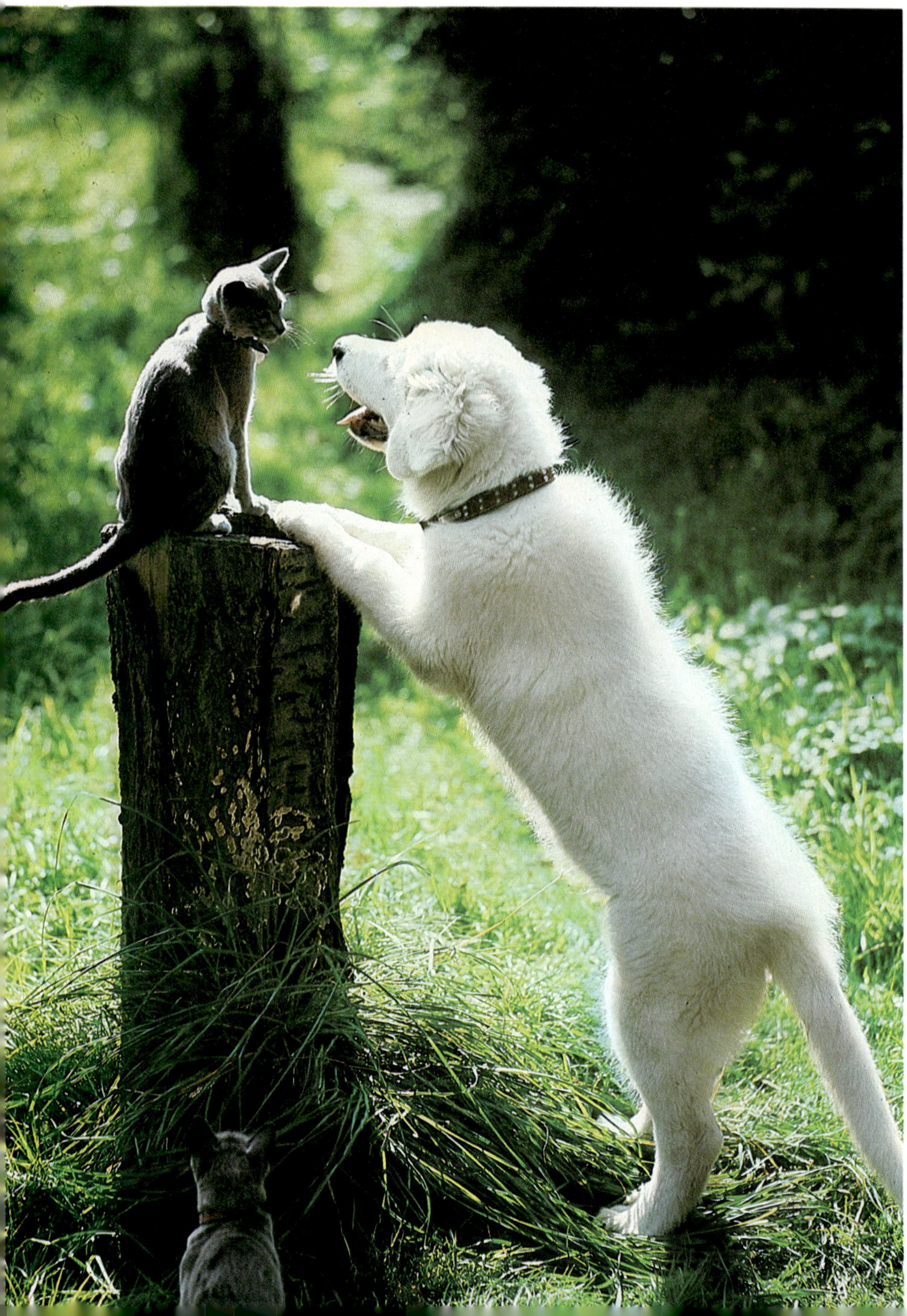

The best photographs are invariably those that show the animal quite tightly framed and well separated from an uncluttered background. A long-focus lens of say 105 mm or 135 mm on a 35 mm camera is a considerable advantage, particularly when taking pictures of small dogs and cats, as to fill the frame with a standard lens will mean approaching them very closely. A long-focus lens will also help to throw background details well out of focus. It is a great help to have some assistance – someone who can help to keep your subject amused and occupied in one place while you are taking the photographs.

Daylight is the easiest method of lighting as it allows you the freedom to follow the pet around and shoot from a variety of positions, and a garden is a convenient location. Bright sunlight is best avoided as the resulting shadows can easily obscure the faces of small creatures; a hazy or cloudy day is better as it produces a softer light with minimal shadows. Indoors, window light is effective, providing it is a reasonably bright day, or you can use the light of a small flash gun bounced from a white ceiling or a wall, and the brief duration of the flash means that you do not have to worry about subject movement. Direct flash is best avoided as it can create hard shadows and will also often produce the 'red eyes' effect when used close to the camera lens. This is caused by the flash being reflected back off the retina in the animal's eyes.

It can also be very satisfying to photograph wild birds in a garden. Elaborate equipment is not essential although, again, a long-focus or telephoto lens is an advantage. Even with a standard lens it is possible, if you set the camera on a tripod quite close to, say, a bird table, prefocus and frame the picture and then leave it there undisturbed for a while. You will find that the regular visitors to your garden will quickly become accustomed to its presence and return to their familiar haunts. When a suitable subject alights in the right position the shutter can be released with the aid of a remote release from some distance away. Of course, if you own an automatic camera and an electric winder you can shoot an entire roll of film without having to go near the camera. Once again, you should remember, when setting up your camera, to choose a viewpoint which provides an uncluttered and contrasting background so that the subject will stand out clearly against it.

If rather more exotic animals appeal to you then obviously a zoo or a wildlife park can provide a wide variety of subjects. Providing you choose your viewpoints carefully and frame your pictures quite tightly it is possible to take photographs that give no indication that the animals are in captivity. It is a good idea to find out the feeding times of the animals you want to photograph as this is when they will be most active and will provide the most lively subjects. A long-focus lens is a particular advantage when photographing animals behind bars, not only because it enables you to obtain a large image of a distant subject, but also because it is possible to shoot through mesh cages without their being visible. Providing the camera is placed as close to the mesh as possible and a fairly wide aperture is used, the wire will be so out of focus that it will not record on the film.

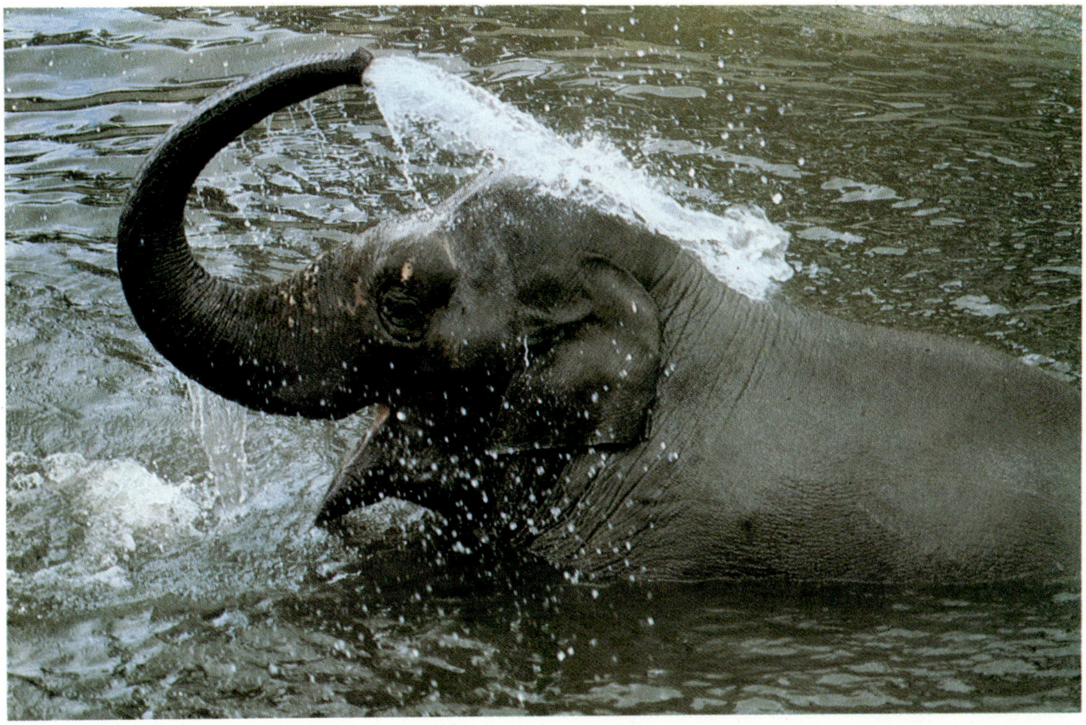

This tightly-framed picture of an elephant at bathtime gives little indication that it is in captivity. A long-focus lens was used to obtain a close-up image from a distant viewpoint.

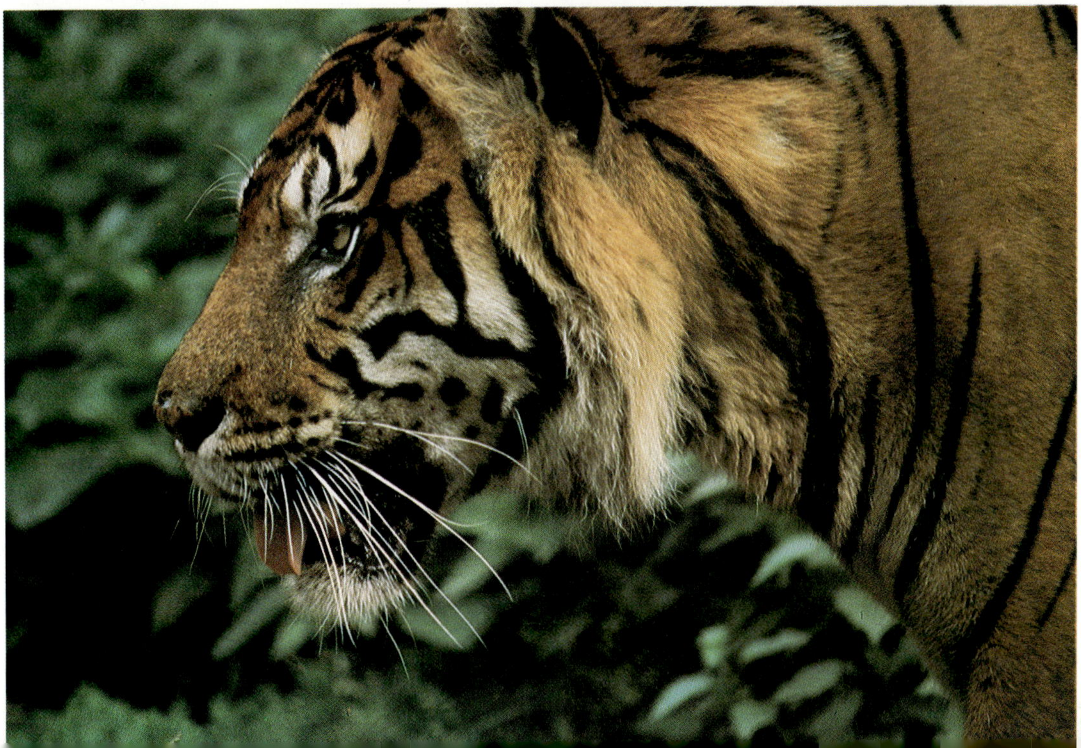

Although a wire-mesh fence was between the camera and the tiger, the use of a wide aperture and a long-focus lens has thrown it so far out of focus that it has become invisible.

The camera on holiday

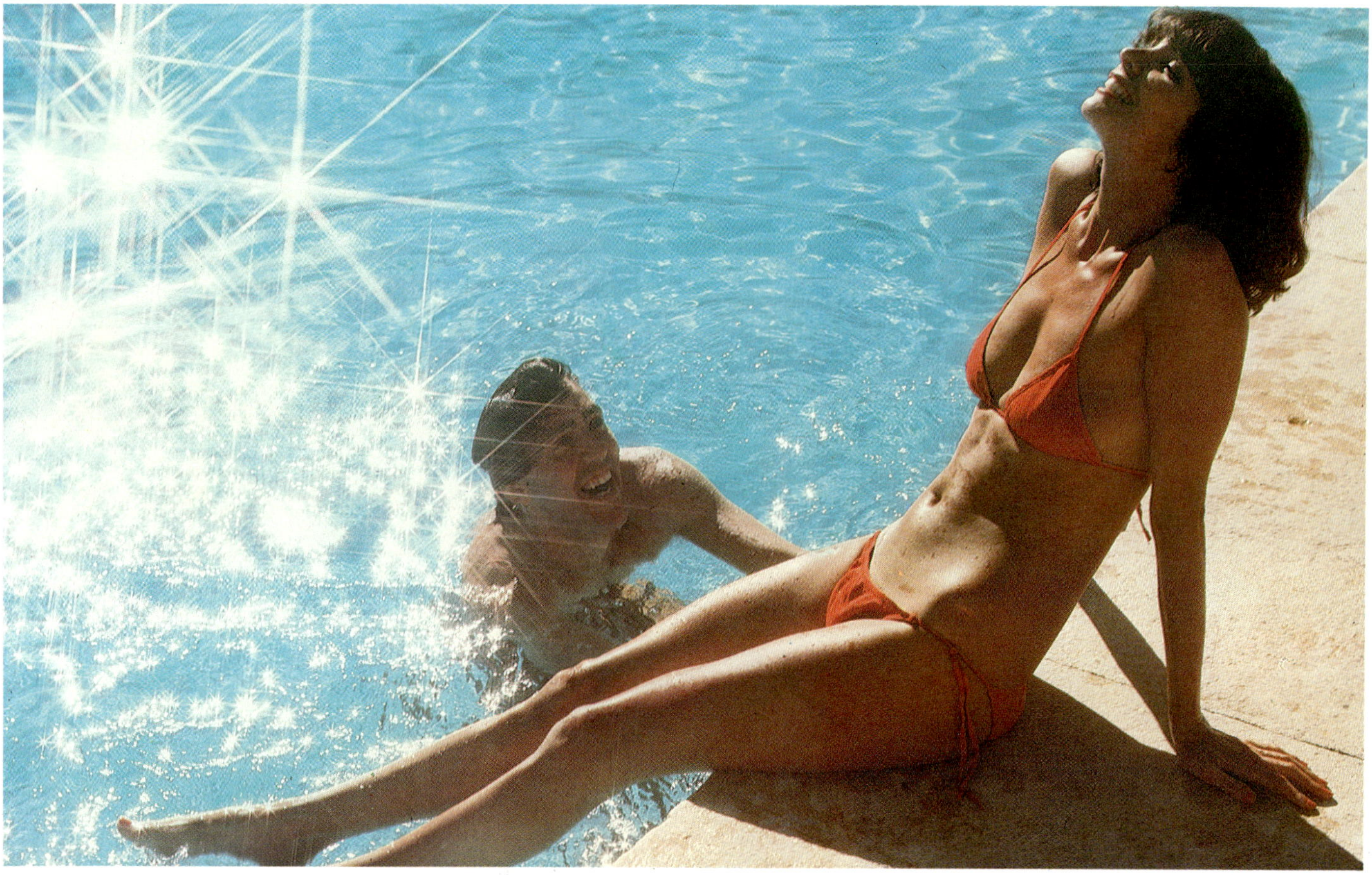

Above: A starburst filter added interest and sparkle to this picture of a couple in a swimming pool.

Below: A distant viewpoint and a long-focus lens have accentuated the scale of these holidaymakers on a beach.

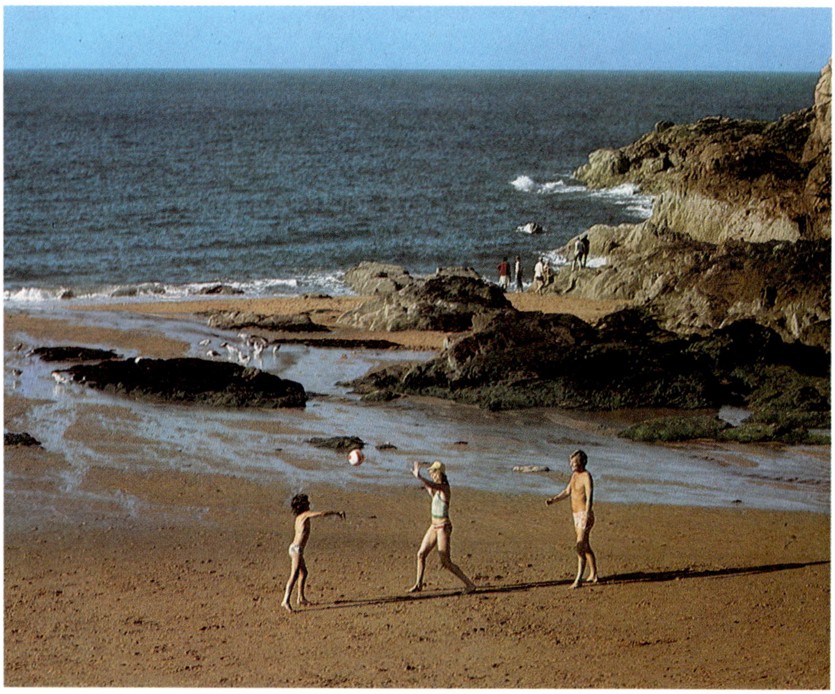

Even the least enthusiastic photographer tends to make a special effort when on holiday. Apart from the visual stimulation of a new environment and the extra time available, there is the additional incentive to produce a good set of pictures to show friends at home and to provide a lasting record of the occasion. Unfortunately, the majority of holiday photographs tend to be very dull indeed, especially for those who were not there. This is usually because either normal care and thought has been abandoned or the photography has been left until the last moment and then a roll of film has been hastily shot. For the little extra effort that is required it really is worthwhile to try and make a complete record – try to shoot a few frames every day; vary the pace a little; don't take all of the pictures in the same way. Try to get as much variety as possible into the pictures you take and then they will be a pleasure to look through – even for your friends who were not there.

A holiday usually means visiting the seaside and here you do need to take a little extra care of both your equipment and the way you take your pictures, as both sand and sea water can cause great damage to a camera. It is a good idea to keep your camera and lenses in a polythene bag inside your camera bag when they are not being used, and try to avoid resting your camera bag on the sand. When you have left the beach you should carefully remove any grains of sand with a blower brush and any smears on the lens can be removed by a *light* wipe with a lens tissue or a selvyt cloth.

Exposure calculations need to be made with some care as the large amount of light which is reflected and scattered from sand and sea can result in unrealistically high readings. A good method is to take close-up readings from your subject, being careful to shield the meter from stray light. Quite often colour pictures taken at the seaside acquire a pronounced blue cast, due to an excess of ultraviolet light which often exists under these conditions and which, although not visible to the eye, will record on the film. An ultraviolet or skylight filter will help to reduce this and as there is no adverse effect can be left permanently in position on the lens. This will also give added protection to the much more costly lens. Often it is preferable to use a stronger filter, such as a Wratten 81A or 81B which are a warm straw colour, and a polarizing filter can also be effective in these conditions. Similar problems exist when taking photographs in high altitudes as mountains and snow scenes often produce excessive ultraviolet. There can be a certain amount of haze in mountain views and although with colour films a haze filter will give some help, it is rather limited. In black-and-white photography, however, a considerable benefit can be obtained by using an orange or a red filter as this not only improves the clarity of the scene but also will provide additional contrast between snow-capped mountains and blue sky. Photographs taken either in the early morning or in the late afternoon when there is haze present will have greater clarity, and the ever useful polarizing filter will produce pictures with a little more 'bite'.

As well as taking extra care with your equipment when travelling, you should also make sure that your film is not exposed to excessive temperatures as this can affect the colour balance both before and after it is exposed. If you are intending to take a lot of pictures and will be away for several weeks it is strongly advisable to ensure that you take an adequate supply of film from your regular supplier. Do not rely upon buying film when you arrive as this may well be badly stored or short dated, especially if you are holidaying in the country or in under-developed areas. One last important point is to avoid having your film subjected to X-ray examination when passing through the security control at airports, as this can cause fogging. Do *not* pack your film in luggage which will be loaded into the aircraft hold and also try to avoid its going through the hand luggage X-rays, as although they claim to be safe this is not always so: if you fly frequently the X-rays can have a cumulative effect.

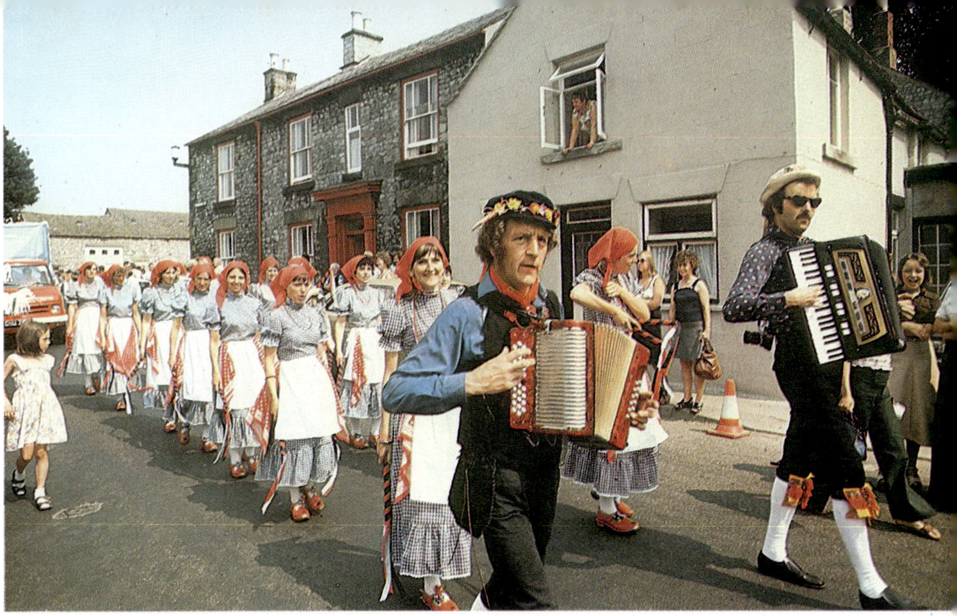

Above: A wide-angle lens was used to photograph this parade in a Derbyshire village. Wide depth of field and angle of view enabled the whole scene to be recorded.

Below: Late afternoon sunlight has added warmth and strength to this colourful scene of a carnival procession in Malta. A long-focus lens was used to isolate a small area.

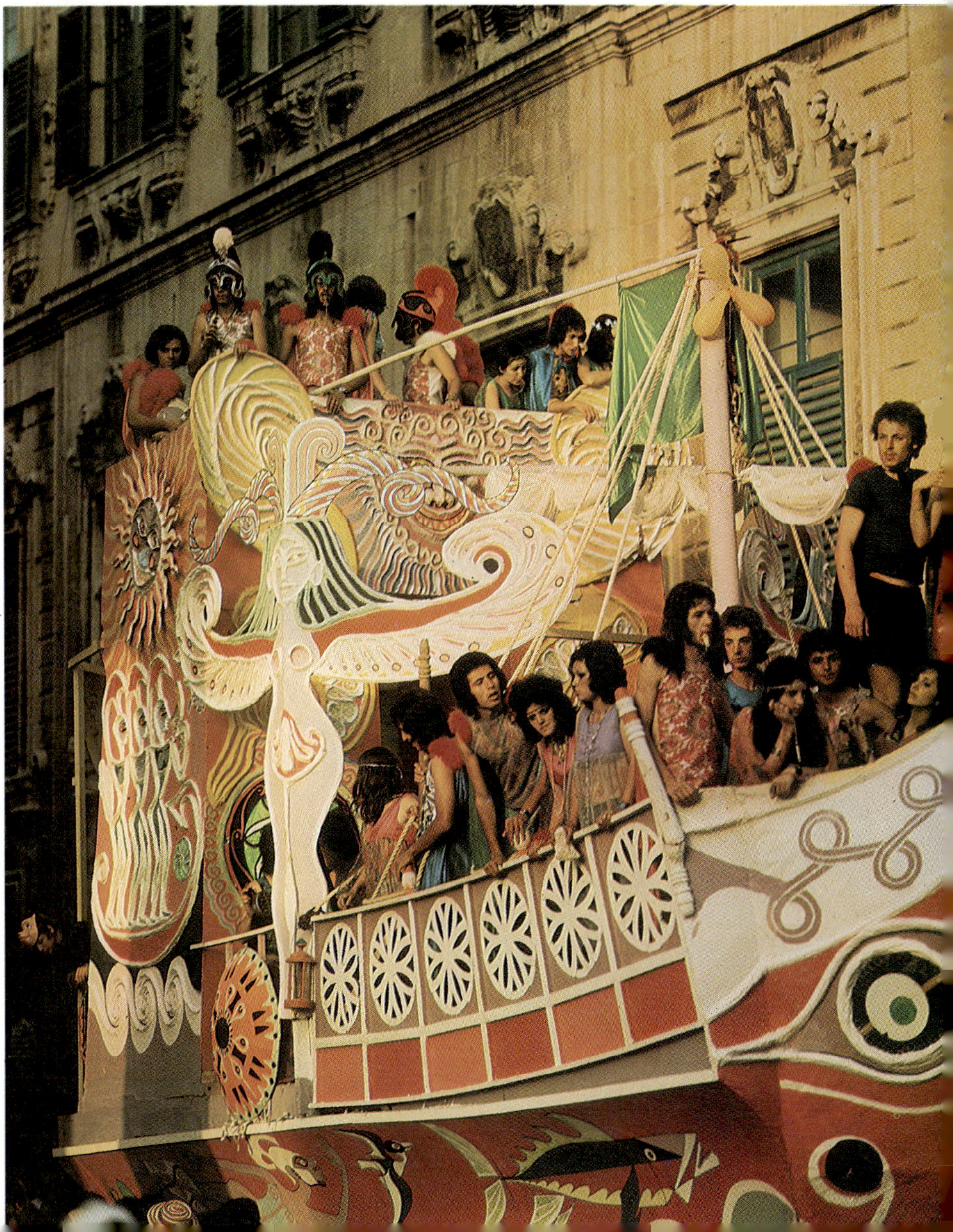

Photographing the sights

For the photographer one of the principal pleasures of travelling is the stimulating experience of seeing new and unfamiliar places. On arrival in an unfamiliar location, it is worthwhile studying postcards and souvenir books to get some idea of possible viewpoints and to work out the best time of day to photograph particular situations. Viewpoints of buildings in an urban setting are often rather restricted and good postcards will usually indicate most of the possibilities. This does not mean you should simply try to duplicate the postcards, rather use them as starting points for your own interpretations.

Perspective is one of the main considerations when shooting from a close viewpoint, and if you want to photograph the whole building a wide-angle lens is an advantage. If you want to avoid converging verticals it is important to resist tilting the camera upwards to include the top of a structure. One solution is to shoot from a more distant viewpoint so that the building occupies the top half of the frame with some foreground interest filling the bottom half of the frame. Another method is to find a higher viewpoint, perhaps a building opposite the one you want to photograph, so that you are able to shoot from a position approximately midway between its ground level and the roof. Even in a city it is usually possible to find distant viewpoints of buildings such as a cathedral, and a long-focus lens will usually enable you to produce a large image of your subject. But you should also

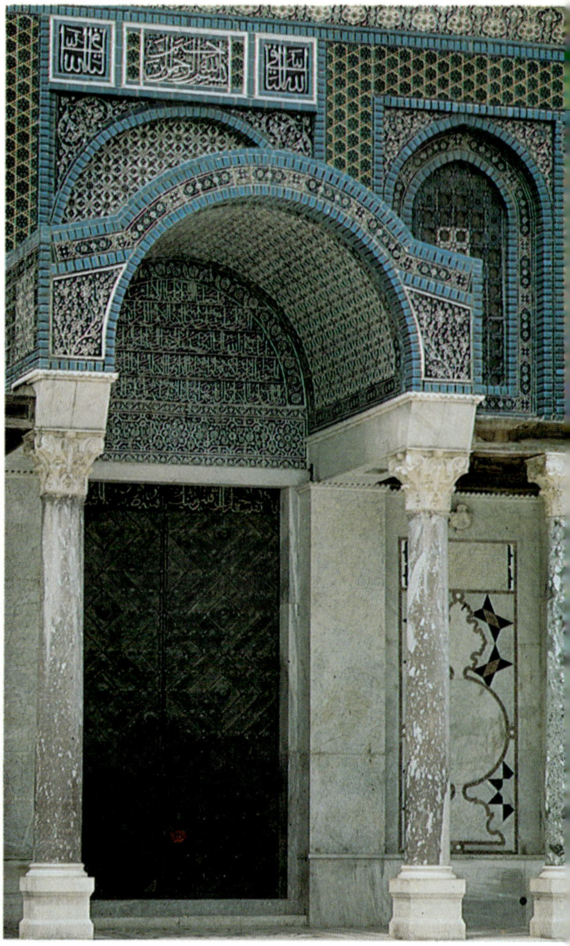

Right: It is often effective to isolate small details of a building, especially when there are interesting shapes and patterns.

Below: When including the whole structure in a photograph a distant viewpoint and moody lighting help convey the atmosphere and setting of the building.

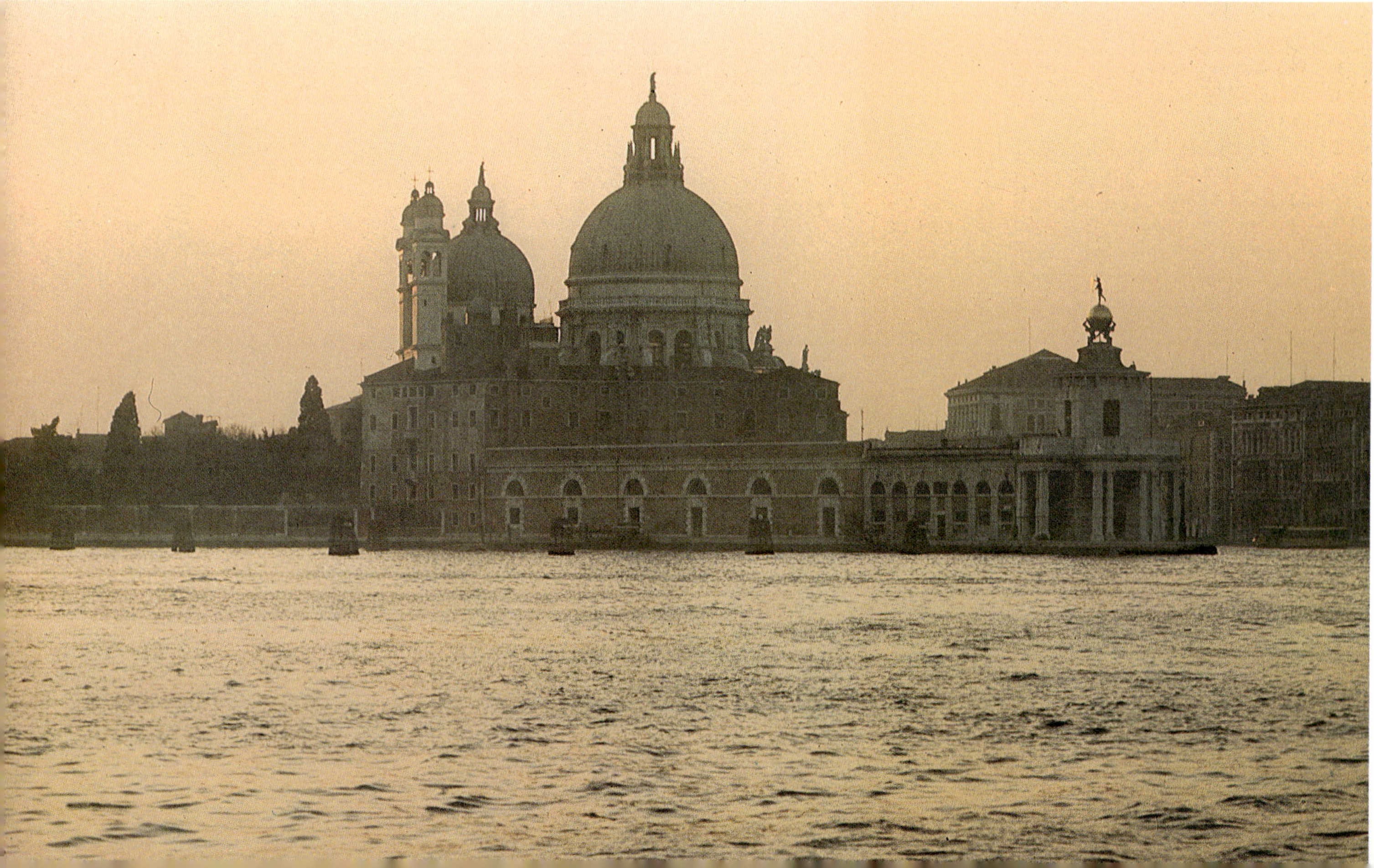

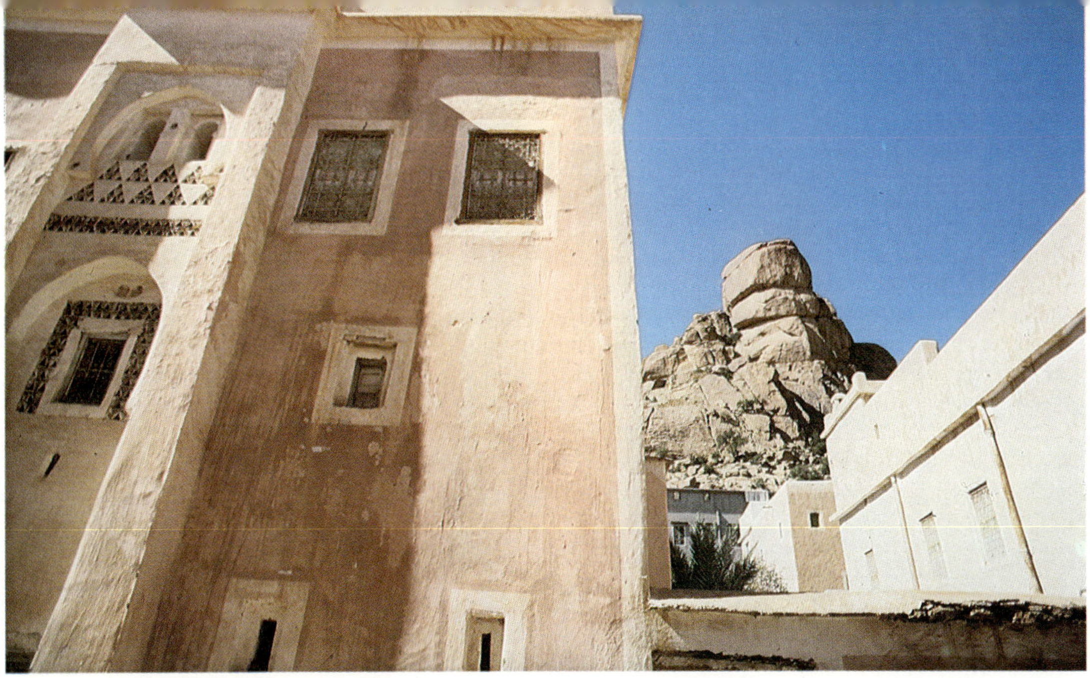

Left: Deliberately tilting the camera upwards to include the top of a building can add a more dramatic quality to the picture. In this case a wide-angle lens has exaggerated the effect.

consider the possibilities of showing such buildings in their setting. It is, after all, with this in mind that they were designed and built, and such views can often be more evocative than the more close-up architectural images, especially with sympathetic lighting.

Deliberate tilting of the camera can produce dramatic pictures. If you decide to do this it is generally better not to include the ground in the picture as this will create the impression that the building is about to fall over. It is also important to use the lines which are created by the converging verticals as part of the composition: sometimes it helps to tilt the camera slightly to one side as well as upwards in order to control the direction of these lines of perspective. It is better to overdo this effect rather than underdo it otherwise the result can easily look accidental; the closer you are to the base of the building and the wider the angle of the lens the stronger the perspective will be.

In addition to photographing a whole building it can also be rewarding to isolate small areas and details. Interesting textures and patterns can be used to create pictures with strong impact. In addition to showing aspects of the building which a wider view would fail to do, such details will help to produce a more personal and interpretative record of a place.

Photographing at night, when buildings are illuminated, is another way of producing pictures that have more impact. It is best to shoot before it becomes completely dark – just after sunset is ideal when there is still enough light in the sky to record a tone or a colour instead of pure black. As long exposures are usually needed a tripod is virtually essential and you should take your exposure readings so that bright light sources are avoided as this will induce under-exposure. Alternatively you can take an average from the lightest and darkest part of the scene. Whichever method you use it is safer to bracket exposures. It is often preferable to use daylight film when shooting in colour, especially when there is still some daylight present – a film such as Ektachrome 400 is ideal as in addition to its greater speed it tends to be rather more tolerant of changes in colour balance.

Photographing the interiors of buildings presents a similar problem to that of floodlit exteriors: a tripod is advisable for the longer exposures that are necessary. When framing your picture you should exclude large areas of window as this will produce excessive contrast. Try to position your camera so that the field of view is lit as evenly as possible and calculate your exposure by the averaging method. Exposures longer than about half a second produce reciprocity failure in the film, which means that the ISO rating of the film becomes less as the exposures increase, so that if your meter indicates a two-second exposure, an *actual* exposure of say three seconds may be needed. This effect varies from one film type to another, but as a general rule allow half as much exposure again from one second to ten seconds and twice that indicated from ten seconds to twenty seconds.

Below: Pictures of illuminated buildings at night are best taken before the sky is completely dark. Daylight film was used in this shot to accentuate the colours.

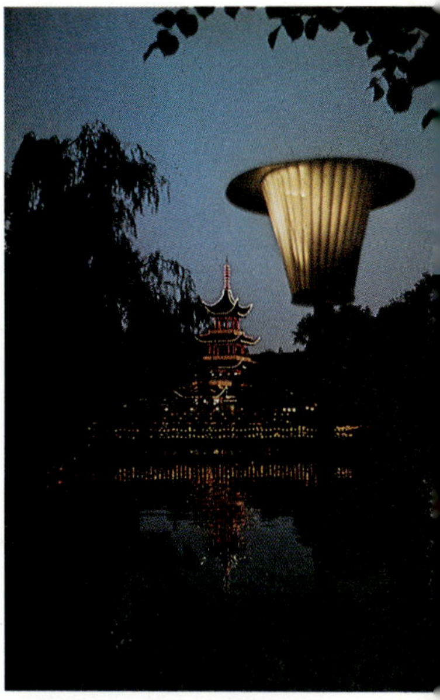

Below: It is often possible to find a high viewpoint from which to photograph large buildings effectively while including their setting.

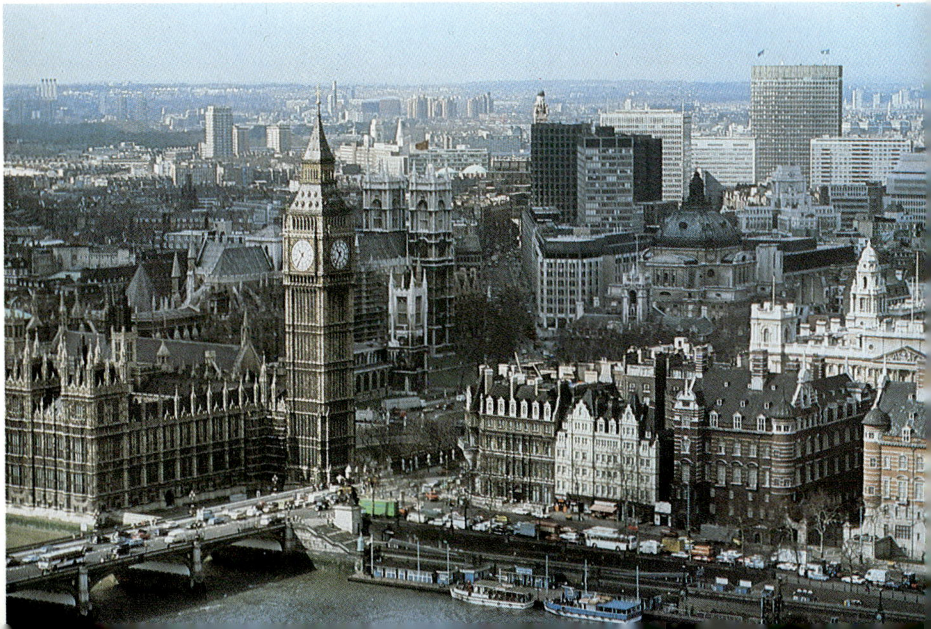

Available light photography

Bottom: An exposure of several seconds, with the camera mounted on a tripod, was used for this picture taken at dusk.

Below: A fast film and a hand-held camera, using an exposure of about 1/15 second produced this shot of an interior of a casino.

Modern films and equipment make it possible to take pictures under a wide range of lighting conditions. There are sometimes occasions, even when the light is at a low level, when, to retain atmosphere or to photograph unobtrusively, it is preferable to make use of the available light rather than use flash or artificial lighting. Of course there are situations when it is simply not possible to use extra lighting.

The main problem that is caused by shooting in low light is that of giving adequate exposure. A fast film such as ISO 400/27 will enable reasonably fast shutter speeds to be used with a wide aperture in all but the poorest light. It is, however, possible to increase the speed of both colour and black-and-white films during processing: ISO 800/30 or ISO 1600/33 is easily achieved. Some increase in grain will result from using these techniques and a corresponding loss in image quality will occur, but this can often enhance the atmosphere. As you will need to use a wide aperture the shallow depth of field which this produces means that focusing needs to be very accurate. It is in these conditions that the advantages of the range finder cameras can be appreciated in preference to the single lens reflex, as even in poor light the focusing remains quite clear and positive.

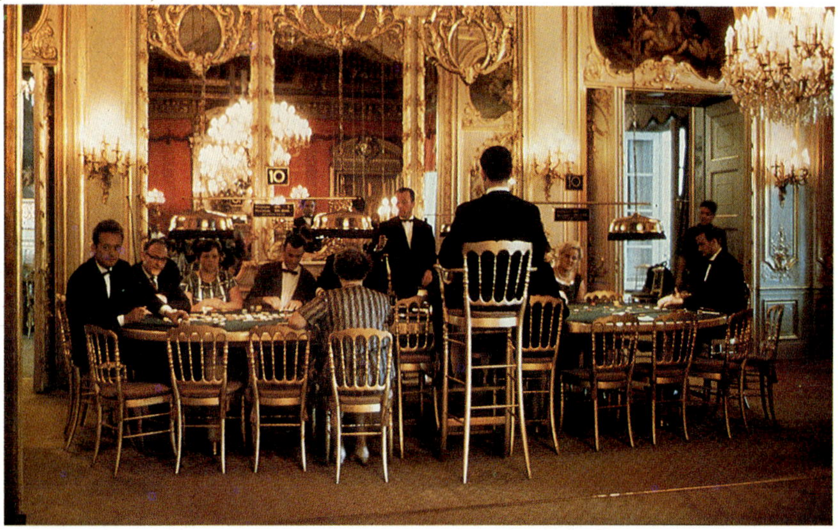

At shutter speeds of less than 1/30 second camera shake is an inevitable problem, and it is vital to hold the camera firmly and release the shutter in a smooth action. Using a tripod is by far the best method of avoiding camera shake, but if one is not available then any form of additional support is worth using.

Exposure calculation also needs to be made carefully, as this type of picture has a high brightness range with dense shadows and often the light sources themselves are within the picture area. In order to reduce the contrast frame the picture in such a way that the image consists predominantly of either darker or lighter tones and expose accordingly. The film will not otherwise be able to record both adequately, and a picture which contains an equal mixture of darker and lighter tones will show little detail in either area.

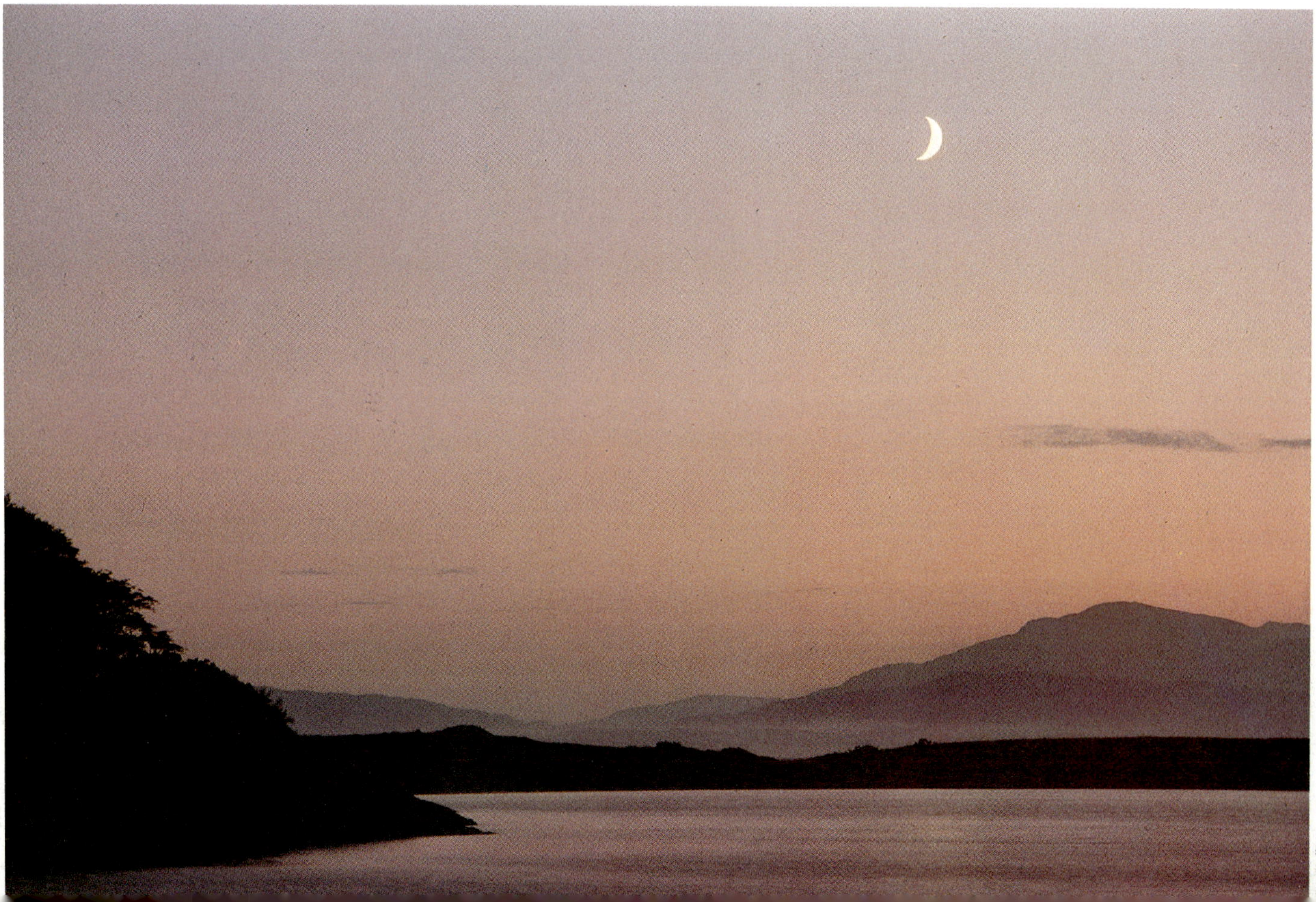

In addition to the level of light it is also necessary to consider the colour quality of the light source when taking colour pictures – for example, when you are shooting a scene which is lighted predominantly by tungsten light. The use of artificial light film is essential to avoid a colour cast, but quite often there is a mixture of light sources and the choice of film can be rather confusing. When taking pictures with a fairly equal balance of daylight and tungsten it may be better to use a daylight film, as the orange cast produced by the tungsten light will produce a more pleasing effect than the blue cast resulting from using artificial light film when daylight is present. A scene which is lit mainly by fluorescent lighting also needs special consideration. Although it may appear to have a similar quality to daylight it tends to produce a very unpleasant green cast on daylight film and quite strong filtration is needed to overcome this. It is possible to buy a special fluorescent correction filter to deal with this problem, or a CC 20 or 30 magenta can be used.

Another rather unpredictable situation is that produced by theatre lighting, such as at a concert or discothèque. Although the basis of such lighting is tungsten it is preferable to use daylight film as the lamps in such places are usually heavily filtered with coloured acetates, and when they are mixed to produce a white light it is closer to daylight in quality. Even if a slight orange colour cast is produced this often adds to the atmosphere of this type of picture.

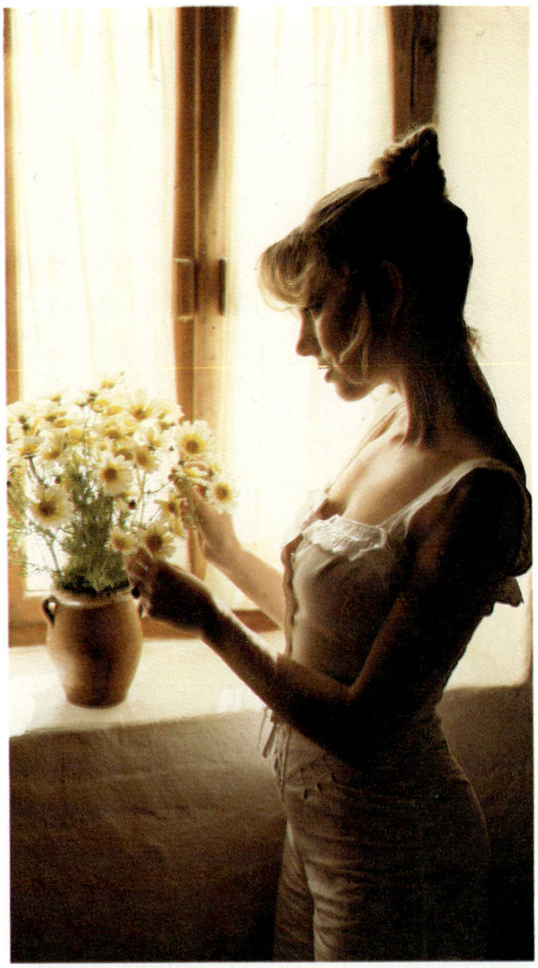

This picture was taken using only the light coming through the window. Sunlight bouncing off the pale walls has reduced the shadows on the girl.

Below: A fast daylight film, a wide aperture lens and an exposure of approximately 1/125 second enabled a hand-held camera to photograph this scene.

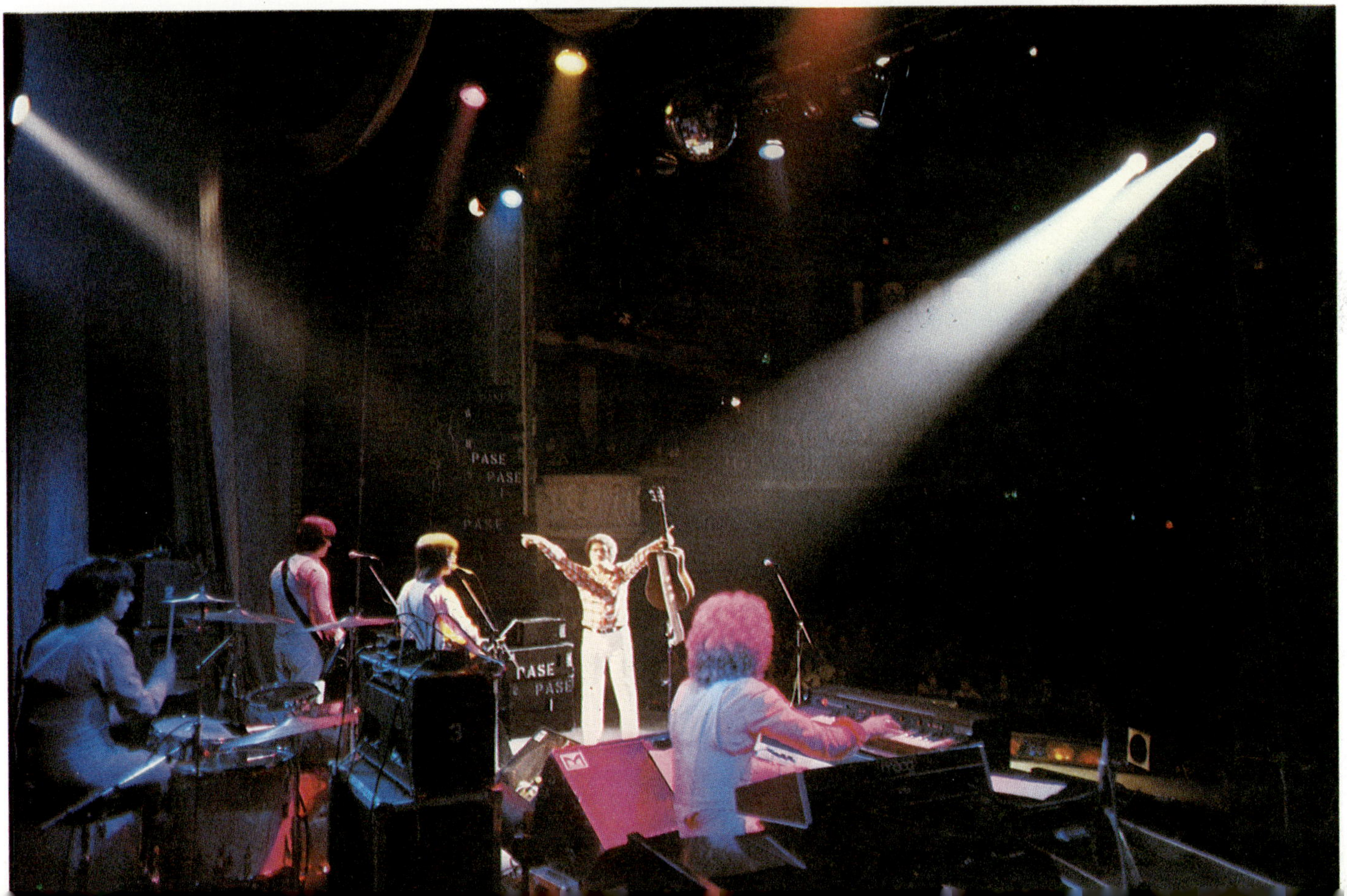

Fault-finder

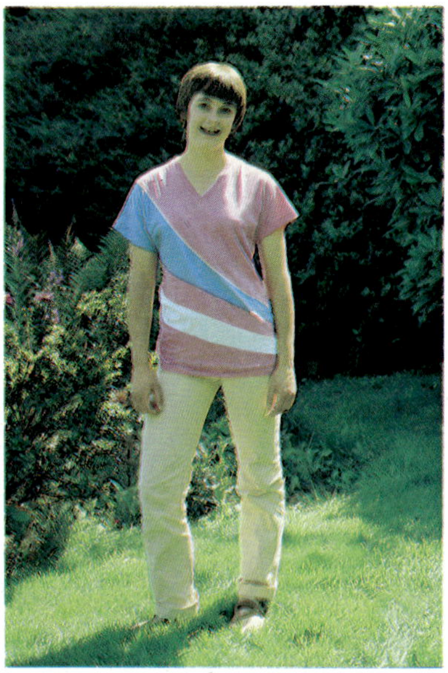

This picture is the result of the camera not being close enough to the subject; the composition is uninteresting because the subject has been centrally positioned; and the model also appears awkward and unrelaxed. The solution is to move the camera closer, compose more carefully and place the model in a more comfortable position.

This is the result of the camera moving during the exposure. The solution is to hold the camera firmly and to release the shutter in a smooth, non-stabbing movement. A fast shutter speed will help to prevent this problem but if this is not possible a tripod or some additional support should be used.

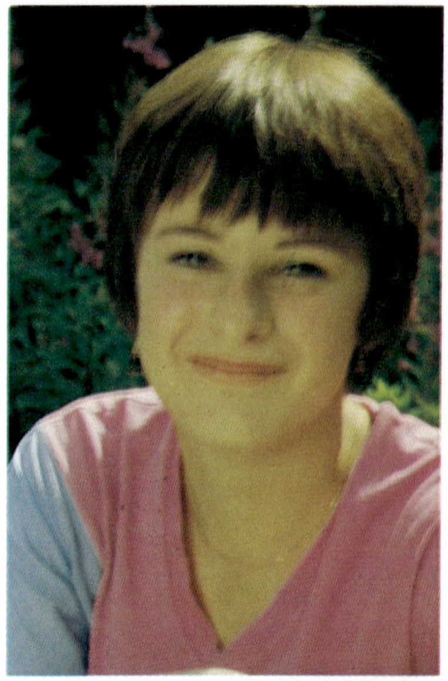

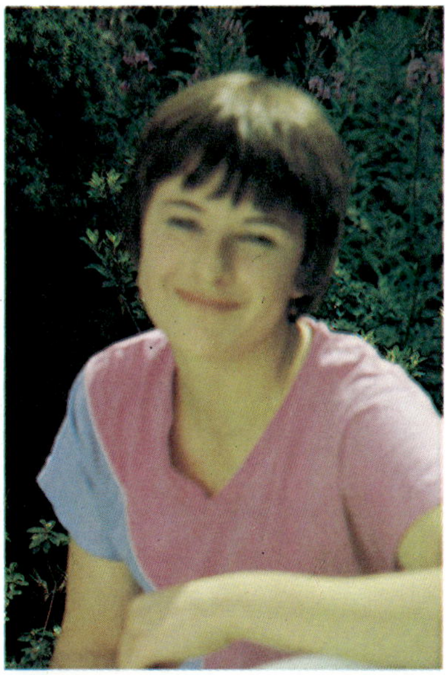

Inaccurate focusing has produced a picture where the background is sharp but the subject is fuzzy. With close distances it is important to be accurate to within an inch or two. This can be measured when using a camera without a range finder or focusing screen. Non-focusing cameras need a supplementary, or close-up, lens for distances of less than 6–8 feet.

This is the result of the film receiving insufficient exposure. Underexposure can be caused by a wrongly set film speed on automatic cameras (too high a number), a badly taken exposure reading, a malfunction of the camera controls or simply inaccurate setting when using a hand meter.

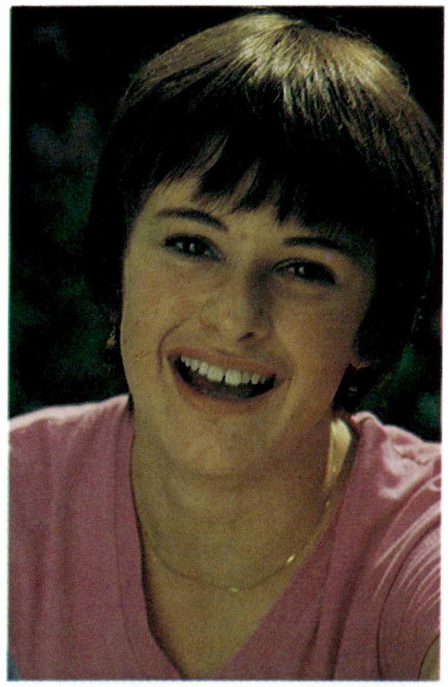

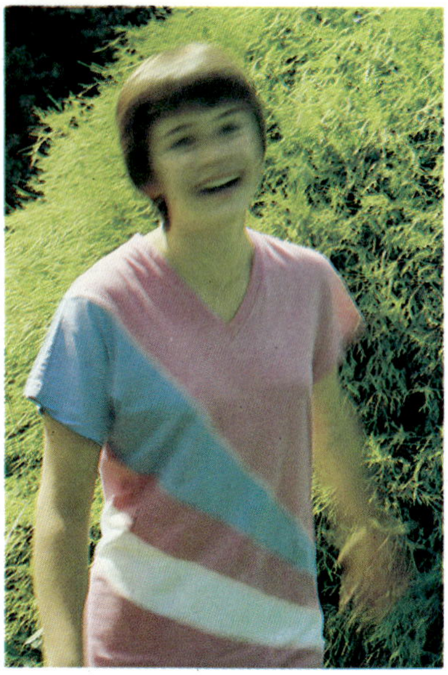

This picture is a result of attempting to photograph a moving subject with a shutter speed insufficiently fast to freeze the movement. The solution is to use a faster shutter speed or, with a simple camera, to avoid exposing until the subject has stopped moving.

This picture shows the result of the film receiving too much exposure. Over-exposure can be the result of setting the film speed wrongly on an automatic camera (too low a number), a badly taken exposure reading, a malfunction of the camera controls or simply setting them inaccurate setting when using a hand meter.

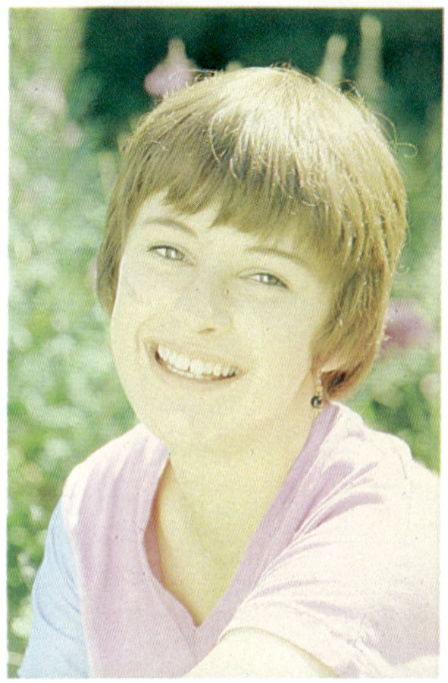

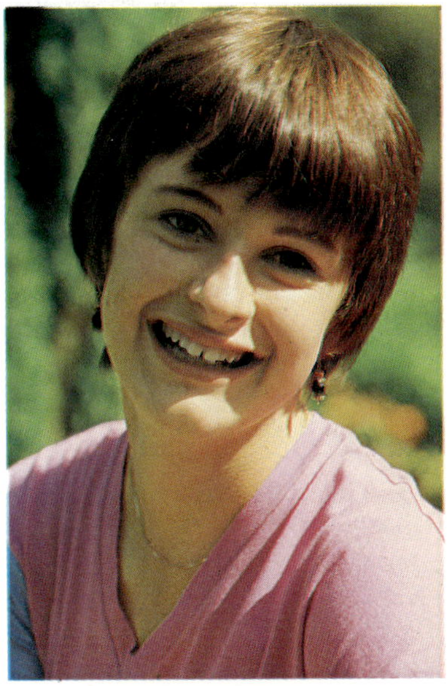

This picture shows the result of shooting when the lighting has produced too much contrast for the film to handle. The solution is to position the camera or the model so that the lighting produces a more even range of brightness, or to use a reflector or a flash gun to reduce the shadows.

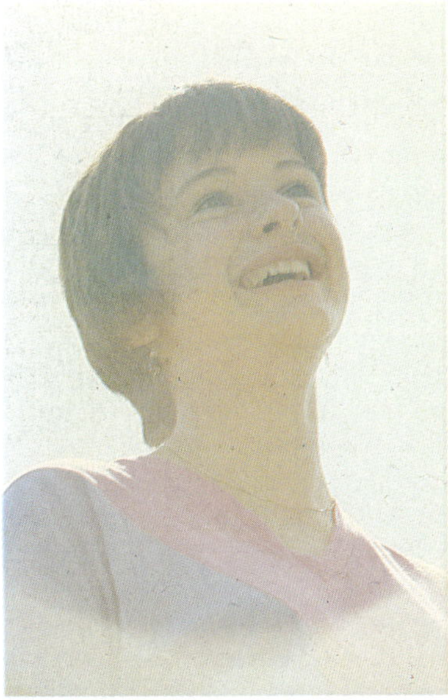

This picture shows the effect produced when strong light, such as direct sunlight or a very bright sky, falls on to the camera lens. The solution is to use a lens hood or to shield the lens with your hand. Alternatively, you could use a natural shadow, such as the branch of a tree, to protect the lens.

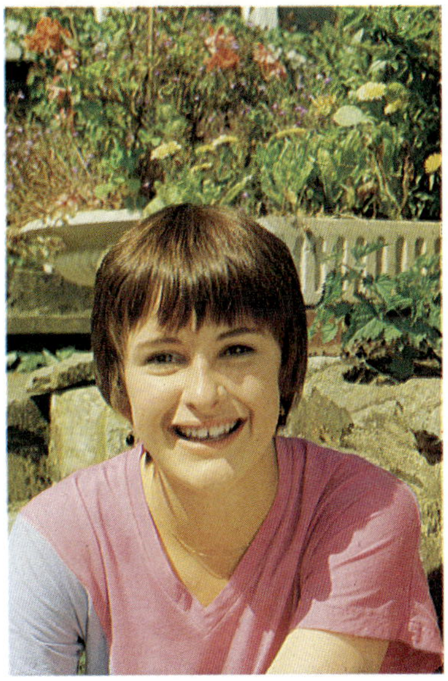

This picture shows the result of allowing the background to become too fussy and obtrusive. The solution is to position the camera or the subject so that a more neutral area is behind him or her, or to ensure that the background is a considerable distance behind the subject. A wide aperture will help to throw it out of focus.

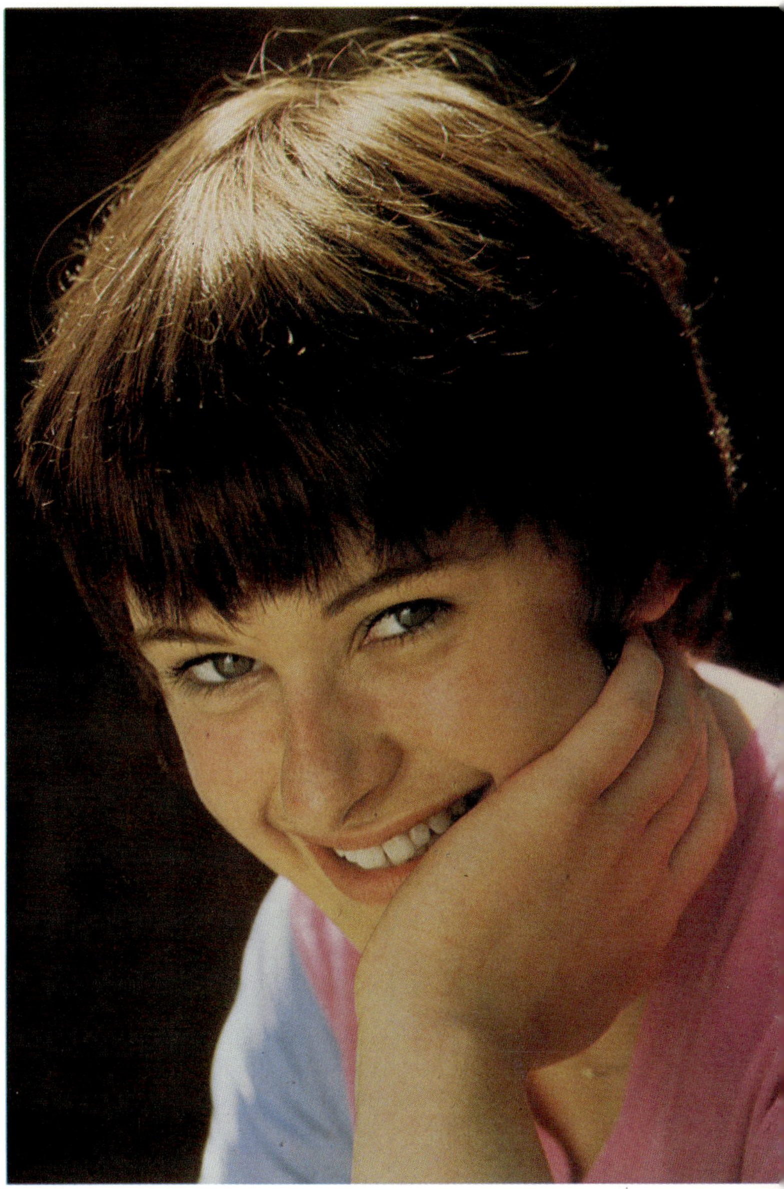

A good one!

Presentation & storage

All pictures benefit from being well presented, and if carefully and thoughtfully mounted and displayed they are also less likely to be damaged.

The most effective way of presenting colour transparencies is undoubtedly by projection, and the extra trouble involved in preparing and showing a sequence of slides by this method will be well repaid by the additional impact that your pictures will have. Plan carefully the sequence in which the transparencies should be shown. Avoid too much repetition of similar images and vary the pace of the screening by interspersing close-ups with long shots, portraits with views and so on. You should also give thought to the colour quality of your slide. For example, the impact of a picture with strong colour will be far greater when shown after a series of pictures with subdued colour tones than in a sequence of images with similar colour strength.

Transparencies that are intended mainly for projection are best mounted in glass and can be stored in the projector magazines, but, in common with all photographic materials, exposed or unexposed, they should be kept somewhere cool and dry.

For those who do not wish to use a projector another effective way of both storing and presenting colour slides is to mount them individually in card mounts and then place them in plastic sheets or view packs which hold twenty or twenty-four 35 mm slides. These provide protection and the frosted backing enables the slides to be viewed effectively against any convenient light source. The sheets can be stored in a ring binder or kept in a filing cabinet using suspension bars.

Negatives need to be stored with care. Whatever size they are they should never be cut up individually but kept in strips. This makes it far easier to handle them and they are consequently less likely to be scratched or finger-marked. The strips can then be kept in specially made divided acetate sheets which will hold a complete roll of film.

An album provides the simplest and most inexpensive method of storing and displaying photographic prints. Small prints such as EN prints can be placed in albums which will hold up to six pictures per page, and can be held in place by self-adhesive leaves with acetate overlays or on plain pages using corner mounts. Either method allows them to be easily removed and changed around but the acetate type does offer some additional protection against scuffing and finger-marking. Resist simply cramming them in. Make some effort to lay them out attractively on the page, juxtaposing pictures which complement and enhance each other, avoiding repetition. Larger photographs of 10 × 8 inches or more are best displayed individually on a page. One method is to mount them on plain, thin card which can then be stored and displayed in an album with clear acetate sleeves, either one to a spread or back to back with one on each page. The simplest method of mounting prints is to use the spray adhesives supplied by most art stores. These have the advantage, because they give a very fine spray of glue, of making the print relatively easy to demount if required. The best method, however, is the dry mounting technique. This involves sandwiching a sheet of special tissue between the print and its mount and then applying heat and pressure to form a bond between them: the result is a beautifully flat smooth print with no mess. A domestic iron can be used to do this with care, but a piece of thin card should be placed between the iron and the surface of the print to protect it from the heat.

Prints of which you are particularly proud can be effectively mounted and framed for hanging on the wall at home. The simplest method is to use self-adhesive polystyrene boards which can be bought from photographic and art supply stores. They are about half an inch thick, very light, easily trimmed to size with a sharp blade after the print has been pressed down into position, and can be fixed to the wall with self-adhesive pads or putty. A more elaborate display can be achieved from the frames sold in kit form, which can be obtained with cut-out overlays for the print to add a professional finish. When displaying prints in this way, particularly colour photographs, you should avoid placing them where they will be subjected to sunlight or even very bright daylight as this will produce fading. It is possible to buy an aerosol spray which gives an ultraviolet protective film to the surface of the print, reducing this hazard slightly, but colour prints intended for permanent display are best made by the Cibachrome process, which is particularly resistant to fading.

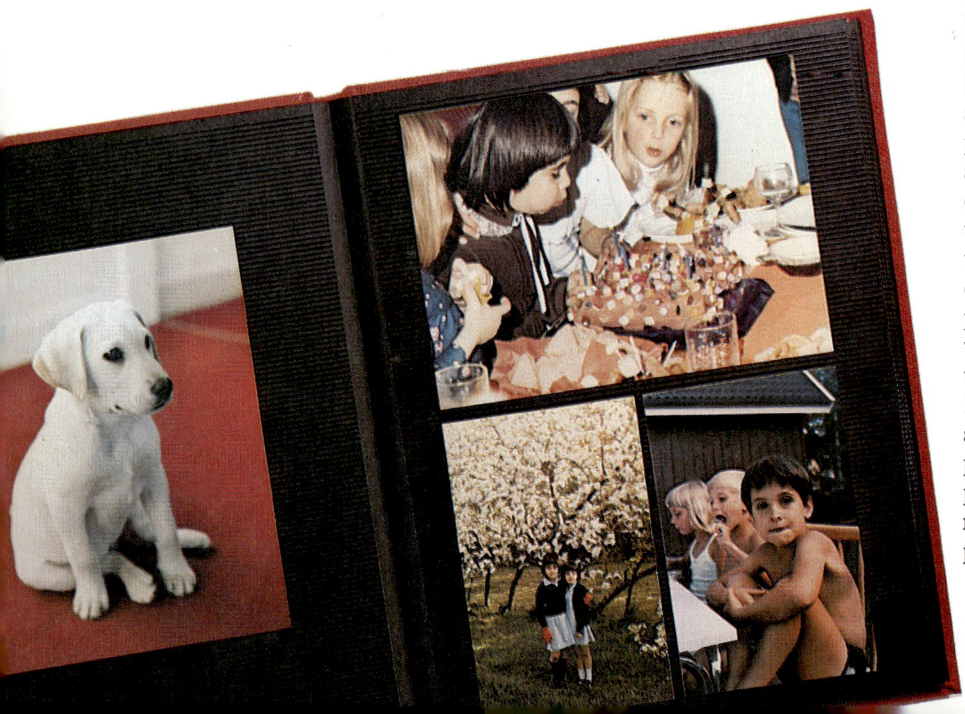

Glossary

Aerial perspective an impression of depth or distance in a photograph created by the presence of mist or haze.

Angle of view the maximum angle of acceptance of a lens. This depends on its focal length and the film format for which it is designed.

Aperture the hole which controls the amount of light passing through the lens on to the film. In all but the simplest cameras this is variable, the sizes of the variable apertures are indicated by *f* numbers.

ASA this stands for the American Standards Association and is one method of rating film speeds.

Blur unsharp areas of the image caused by movement, inaccurate focusing or limited depth of field.

Brightness range the difference between the lightest and darkest tones of the subject or image.

Cable release a flexible extension to enable the camera's shutter to be released with minimum risk of camera shake, designed for use with longer exposures when using a tripod.

Contrast a term which describes the difference between the brightest and darkest areas of a subject or an image.

Coupled rangefinder a method of accurate focusing for non-reflex cameras.

Definition a term used to describe the degree of sharpness produced by a lens and film when recording fine detail.

Depth of field the distance either side of the point at which the lens is focused which is recorded with acceptable sharpness.

DIN a method of designating relative film speeds widely used in Europe.

Exposure the total amount of light allowed to reach the film. This is a combination of the subject brightness, the aperture and the shutter speed.

Exposure meter an instrument for measuring the amount of light which is reflected from, or falls on, the subject.

Extension tubes an accessory which fits between the lens and camera body allowing much closer focusing distances to be achieved.

Filters tinted glass, acetate or gelatin discs or squares which can be used to control the way the image forming light affects the film.

Fisheye lens lens of extreme wide-angle view, up to 180 degrees, which produces a distorted image of the subject.

Fixed focus a simple camera with a lens which can not be focused on selected distances but remains permanently set, usually at around fifteen feet.

Flare the result of light which is scattered indiscriminately inside the lens or camera causing a flat foggy image.

***f* numbers** a method of designating the relative apertures of a lens. They are found by dividing its focal length by the diameter of the aperture, i.e. an aperture of 10 mm with an 80 mm lens would be called *f*8.

Focal plane shutter this type of shutter is used with most SLR cameras. It consists of a flexible blind with a slit which travels at a variable speed across and directly in front of the film.

Guide number a number which enables exposure calculations to be made when using a flash gun. It is also called a flash factor.

High key a photograph which consists of predominantly light tones.

Incident light reading a term used to describe the method of using an exposure meter to read the light falling on the subject rather than that being reflected from it.

Infra-red film film which is sensitive to the non-visible rays beyond the red end of the spectrum. It can be obtained both in black-and-white and colour emulsions and can be used to produce unusual effects.

Joule unit of measurement of light output of electronic flash equipment.

Latitude the amount of exposure variation with which a particular film will still produce an acceptable result.

Long-focus lens a lens which has a focal length somewhat greater than the diagonal measurement of the film format in use, producing a narrower angle of view than a standard lens.

Low key a photograph in which dark tones predominate.

Mirror lens a long-focus lens in which mirrors are used to enable a more compact design.

Negative a photographic image where the tones are in reverse to the subject. This is the first stage in all processes and a photographic print or transparency is a re-reversal of these tones.

Orthochromatic film this describes a film which is sensitive to blue and green but not red.

Panchromatic film black-and-white film which is sensitive to all colours and must be handled in total darkness.

Stop the aperture or *f* number of a lens.

Telephoto lens a design which enables a long-focus lens to be made more compact.

Tungsten light an artificial light source with a filament-type bulb for which a specially balanced film must be used when shooting in colour.

TTL stands for through-the-lens metering. A system used in SLR cameras where the exposure reading is taken after the light has passed through the lens.

Uprating using special processing techniques to gain more than the manufacturer's recommended film speed.

Wide-angle lens lens which produces a wider field of view than that of a standard lens and has a shorter focal length.

Zoom lens a lens which has the facility to vary its focal length.

Index